Praise for `Championship Rounds, Round 2'

"Boxers are crazy. We know this. But they're immersed in that mystical, macho web known as the sweet science, and their dreams and failings and victories are so full of human yearning. Bernard Fernandez gives them all the sweetest of touches. As fascinating as it is real, this book is a knockout."
*Rick Telander, sports columnist for the *Chicago Sun-Times* and author of *Heaven is a Playground*

"If Bernard Fernandez was a fighter instead of a writer, he'd have all the qualities to be a champion and hold onto the belt for a long time. A great read by a terrific writer! I recommend this book to every boxing fan."
*Ray "Boom Boom" Mancini, former WBA lightweight champion and 2015 inductee into the International Boxing Hall of Fame

"Like the boxers themselves, boxing writers have their own style, and no boxing writer's style is more enjoyable to read than that of Bernard Fernandez. He wins every round in his most recent story collection titled `Championship Rounds, Round 2.' Buy this book!"
*Tom MacDonald, adjunct professor of the Woods College of Advancing Studies at Boston College and author of the Dermot Sparhawk mystery novels

"Philadelphia has produced many great boxers and many great boxing writers. Read this collection of columns and you will see why Bernard Fernandez is a Hall of Famer."
*Ray Didinger, award-winning sports columnist and author

"There are few things in life better than great storytelling. Bernard Fernandez's `Championship Rounds, Round 2' is just that. The variety is stunning, and intoxicating. This is can't-put-the-book-down reading."
*Bill Dwyre, retired sports editor and columnist for the *Los Angeles Times*

"If boxing is analogous to hip-hop, then Bernard Fernandez is an OG. He's an old-school newspaperman, one who knows all the characters and how to colorfully tell their stories, with the keen eye of an insider."

*Lou DiBella, boxing promoter and 2020 inductee into the International Boxing Hall of Fame

"In his second published anthology, Bernard Fernandez delivers a knockout journalistic feat. He brings you directly into the ring, but also outside of it, where these fascinating fighters live like royalty, paupers or somewhere in between. This is a book that's hard to put down."

*Chuck Bausman, Professor of Journalism, Rider University

Bernard's amazing stories put you at ringside where you can hear the punches pound, see the sweat fly and duck the spilling blood."
*Joseph Santoliquito, president of the Boxing Writers Association of America

"Unlike the original 'Championship Rounds,' Round 2 contains several admirable chapters about other sports Bernard has covered during his distinguished career. It is, however, boxing and its practitioners that are closest to his heart, which is evident by his depth and knowledge and the elegance of his prose."
*Nigel Collins, former editor of The Ring, author and 2015 inductee into the International Boxing Hall of Fame

Championships Rounds
Round 2

Bernard Fernandez

RKMA Publishing—Drexel Hill, PA
ISBN: 978-0-578-31501-0
Title: *Championship Rounds, Round 2'*
Author: Bernard Fernandez
Digital distribution | 2021
Paperback | 2021

Cover art by Richard T. Slone.

Published in the United States by New Book Authors Publishing

Dedication

To Carmen Basilio, Stan Musial, Billy Cannon and Bob Pettit:
The first sports heroes of my childhood, they ignited my passion for the games people play and the battles they wage, which ultimately birthed my desired to write about the rises and falls of their successors in the competitive arena.

Table of Contents

Foreword by Jim Lampley vii
Section A: *Tales Worth Telling*..1
  Pryor, Quarry Create a State of Turmoil 1
  Boxing Still Thrives in the Service Academies.................5
  Jim Lampley Recalls the Roy Jones That Was................. 12
  *Teddy Atlas and His Dad Really Have Served to Help Hold
  Up The World*...17
  All That Czyz... 22
  A Fistful of Kindness.. 28
  Jimmy Lennon Jr., In His Father's Image 31
  Marv Marinovich Had a Son, Not a Science Project 36
  One Joe's Helping Hand to Another................................ 43
  *Ringling Brothers Throws in the Towel; Boxing's
  Ringmasters Next?* 49
  The Fonz in Bronze 53
Section B: *The Heavyweights* 56
  Remembering the Mike Tyson Rape Trial 56
  Gridiron Greatness No Sure Path to Gloved Glory..................... 62
  *Riddick Bowe: Really Good, But Could've Been Even Better
  Shavers Rates Himself – Who Else? – Hardest-Hitting
  Heavyweight*.. 69
  Tyson Fury Gets Offensive for Rematch with Wilder.................. 79
  Foreman-Holmes Would Have Been One for the Aged 82
  Butterbean Turns 50: Pass the Cake (and a Slab of Ribs).......... 88
  A Salute to the Razor Ruddock That Might Have Been.............. 92
Section C: *2016 Olympic Boxing Redux* 97
  When Will the Corruption End? 97
Section D: *The Non-Heavyweights* 110
  Oscar & Felix: Boxing's Odd Couple............................ 110
  Mayweather's Lifestyle of the Rich and Famous 114
  A-Ward Winning.. 120
  Remembering Joe `Old Bones' Brown 124

132,000-Plus ... An Attendance Record Unlikely to be Broken 128

When Carbajal-Gonzalez I Made Ounce-For-Ounce Magic ... 132

Luck of the Non-Draw 137

Section E: *Screenings* 140

Rocky's Legacy Complete 140

Joey Giardello: The Reel Victim 143

Section F: *Farewells* 147

Emile Griffith's Veil of Drama Often Overshadowed His Deeds 147

Floyd Patterson: a Gentlemanly Champion 151

Edwin Pope's Death Further Contracts Fraternity of Great Boxing Writers 160

Angelo Dundee Was Boxing's Will Rogers 163

Sad Final Chapter for a Great Action Hero 167

RIP, Toby Gibson 172

Section G: *Personals* 177

The Night Smokin' Joe Fought Terry Daniels (But I Missed It) 177

Marvis Frazier, Bikers and Hot Dogs in the Ring 182

The Bite Fight ... And the King of the Cowboys 188

ESPN The Magazine's `Cuba' Issue 194

Section H: *Other Sports* 200

The Wrong Goodbye? Jordan Wanted More from Last 200

Go-Round Rising From the Floodwaters 205

Off to See the Whizards 209

`I'm Not Down One Bit' 215

Cold War: Hockey Divides Quebec 221

Agassi Prepared for One Last Run 227

Acknowledgements 231

Foreword
By Jim Lampley
Longtime blow-by-blow boxing commentator for HBO Sports

Possibly the most striking general phenomenon which developed before my eyes in 33 years of calling fights on television was the degree to which the sport mirrored the inexorable process of globalization. Boxing's business changed, the nature of its audience attractions changed, the structure of its competitive hierarchies changed and to a certain degree you can synthesize all that in terms of the differences between, say, Mike Tyson and Wladimir Klitschko or Sugar Ray Leonard and Manny Pacquiao. Those are big differences. But within overarching change there are always constancies, and in boxing a durable constant has been the identity of Philadelphia, Pennsylvania – not just Fight Town USA, but in terms of cultural consistency and audience devotion, the No. 1 fight town on the planet. Ask an aspiring post-Olympic professional from Khazakstan or Thailand or Ghana what he knows about Philly and chances are he will rhapsodize at length about Joe Frazier, Bernard Hopkins, George Benton or the Blue Horizon. They *know*. So it is, and so it has been for a long time.

Another constant has been the significance and power of the storytelling that continually advances the narrative of boxing in the minds of its followers. Because for decades prior to the 1980s boxing had no commonly observed statistical model to provide a framework for fans to understand exactly what happened in a fight, the sport has long been a platform for the most subjective, the most literate, and often the most lyrical modes of expression to be found in the general art of sports writing. And though over the past three-plus decades the numerical profiles of CompuBox have given boxing writers a method for delivering reporting that more directly mimics what their counterparts turn out from watching football, basketball and baseball, the poetry, the passion and the literary license still survive. No city has produced more meaningful boxing writers than Philadelphia, both pre-

CompuBox and post-CompuBox. And none have been more meaningful to the preservation and curation of that art than Bernard Fernandez.

As the son of a journeyman left hooker from New Orleans named Jack Fernandez, Bernard grew up casting a closer eye toward the ring than was the case for his bayou classmates. Destined to write, he snagged a gig as a copy boy for the sports department of the New Orleans *Times-Picayune* in the summer before his senior year of high school. Later the characteristic peripatetic evolution of a newspaper sports writer began at the *Houma (Louisiana) Courier*, and took him to the *Miami Herald, Jackson (Mississippi) Daily News* and the *Pittsburgh Post-Gazette* before he eventually landed at the *Philadelphia Daily News*, some years after a budding legend of a sports editor and columnist named Larry Merchant had assembled perhaps the most talented daily newspaper sports department in the United States.

In Philadelphia, a boxing writer could compare his developing skills to those of the likes of Jack McKinney, whom Merchant had converted from his previous identity as a classical music critic; of Sandy Grady and Stan Hochman and Tom Cushman and Elmer Smith, all great talents whose love of boxing had brought them to the right place to write about it. Ultimately Bernard succeeded Smith on the *Daily News* boxing beat, and a great career that continues to this day had been solidified.

This is the second edition of *Championship Rounds*. The foreword for the first was written by my former broadcast partner George Foreman, so naturally it is unique and a knockout. So was the collection of articles in the book, including profiles of several of the sport's most famous fighters, and a fair number of its most obscure. A small sampling of paragraphs attests to why it is a volume, and now its follow-up anthology, that goes by quickly and leaves indelible images in the mind.

Tyson's favorite video – he had several in his plush suite – was about an Asian clan leader named White Lotus, whose kicks to the stomach caused his enemies to bleed to death slowly from internal injuries.

"I love the loyalty of the clans," Tyson continued. "I've got a tape in which one of those guys says to his clan, `You must go out and you will surely die.' And they're like, `OK, we'll die then.' I love that."

It probably never occurred to Tyson that in a professional sense, he was about to die a few days later, or at least begin the slow internal bleeding that would culminate in those ass-whippings from Evander Holyfield and Lennox Lewis, much less the ignominious defeats to Danny Williams and Kevin McBride.

*Fight fans are left to debate whether Wlad could have or would have spanked Joshua prime on prime, but such exquisitely timed confrontations of elite boxers are relatively rare. Someone is always on the way up, someone is always on the way down. Having lost back-to-back scraps for the first time as a pro, and already affluent enough to consider the move into a rewarding next phase of his life, the erstwhile "Dr. Steelhammer" again chose the safe course. Who knows? Maybe he was influenced by last week's report issued by the American Medical Association that, of 111 deceased NFL players who had donated their brains for scientific research, 110 had varying degrees of Chronic Traumatic Encephalopathy (CTE).

Passages like these underscore Bernard's capacity for the overall vision and comprehensive understanding necessary to properly cover the sport which demands more of its human participants in more different physical and psychological departments than any other. They set the table for the article which was for me the *piece de resistance* of Volume 1, a lyrical ode to the greatness and vulnerability of Manny Pacquiao which employed a compelling use of Elizabeth Taylor as a comparative metaphor for the Filipino superstar, then frankly and unequivocally predicts his upset loss to lesser-known Australian Jeff Horn. It's a classic.

Along with a fellow Philadelphia boxing scribe named Joseph Santoliquito, Bernard Fernandez throughout each year performs the time-consuming and essential task of administering and preserving the Boxing Writers Association of America, whose annual awards dinner is in effect the Academy Awards of boxing. In his role with the BWAA, Bernard is an indispensable bulwark for sustaining and publicizing the celebration of sport writing's most literate and artistic corner. In *Championship Rounds, Volume 2*, he again affirms that he is as deserving of plaudits as anyone in the fraternity. Now read and enjoy. It was a privilege for me to write on behalf of this book.

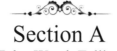

Section A
Tales Worth Telling

Pryor, Quarry Create a State of Turmoil
Philadelphia Daily News, May 16, 1990

MADISON, Wisc.

In 1979, a group of University of Wisconsin students constructed a partial replica of the Statue of Liberty on frozen Lake Mendota.

The 3,000-pound wooden edifice was of the top half of Lady Liberty's head, along with her familiar torch. From a distance, it appeared as if the base of the statue might be resting on the lake bottom, with just the upper part poking through.

But the startling visual effect had a deeper purpose: It was meant to signify that America's cherished ideals were frozen forever in time in Wisconsin, a state that has long viewed itself as a bastion of progressive politics and protector of civil liberties.

Wisconsin's idealism, rooted in some of the strongest anti-discrimination statutes to be found anywhere, now is being put to the test by an influx of aged and infirm boxers who have been turned away virtually everywhere else.

Aaron Pryor, whose vision problems have caused him to be rejected on medical grounds by state boxing commissions in Nevada, New York and California, becomes the first fighter to benefit from a somewhat peculiar application of Wisconsin's tough anti-discrimination statutes when he takes on Daryl Jones tonight at the Masonic Temple. And if you think a howl of protest has gone up over Pryor's appearance, just wait until 45-year-old former heavyweight contender Jerry Quarry launches his comeback June 2 in Lake Geneva.

Professional boxing heretofore has had a low profile in Wisconsin, the site of only 12 fight cards in 1989, but the granting of permits to Pryor and Quarry by the Wisconsin Department of Regulation and Licensing has ignited a firestorm of controversy that

1

could result in either the amending of existing laws or the abolition of the sport in the state.

On one side are boxing officials in Nevada, New York and California, who have appealed directly to Wisconsin Governor Tommy Thompson to intercede and have the Pryor fight stopped. Aligned with those officials are assorted critics of boxing in general and specifically Pryor's appearance in the state.

"This is bad for boxing and bad for the state of Wisconsin," said Dr. James Nave, chairman of the Nevada State Athletic Commission, which voted, 4-1, last month not to allow Pryor to box in that state. "We spent a tremendous amount of time researching this case and I don't think Wisconsin looked at what we did before coming to a decision."

Added Madison mayor Paul Soglin: "I would just as soon see boxing abolished in the state. But if it is to exist, it has to be regulated with some integrity. What is happening here with the Aaron Pryor situation is a complete and utter travesty."

Taking a somewhat different viewpoint is Marlene Cummings, secretary of regulation licensing in Wisconsin, who said she had no choice but to approve of the applications submitted by Pryor and Quarry.

"Everyone has due process in this state," Cummings said. "Aaron Pryor and Jerry Quarry met all the standards required to be allowed to box here. I'm certainly aware that officials in other states have arrived at other decisions, but I am obligated to follow the laws of Wisconsin. I can't take one law and hold it out by itself. We're very serious about being fair in this state."

Falling somewhere in between are Pryor and Quarry, whose hopes of resuming their careers hinge on the outcome of the tug-of-war involving them that now rages within Wisconsin's borders.

"I think Wisconsin is a wonderful place for humanity, for a person to have justice even if you are disabled," Pryor said, perhaps hoping to influence the debate in his favor. "I don't have a medical problem, I have a disability problem."

Some might say that Pryor, 34, is splitting hairs, but the line between a medical problem and a disability isn't as fine as it might appear, at least not in Wisconsin.

It is Pryor's contention that the impaired vision in his left eye is not so severe that it would prevent him from fighting again.

"I can see fairly well," said Pryor, who underwent surgery January 31, 1989, in Rochester, New York, to repair a detached retina and for cataract extraction. "My vision is kind of like what you would have if you wore glasses and took them off."

To back up his claim, Pryor arrived in Wisconsin several weeks ago with two out-of-state ophthalmologists who testified that his left eye could indeed withstand the rigors of a boxing match. A Madison ophthalmologist, Dr. Suresh Chandra, also examined Pryor and found that while there was "some impairment," the fighter was not legally blind in his left eye.

"(Chandra) said the choice (whether to fight or not) should be Aaron's," Cummings said. "Aaron Pryor clearly has a disability, but while some people say you must protect other people from themselves, by Wisconsin law he has the option of making that choice himself.

"I've seen the man spar, jump rope and shoot baskets, and he seems all right to me."

That last statement was met with derision by Randy Gordon, head of the New York State Athletic Commission, who said Cummings "doesn't know a fish hook from a left hook. So she went out to the gym and saw him spar. Is that cause enough to give a man who is under medical suspension a license?"

Quarry's turn in the eye of the hurricane is coming soon enough, but for now Pryor stands alone in what, for him, has become the latest in a series of controversies great and small.

When he was in his prime, Pryor (37-1, 33 KOs), a former World Boxing Association and International Boxing Federation junior welterweight champion, was a fighting machine, a non-stop dispenser of punches who could take as well as he gave. A *Daily News* poll of boxing experts rated his November 12, 1982, battle royal with Alexis Arguello, in which Pryor defended his WBA title on a 14th-round technical knockout, as the best fight of the '80s.

"I'm not bragging or anything," Pryor said, "but I was a great fighter once – not just good, *great.*"

That aura of greatness began to fade as Pryor, from Cincinnati, began losing his personal struggle with cocaine addiction. By his own admission, Pryor, who earned in excess of $3 million in the ring, snorted or smoked away $500,000 of his fortune. The rest, he said, evaporated in divorce settlements and bad business deals.

3

"I went from having everything to having nothing," Pryor said.

Even his talent began to fail him when, on August 8, 1987, he suffered his only loss, a seventh-round knockout to Bobby Joe Young. The Aaron Pryor on display that night was only a shadow of his former self.

In his most recent bout, on December 15, 1988, Pryor knocked out Herminio Morales in the third round, but came away with retinal damage that, insofar as most state boxing commissions were concerned, effectively ended the ring career of the man known as "The Hawk."

Pryor, whose checkered past includes a shooting that left him with a scarred left hand and arrests for rape, kidnapping (charges later were dropped) and assault against his own mother, has spent the interim trying to get his life back in order. It often seemed as if he were taking one step forward and two backward until World Boxing Organization junior welterweight champion Hector "Macho" Camacho suggested that he just might like to swap punches with Pryor. That served as an impetus for Pryor to go through a 28-day drug rehab program in Cleveland recently.

Camacho and Pryor actually signed a contract that called for a $1 million payday for Camacho and $500,000 for Pryor, but it went by the boards when a succession of state boxing commissions refused to grant Pryor a license.

"They discriminated against me in Vegas because of my past, and sooner or later they're going to have to pay for it," said Pryor, who has a lawsuit pending against the Nevada commission. "They want to take my livelihood away from me because of some of the mistakes I've made.

"I keep hearing that it's my eye that's the problem, but I can't see how that can be the case when all these doctors have certified I'm all right to fight. And if they're trying to hold me back because of my history of drug use, that's discrimination. How can you be rehabilitated if you're forever going to be haunted by your past? I'd like to think I've paid for my mistakes."

And so Pryor, who still hopes for a big-bucks meeting with Camacho, has turned up in Wisconsin.

Even if the fight goes off without a hitch – hardly a certainty, considering that he had to undergo still another medical examination and urine test yesterday and that part-time promoter Diana Lewis

4

reportedly might not have met all of the state's requirements – Pryor's Wisconsin sojourn will have been anything but blissful. Only 400 seats in the 1,200-seat arena have been sold, and Lewis has had to refute published reports that Jones (13-12, no KOs) actually is Jerry Strickland, a notorious loser whose record, under his name and a number of aliases, is 11-74 with 38 KO losses.

"I don't see how they could have got me mixed up with that other guy," said an indignant Jones, whose own credentials are hardly impeccable. He is 37 and hasn't fought in seven years.

Meanwhile, Governor Thompson speaks of reinstating a boxing commission, which Wisconsin hasn't had since 1980, and Madison boxing promoter Bob Lynch, who is not involved with either Pryor or Quarry, wonders if the state can recover from all the negative publicity.

"Good, clean boxing still exists in this country and we've kept the flame flickering a little bit here," Lynch said. "Then something like this comes along and ruins everything we've worked so hard to preserve. It's a crying shame."

Epilogue: Disabled or not, Aaron Pryor knocked out the clearly inferior Jones in three rounds. A 1996 inductee into the International Boxing Hall of Fame, he fought just once thereafter, a seventh-round stoppage of Roger Choate on December 4, 1990, in Norman, Oklahoma, to finish with a career record of 39-1 with 35 KOs. He reportedly kicked his drug habit in 1993 and remained drug-free until his death, at 60, on October 9, 2016. Jerry Quarry never did fight in Wisconsin; beset with CTE (chronic traumatic encephalopathy), he was just 53 when he passed away on January 3, 1999

Boxing Still Thrives in the Service Academies
The Ring, April 2014 issue

Upon the fields of friendly strife
Are sown the seeds that,
upon other fields and other days,
will bear the fruits of victory.
*General Douglas MacArthur

5

I have not yet begun to fight
*John Paul Jones

General MacArthur, former superintendent of the United States Military Academy and supreme commander in the Pacific theater during World War II, and Jones, the Revolutionary War hero who is widely regarded as the "father of the U.S. Navy," surely would have understood what had just taken place in the Pennsylvania Convention Center on a chilly evening in mid-December. So did a more recent shining light of the American military, Sergeant 1st Class Leroy Perry, a veteran of *seven* deployments to Iraq and Afghanistan and recipient of the Congressional Medal of Honor.

Boxers representing West Point and the U.S. Naval Academy had hurled themselves at one another with typical tenacity during the nine-bout Army-Navy Boxing Classic in Philadelphia. Depending upon one's point of view, Army had emerged victorious, winning four of the seven bouts televised by the CBS Sports Network, although Navy coach Jim McNally and the Middies were claiming a 5-4 team triumph on the basis of two other matches that preceded the TV fights. Much to McNally's indignation, color analyst Sean O'Grady, the former WBA lightweight champion, and West Point officials opted to count only the televised bouts.

As an enthusiastic crowd of about 1,500 spectators began to file out, a man wearing a Naval Academy hoodie approached Sergeant 1st Class Petry with a request. "Please allow me the privilege of shaking the hand of a Medal of Honor recipient," said the guy in the hoodie, who then grasped the prosthesis that occupied the space where Petry's right hand should have been. Petry's arm had been blown off below the elbow by a Taliban grenade he attempted to throw away after stepping protectively in front of two other soldiers.

It is that commitment to duty, honor, country, as much as anything, that explains why Army, Navy and the Air Force Academy have dominated the National Collegiate Boxing Association, winning a combined 29 of 38 team titles since the NCBA was formed in 1976. Air Force, behind 38-year veteran coach Eddie Weichers, leads the way with 19 of the big trophies; Navy has won five under 28-year coach McNally, and defending champion Army has claimed five – all since 2008 – under Dr. Ray Barone, a retired lieutenant colonel in his 16th year as coach of the Black Knights.

West Point's boxing focus had been on its highly competitive intramural program until its entry into the NCBA in 1998.

The University of Nevada in Reno, with four, and West Chester (Pa.) University, with two, are the only other teams in the now-33-school organization, spread over three regions, with more than one title.

Unlike at other NCBA-affiliated schools, boxing – which has not been an NCAA-sanctioned sport since 1960 – is a mandatory class required of all male students at Army, Navy and Air Force, as well as of all female midshipmen at Navy. There is a reason for that, and it carries potential life-and-death connotations.

"The core courses here include combatives and aquatics," noted Weichers, a graduate of West Chester whose stellar career at the Air Force Academy has to date produced 316 NCBA All-Americans and 111 individual national champions. "Cadets are trained to fly, to fight and to win. We have an ethos that resounds throughout the entire academy, as well as our sister services. These young people are preparing to do things that students at 'civilian' schools are not preparing to do, and that's to lay down their lives for their country if necessary.

"The combatives and water-survival courses are necessary because of what is required to go out and lead troops in combat, and to make quick and good decisions under pressure. Boxing classes are not just designed to teach you how to box, but to help you, internally, to handle stress, fear and anxiety so that you're better able to not get yourself or your wingman killed. That's the mission and the purpose of the Air Force Academy, although Army and Navy have almost identical missions and goals. One's primarily on land, one's primarily at sea and one's primarily in the air."

Barone said that the 60 to 80 cadets who seek to refine their skills under him in any given years never lose sight of what they're there for.

"The academy certainly presents those who are more interested in boxing with that opportunity," he said. "It's a useful tool to help prepare them to lead soldiers as officers in the United States Army. Soldiers, like boxers, lead highly disciplined lives. They're on a schedule, they are very physically fit, and they train to be experts at what they do."

The service academies are unique because while they are prestigious academic institutions – the 2014 edition of *Best Colleges* rates the Naval Academy at No. 14 among American universities, while West Point is 17th and the Air Force Academy 25th – there is a requisite physical component that is not nearly so prevalent on other campuses. Which is not to say that every cadet or midshipman who is required to take boxing classes is naturally suited to opening a can of whup-ass.

"It has some validity," McNally, a former NCBA semifinalist at Lock Haven (Pa.) University, said when asked of the Naval Academy's express purpose of developing fighting men and women produces optimal results in the ring. "But there are plenty of students here who would not be disposed to becoming good boxers, regardless of the amount of physical training they receive.

"Now, when most people think of the Army, they probably think of the infantry. Here at the Naval Academy, members of the Brigade who are most attracted to boxing tend to go into the Marine Corps or the SEALs. They have more of what you might call that warrior mentality."

Boxing has always played an integral role in the overall development of cadets and midshipmen, particularly at Army (the U.S. Military Academy in West Point, New York, was established in 1802) and Navy (Annapolis, Maryland, 1845), which far predate the 1954 founding of the Air Force Academy in Colorado Springs, Colorado. When boxing was still an NCAA sport, Navy won six national championships under legendary coach Hamilton "Spike" Webb, who oversaw the U.S. Olympic boxing teams between 1920 and '32, with more than a few Navy men dotting those rosters. Boxing became a part of the curriculum at Army in 1905, under the direction of President Theodore Roosevelt, and its intercollegiate program, started in 1921 by coach Billy Cavanaugh, fielded seven undefeated squads over 28 years.

But Army and Navy hardly stood alone as national powers during a decades-long golden era of college boxing when many schools fielded teams with large and enthusiastic followings. More than 200 universities had NCAA boxing in the early 1950s, and the dynastic program at Wisconsin, which won eight team titles from 1939 through '56, was so popular that a home match against Michigan State on March 29, 1940, drew more than 15,000 fans, easily topping the 11,620 who came out that same night to watch heavyweight champion Joe Louis defend his title on a second-round stoppage of Johnny Paycheck in Madison Square Garden.

But the end of NCAA boxing came in 1960, when Wisconsin middleweight Charlie Mohr was stopped in two rounds by San Jose State's Stu Bartell. Mohr was hospitalized with a massive subdural hematoma and he died eight days later. His passing gave the NCAA, which had already been wavering in its support of the sport, a reason to withdraw after that season. Subsequent studies showed that an undiagnosed aneurism, not boxing, might have caused Mohr's death, but by then the fight game's separation from the NCAA had been finalized.

From 1960 until 1976, when the NCBA came into existence, college boxing barely hung on, with a handful of schools fielding club teams coached almost exclusively by unpaid volunteers. Weichers, who went to West Chester to play football, gravitated to boxing through the influence of two men, Al McChesney and Dean Plemmons, who started the university's boxing team (the Golden Rams were NCBA team champs in 1979 and '82) and later were co-founders of the organization that has kept college boxing alive and, all things considered, reasonably healthy.

As might be expected, the competition among the service academies is heated, although at a markedly different level than football. McNally, who notes that he, Weichers and Barone are all faculty members in their respective schools' departments of physical education, said he and his fellow boxing coaches enjoy the sort of job security their football counterparts do not.

"You have to understand that boxing here is not like football or basketball," McNally said. "These kids were not recruited to be boxers. There's no recruiting by the NCBA in any case. A lot of our team members had never put on a boxing glove until they got to the Naval Academy.

"For the coaches in many of our sports, and most particularly football, their job security depends on how they do against Army. It's the same at Army, maybe not so much at Air Force because most of our sports teams don't compete against Air Force. But Army and Navy are both in the Patriot League, except for football. The brass keep a running total every year of how Navy does against Army.

9

You can lose to them once, but if you lose two, three, four in a row, you're probably looking for another job."

As proof of McNally's assertion, within days of Navy's 12th straight conquest of the Army football team, a 34-7 rout the day after the Army-Navy Boxing Classic, Army coach Rich Ellerson – 0-5 against the Midshipmen – was fired. But even in presumably lower-profile sports like boxing the competition is nothing short of intense.

"Why is Army-Navy so big, in everything?" Barone asked, rhetorically. "Why is Michigan-Ohio State? Or Yankees-Red Sox? Army-Navy is big because, well, it just is. It's been inbred in our culture, in our values, in our tradition."

Weichers said that his team's matches with Army and Navy come relatively early in the boxing season, always the night before football games, thus limiting his options until he has a better feel for who his top guys are. And that's all right with him.

"If we had something like the Commander-in-Chief Trophy (which is awarded to the top academy football team each year) in boxing like we do in football, we'd have to put our best fighters up against the best fighters from Army and Navy too soon, before they'd probably be ready," he said. "It's not a true indicator of team strength. Sometimes we put our second- and third-line guys up against their second- and third-line guys, matching them up according to size and ability.

"We don't want to have a situation where the pressure to win these (inter-service) competitions is overwhelming. We don't want to create that monster and make those matches more important than the nationals."

The national NCBA tournament is scheduled for April 3-5 at West Point, with the host Black Knights seeking to retain their team championship and take the top prize for the sixth time in seven years.

The academies' boxing coaches are in agreement that their function is not to produce future professional boxers or even elite amateurs capable of making an Olympic team, although all branches of the service have been or at least have a chance to be thus represented. Ken Norton and Leon Spinks got their boxing starts in the Marines, two-time former IBF cruiserweight champion Steve "USS" Cunningham in the Navy and 1988 Olympic heavyweight gold medalist Ray Mercer in the Army.

"Back then we – I mean the Army – would go to the Armed Forces Championships and win, like, 11 of the 12 individual finals," recalled Mercer, a two-time titlist. "I'm not sure people who have never been in the military understand when you talk about *esprit de corps* and all that, but it's very important to us that have been there. You want to uphold the honor of your branch of the service.

"Look, we're brothers in arms and all that good stuff every day of the year – except when you go against one another. We love each other, but it's all about winning. It's about pride. The way I look at it, boxing and the military have a lot in common. They kind of go together."

O'Grady, who did the commentary for those seven bouts at the Army-Navy Boxing Classic, knows where Mercer is coming from. He said he didn't go to Philly "expecting to see the next Floyd Mayweather, but I did expect to see guts, determination, Army strong and Navy pride. I expected to see our country's future heroes, and I did. I came away with restored faith in the youth of America."

The cost of producing those newly minted ensigns and second lieutenants is high, and getting higher. Weichers said that when he first went to the Air Force Academy in 1976, the price tag to taxpayers for educating each cadet over four years was $80,000. It's now up to $417,000, which must be multiplied by more than 12,000 attendees spread over the three academies.

"Our country has invested so much into training these guys to be pilots or navigators or whatever," he said. "They're not here to go to the next level of boxing after college. They're here to serve in defense of the nation. If any of my guys is even thinking of the Olympics or something like that, I squash that idea pretty quick. I say, 'When you're done here, hang up your gloves and go serve your country. Oh, and I'm proud of you.'"

Epilogue: The author of this story was asleep at the wheel in one important respect. While paying tribute to the three cited service academies, I neglected to mention the competitive boxing program at the Coast Guard Academy, located in New London, Connecticut. I now offer a belated *mea culpa* to those who have represented the USCGA in the ring.

Even Superman was not wholly impervious to danger and the specter of defeat. Kryptonite could bring the Man of Steel to his knees. Greek mythology's Achilles was virtually unconquerable in battle, but he could be felled if struck with a strategically placed blow to an unprotected heel.

The only two boxers that longtime HBO blow-by-blow announcer Jim Lampley has observed who were so preternaturally gifted that they superseded the normal boundaries of human excellence were the younger, nearly-perfect versions of Muhammad Ali and Lampley's current HBO broadcast partner, Roy Jones Jr. But each of those superheroes of the ring eventually encountered a relentless opponent that incrementally stripped away the insulating layers that had made them such very special fighters. It was not so much another living, breathing human being who served as the kryptonite that revealed their fallibility as the unseen thief that comes silently in the night, stealing tiny bits and pieces of their exquisite talent until only a shell of what had been remained.

On February 8, in his hometown of Pensacola, Florida, the 49-year-old Jones (65-9, 49 KOs) presumably brings down the curtain on his 29-year professional boxing career when he takes on a carefully selected designated victim, Scott Sigmon (30-11-1, 16 KOs), in a scheduled 10-round cruiserweight bout. The plan is for Jones, a world champion in four weight classes and a surefire first-ballot International Boxing Hall of Fame inductee whenever he becomes eligible, to go out in a blaze of out-of-the-spotlight glory. But if boxing history tells us anything, it is that not everything goes according to plan even for those who have enjoyed the panoramic view from the summit of Mount Pugilism. Mike Tyson, 19 days from his 39th birthday, never fought again after he was stopped in six rounds by plodding Irishman Kevin McBride on June 11, 2005, and Bernard Hopkins, 29 days from his 52nd birthday, was finally obliged to acknowledge the natural laws of diminishing returns when he was knocked out in eight rounds by Joe Smith Jr. on December 17, 2016.

"I have read reports that he is saying this will be his last fight and that's very encouraging and gratifying to me," Lampley said of his friend's farewell appearance, which by any reasonable criteria is coming a good dozen years after what should have been his career's optimal expiration date. "I don't know of a single soul in our little universe of boxing who wants him to keep doing this. We all know realistically that it's certainly of no value to his legacy as a fighter.

"I'd be lying if I said that I never once made a comment to him or tried to engage him in a conversation as to why he was still doing this. The last time I did so he made clear to me that, in his view, it wasn't something he had to defend to me. He was going to do what he was going to do and that within our friendship it was important to me to accept that. I accepted it. Probably five or six years have gone by since the last time I had a discussion with him about it."

The most revered gods of war are held to a higher standard than fighters of a lesser pedigree. It thus should come as no surprise that those members of boxing's most exclusive club are sometimes resistant to step away from something that always has defined them more than anything they could ever do outside of a roped-off swatch of canvas.

"You always think of yourself as the best you ever were," Sugar Ray Leonard, he of the four announced retirements that didn't stick, once said. "Even if money is not an issue, and you have other options, you never lose that belief in yourself as a fighter, particularly if you've been to the very top of the mountain. (Being retired) eats at you. It's hard to find anything else that gives you that high."

Ali lost three years of his prime to his banishment for refusing to be inducted into the Army during the Vietnam War, but, unlike the stop-and-start Leonard, Jones' response to every warning sign that he was on the downward slope of that figurative mountain was to keep fighting, all the while holding fast to the distinctive style he shared with Ali. It was those non-traditional mannerisms, which worked so spectacularly well when Ali and Jones were at their best, that sometimes produced disastrous results when their fundamental deficiencies were exposed.

"The direct comparison is Ali," Lampley said of the closest thing to Jones he has known, both in good times and not so good. "I've said a thousand times that there were only two fighters in the history of the sport, certainly since I've been watching boxing, whose physical talents were so overwhelming that they could take apart the tool kit and put it back together in any way they wanted – lead with a hook, lead with a straight right hand, dispense with the jab, back away from punches rather than duck and slip. Ali could do that *for a while.* Roy could do that *for a while.* But nobody can do that forever.

"That is why the tool kit is what it is, for normally talented human beings. It's your protection in the ring. For a long time Ali and Roy didn't need that protection. Then, when their bodies lost something and they weren't so overwhelmingly physically superior, they didn't have that tool kit to protect them.

"The perfect and most graphic example is if you watch the first Roy Jones-Bernard Hopkins fight (on May 22, 1993). It's all Roy Jones. If you watch the second Jones-Hopkins fight (on April 3, 2010), that's all Bernard Hopkins. The difference is that, during the passage of time, Roy felt he never needed to employ the tool kit. Bernard, of course, was passionate about learning and amplifying and exercising everything in the tool kit. The amazing thing to me is that Roy *knows* the tool kit. He knows it as well as anybody. He demonstrates that as an expert commentator. He sits there and talks about what normal fighters should do, using the normal craft of boxing. But he never felt compelled to use any of that throughout his own career."

For some, the best of Roy Jones Jr. was on display the night he picked apart fellow future Hall of Famer James Toney to win a wide unanimous decision on November 18, 1994. For others, it was his utter domination of Vinny Pazienza en route to scoring a sixth-round stoppage on June 24, 1995. The highlight of Jones' deconstruction of Paz was a sequence in which, holding onto the top ring rope with his right glove, he fired eight consecutive left hooks in a machine-gun burst, all eight connecting with the target's increasingly busted-up face. It was an expression of creativity akin to a musical genius who spontaneously reproduces a rhythm in his head only he can hear. Think Miles Davis at the Newport Jazz Festival, Ray Charles at the Apollo, Count Basie at Carnegie Hall.

Said Seth Abraham, then-president of HBO Sports: "George Foreman (who did color commentary for Jones-Pazienza) told me after that fight only Roy fights like a great jazzman plays. He improvises. He does riffs. I thought that was such an insightful way to describe Roy Jones."

For a majority of fight fans, however, the most lasting memory of Roy Jones Jr. came on March 1, 2003, when the man who began his pro career as a middleweight and won a world championship in that division, later adding super middleweight and light heavyweight titles, boldly moved up to heavyweight to challenge the much-larger but less-skilled WBA champion, John Ruiz. There was a school of thought that Ruiz was too big and strong for Jones and another that Jones' speed and mobility would surely carry the day because talent is usually a more precious commodity than size.

It was, of course, no contest as Jones – who went off as a 2-1 favorite – darted in and out, pounding on the bewildered Ruiz as if he were just another heavy bag in the challenger's Pensacola gym. The margins of victory on the official scorecards – eight, six and four points – scarcely reflected the level of Jones' dominance.

But, as is sometimes the case, the showcase conquest of Ruiz actually marked the beginning of the end of Jones as a larger-than-life source of wonderment. Curiously, at age 34 he elected to return to light heavyweight instead of a more sensible reduction to cruiserweight. While it had been a bit of a chore to bulk up the right way to 193 pounds for the weigh-in for Ruiz (he was 199 the morning of the fight), paring 20-plus pounds of muscle was infinitely more taxing. In retrospect, it now seems apparent that Jones was never the same after the happy glow of his rout of Ruiz subsided.

"He took 31 pounds of muscle off (that figure might be a tad excessive) and that can't be done without a residue of damage," Lampley said. "It just can't be done, and he suffered from that, maybe permanently. I don't know what his thought process was, why he thought it was important to come all the way back down to light heavyweight. I certainly get it that he was never a natural heavyweight. For him to remain in the heavyweight division would have been an aberration. I guess he figured that, as a big-name fighter, for him to fight at cruiserweight, which was not a prestigious weight class at the time, would be like saying, 'I'm going to go over here in the back closet and fight where you won't see me.' Maybe that was an option that was not acceptable to him."

In his first post-Ruiz fight, Jones retained his light heavyweight titles on a disputed majority decision over Antonio Tarver. He followed that with a two-round TKO loss to Tarver in the second of their three fights, but that could be dismissed as a bolt of lightning that occasionally can fell even elite fighters. But it was in his next

15

outing, on September 25, 2004, against Glen Johnson, that it became apparent to all that Roy Jones Jr. had descended from on high into the ranks of the merely mortal. Johnson, a fringe contender whose willingness to mix it up superseded his good but hardly remarkable talent, gave Jones a taste of his own butt-kicking medicine until he literally knocked him cold to win on a ninth-round KO.

For Lampley, it was like a repeat of another fight from another time, when Jones' magnificent stylistic predecessor suffered a similar head-on crash with boxing's crueler realities.

"The night that Ali fought Larry Holmes (October 2, 1980) at Caesars Palace in Las Vegas) I heard – and I'll never forget it – the greatest single line of boxing commentary ever, and it came from someone who wasn't involved in boxing," Lampley recalled. "I was in the executive suite at ABC in New York, watching the fight, which was one of the sport's rites of passage. We all know the culture of boxing, the old giving way to the new. Ali vs. Holmes was just such a rite of passage. It had to happen the way it happened.

"In the late rounds, when Holmes was beating Ali to a pulp, I got a little jab to my rib cage. I looked to my right and it was Mick Jagger. Mick said to me, `Lamps, you know what we're watching?' And I said, `No, Mick, what are we watching?' He said, `It's the end of our youth.' And it wasn't just that for us, but for the whole audience."

The night that Jones, who once had towered over boxing as if he were the Colossus of Rhodes, was pummeled by Johnson reminded Lampley as no fight ever had of Ali-Holmes. Nothing would ever be quite the same again.

"How else could a relatively ordinary fighter, albeit one with a big heart and a big motor like Glen Johnson, knock the great Roy Jones into next week the way he did? That was not the Roy Jones we had seen before. It was a different person."

But, as Sugar Ray Leonard noted, it is human nature to think of ourselves as the best we ever were. The Roy Jones Jr. who will answer the opening bell against Sigmon will have his hands low, leaning back from punches instead of stepping to the side because that is who he was at his best. To do otherwise would be a concession to mortality, an acknowledgment that all glory is fleeting, and perhaps his last waltz around the ring will turn out better than it did for Tyson and for Hopkins. But whether it does or doesn't, his enshrinement into the IBHOF in Canastota, New York, is assured.

"What I don't understand is why, once the handwriting was on the wall – Glen Johnson, Danny Green, Denis Ledbedev – he kept going after that," Lampley said of Jones' refusal to leave the arena when so many were urging him to do so. "That's what I don't understand, and never will. He's never tried to explain it to me and I'm too respectful of him to have pressed the issue. I did at one point say to him, 'I think you're hurting your legacy and you're not accomplishing anything here.' He basically said to me, 'That's my business, not yours.' So I said, 'OK.'

"When it comes right down to it, I think there's a part of Roy Jones who still thinks, and always will, that he's still *that* Roy Jones, despite all evidence to the contrary. And he's earned the right to think that way."

Teddy Atlas and His Dad Really Have Served to Help Hold Up The World
TheSweetScience.com, November 25, 2014

STATEN ISLAND, N.Y.

Marcus Welby was a doctor who knew his patients on a first-name basis, regularly made house calls and never seemed to be concerned about getting paid for his ministrations. He was, of course, a fictional character, portrayed by *Father Knows Best* actor Robert Young in the television series that ran from 1969 to '76.

But there was a real-life Marcus Welby, and he dispensed his time, more than a little of his own money and especially his genuine concern for his patients, especially the poor, and even more especially the children of the poor. His name was Dr. Theodore A. Atlas Sr. and his well of compassion must have seemed bottomless to those residents of this comparatively unglamorous borough of New York City who seldom are served much when life's better things are handed out.

Here are some facts about Dr. Atlas that weren't glimpsed even on episodes of *Marcus Welby, M.D.* He waded through snow drifts and climbed through windows to deliver babies during winter's worst storms; he went into the projects to provide needed medical services while other physicians refused to go there, and on Wednesdays he used blankets and pillows to make makeshift beds in his office and performed tonsillectomies on patients who could not afford to pay for surgery. It was not unusual to see him with pajamas under his working clothes because he never made it home after a late-night emergency house call.

And when even those efforts proved to be inadequate to care for the masses that had come to depend on him, Dr. Atlas founded two hospitals whose first mission is not to ascertain how much and how soon their patients will be able to pay for the treatment they receive.

It would be easy to surmise that, in this cynical world, there isn't anyone around with a heart and a purpose as pure as that demonstrated in the 55 years in which Dr. Atlas, who was 88 when he died in 1994, served humanity in general and specifically his fellow citizens of Staten Island. But such a supposition would be incorrect.

Theodore A. Atlas Jr. – most people know him as Teddy – is not a physician, but through the magic of TV he is better known than his father ever was, and maybe even more so than Dr. Welby was when the late Robert Young was delivering scripted lines of dialogue instead of babies, and making viewers wish their own doctor was somehow more like the kindly guy who came into their living rooms on the small screen each week.

Teddy Atlas, 58, has been inducted into three Halls of Fame (the New Jersey Boxing Hall of Fame, World Boxing Hall of Fame in California and the Staten Island Sports Hall of Fame). He has been a noted trainer of world champion boxers (Mike Tyson, Michael Moorer, Wilfred Benitez, Barry McGuigan, Junior Jones, Joey Gamache, Simon Brown, Donny Lalonde, Alexander Povetkin) and, since 1988, is the heavily accented voice of ESPN's *Friday Night Fights*. The Boxing Writers Association of America named him Trainer of the Year in 1994, as well as the recipient of the award for excellence in broadcast journalism in 2001.

But, more than anything, Teddy Atlas is proud to be the son and namesake of a man whose greatness was achieved out of the spotlight, and who performed his countless good deeds without much, if any, thought as to how much credit he would receive.

The Dr. Theodore A. Atlas Foundation, established in 1997, has continued to make Staten Island a better place for those who sometimes find themselves in desperate circumstances. And Teddy

Atlas, whose youthful indiscretions – dropping out of high school, occasional brushes with the law – were not reflective of the upbringing of which he is now so fiercely proud, has embellished his father's legacy by continuing to serve the community he loved with humility, devotion, and the sincere belief that what is bad can often be transformed into something good.

They held the 18th annual "Teddy Dinner" here Thursday night at the Staten Island Hilton Garden Inn, and as usual the big banquet hall was filled by those who want to share in and contribute to the vision of Dr. Atlas and the son who has made it his own. The Dr. Theodore A. Atlas Foundation has funded wheelchair ramps for the elderly and disabled, purchased medical equipment when a person's health insurance has refused to cover it, and paid for a sick child's parents to travel with the child when the right medical care can only be provided away from home. The Foundation also has created and operated the Atlas Cops & Kids Boxing Program, run incentive programs in schools to encourage and motivate students, and distributed turkeys on Thanks giving and toys on Christmas to families who do not have the financial resources to properly celebrate the holidays.

The swells were there, as usual – athletes (John McEnroe, Iran Barkley, Al Leiter, Sean Landeta, Amani Toomer, et al), actors (Rosie Perez, Holt McCallany, Tony "Paulie Walnuts" Sirico, Carmine Giovinazzo), politicians and captains of industry – as well as just plain folks who considered their $200-a-plate ticket price to be an investment in the future of their community. But whatever their status, they came in part because of Dr. Atlas, who has become a local legend, and more so because of Teddy Atlas, who refused to allow that legend to fade away.

"I just figured that a man who cared that much about people should be remembered after dedicating his life the way he did after all those years," Teddy has said of his father. "If you live the right life, you're remembered, and in that way you're never gone."

In addition to the aforementioned charitable acts, the Atlas Foundation also has founded and paid the operating expenses of seven boxing gyms in New York, which is Teddy Atlas' way of putting his own imprimatur on the mission his father undertook so many years ago. But, while those gyms have produced some excellent prospects – chief among them light heavyweight Marcus

Browne, who represented the United States at the 2012 London Olympics and is now 12-0 with nine knockouts as a pro – Atlas stressed that the gyms' primary purpose is to create champions in life, not necessarily champions in the ring.

"A lot of years ago there was a kid, he was 15 years old," Atlas said. "He got lost. People get lost sometimes. He was a great kid, but he got lost and he got into a bad place. He got killed in the streets. So it doesn't matter if he was a great kid, 'cause he's dead.

"I was at his funeral. A few years after that, somebody came up to me and asked if I'd subsidize boxing gyms. It cost a bit of money. I said yes – not to make champion fighters, (although) we do have a kid I'm so proud of, and I love him, Marcus Browne, who went on to the Olympics. But that's not why I subsidize the gyms. I do that because of the day of that funeral. I always thought that if they had gyms back then, and I had gotten that kid into a gym, he wouldn't have gotten lost. He might have gotten found.

"That's what our gyms do. They find people. They help good kids that wind up in bad places. They help them find themselves through the direction, through the confidence, through the pride (of boxing). It gives them a reason to care about themselves when they've lost that reason. It makes them feel good. It makes them understand that they can depend on themselves, that they have that kind of inner strength."

Words, of course, mean so much. But a living, breathing example of what you're speaking about means even more.

"We had a kid who, two years ago, he was lost," Atlas continued. "Through his own words he was drinking a bottle of vodka a day, and his only friends were drug dealers and gang members. Another good kid, but it didn't matter. He was lost. But then he walked into one of your gyms -- I call it your gyms, because they are. And he got found. He's a kid who would make any father in this room proud of who he is, and who he's become. His name is Matty. I'm so proud of you, Matty, because you validate the reason we spend the money on those gyms. You make us right."

Asked to stand and take a bow, Matty, the lost kid who got found, received an ovation that seemed likely to forever keep him from the downward spiral in which he once seemed trapped.

"When you look around today's world and this country, there's a lot to be concerned about," Atlas continued. "Maybe the biggest concern is not knowing what you can depend on anymore. Even our pastimes, the things that are supposed to distract us and give us a temporary escape, like our sports, can give us concerns sometimes. My sport, as powerful and as honest and as testing as that squared circle, the ring, can be, it also can leave you wondering at times. But then comes nights like this – 18 years of nights like this. And what does that tell you? Actually, nothing new. Sometimes you don't really learn nothin' new. You just need to be reminded of something old.

"For me, it's about my business – boxing. If you're in it long enough, you learn it's really not the speed or the power or how good your chin is that decides how great you're going to be. It's something else. It's something that has nothing to do with genetics, race, ethnicity, even religion. It's something that's been here since man has been here. It's something that's available in the richest and the poorest neighborhoods, in double-parent homes and in single ones, on Park Avenue or in the Bowery. It's our ability to decide how we're going to behave. No matter how difficult the fight, it's always your choice. Do we behave like a winner, or behave like a loser? Pretty simple, pretty powerful.

"Once again, on display here tonight, is a room of people who always decide to be champions. I love you all. You do so much."

I turned to see a tear forming in the corner of the eye of a lady seated to my left. And I suspect she wasn't the only one to get misty. As an orator, Teddy Atlas might not have just delivered the Gettysburg Address, but his words nonetheless carried a significant impact. Those words strengthened the Foundation, and touched a spot in the hearts of attendees that can only result in a stronger, more caring community.

In Greek mythology, Atlas was the Titan who held up the weight of the world on his broad shoulders. In that context, Dr. Theodore A. Atlas Sr. and his son are as aptly named as anyone ever has been. But the weight they have borne and are still bearing isn't so terribly heavy because, when you think about it, what could be more uplifting that helping others?

That which does not kill us makes us stronger.
*Friedrich Nietzsche

Boxers, even those who never heard of Nietzsche, the 19th century German philosopher/existentialist, are at least somewhat familiar with the aforementioned precept. To survive in that most unforgiving of sports cauldrons, the ring, a boxer has to physically and mentally condition himself to accept pain of all sorts and to battle through it. Those who can combine skill with a high tolerance for discomfort are venerated not only by action-craving fight fans, but by other scarred practitioners of the pugilistic arts. They understand, more than anyone, that those who can take it as well as dish it out have a chance to develop into something special.

At 50 and with a still-handsome face that has taken on a rugged quality with the passage of time and the addition of the obligatory professional nicks, three-time former world champion Bobby Czyz bears as least some semblance to the unmarked visage of the teenaged "Matinee Idol" who so captivated the public in the 1980s. That Bobby Czyz had it all, or seemed to. He was being groomed for superstardom and all that goes with it – the television exposure, the hefty purses, the parade of attractive women who sought to lay him out, in their own fashion, as much as did his gloved opponents.

It wasn't until much later, when he chose to discuss the dysfunctional childhood he and his younger brothers, Vince and Tony, had to endure at the hands of a compulsively demanding father, that the flip side of Czyz's feel-good story was finally revealed. But, in retrospect, could the satisfaction of the future champion's greatest successes even been possible without the terror that preceded them?

"There's nothing you can throw at me that I can't handle," Czyz said of the hard edge he developed from the ongoing ordeal he was obliged to endure on an almost daily basis from Robert Edward Czyz Sr., who committed suicide on June 12, 1983. "Is that a good thing for me? Probably, but look what I had to go through to get to where I am now."

Czyz now has no problems revisiting less savory aspects of his past, but, understandably, his preference is to harken back to happier times. Those memories aren't just pleasant, they're probably therapeutic.

"My first pro fight was on TV, which is normally not the case," recalled Czyz, who compiled a 44-8 record, with 28 victories inside the distance, in a career that ran from 1980 to '98. "ESPN was still fairly new; they had done an interview with me and somebody there said they were going to hitch their cart to Bobby Czyz's tail, or maybe vice versa. Their thinking was, here's this middle-class kid from the suburbs, a straight-A student, who probably shouldn't even be a fighter. Fighters are supposed to be minorities, from the wrong side of the tracks, downtrodden, trying to rise above their circumstances. It was just a story they bought into."

It was a story that had a nice long run, too. Czyz, the North Jersey boy who was as erudite as a college professor but could bang like Jake LaMotta, was fortunate enough to have come along when there were three or four fight cards in the state almost every weekend. Boxing was huge in New Jersey then, and Czyz was its favorite son. He was an Arturo Gatti-sized drawing card in Atlantic City before Gatti bloomed into the full flower of his popularity there a decade and a half later.

"Gatti probably was a little more exciting, but Bobby was right there with him in terms of having an incredibly loyal fan base," said Henry Hascup, executive director of the New Jersey Boxing Hall of Fame, which inducted Czyz in 1998. "I remember when Bobby was coming up in the amateurs. Even then, he had girls all over him. There was a reason why he was known as 'The Matinee Idol.' But let's not forget, he could really fight. Nobody could make Bobby Czyz quit."

As might be expected, Czyz remembers his halcyon period fondly. "My favorite day is September 6, 1986, the day I won my first world title," he said of the night at the Las Vegas Hilton when he captured the IBF light heavyweight belt on a fifth-round stoppage of Slobodan Kacar, who had won an Olympic gold medal for Serbia at the 1980 Moscow Games.

"In 1986 and '87, wherever I went, I was recognized. I was pampered, catered to. People were sucking up to me all over the place. It was great."

But fame is like a drug, and the high produced by any drug doesn't last forever. "You can lose perspective sometimes," Czyz admitted. "I remember one time I was in Haledon, New Jersey, near Paterson, not too far from where I grew up. Everybody in the area knew me. I walked into this restaurant and said, `I'm Bobby Czyz. I have a reservation.' The maître d' says, `It'll be about 20 minutes. You can wait over there.' After about 30 minutes, I went back and the guy tells me he's sorry, but it'll be another 10 to 15 minutes.

"For a split second I thought, `Don't they know who I am?' Then I said to myself, `You asshole. You're an asshole when you start to think you're better than everyone else. Even if you're a world champion.'"

And especially if you have been bullied almost from birth by someone who is supposed to love you, someone who has made it clear in any number of ways that no matter how highly you achieve, it's not good enough.

If you gaze for long into the abyss, the abyss gazes also into you
*Nietzsche

Bobby Czyz remembers the two filled bookshelves in his childhood home in East Orange, New Jersey. It was there that his father, a bright, compulsive individual without a matching academic resume, thought that he could unlock the secrets of the universe and will what he had learned upon his young children.

"We had two complete sets of encyclopedias, volumes one through 28 for each," Czyz noted. "We had books by Nietzsche, a ton of biographies of great people, great philosophers. And my dad read them all – *twice*. He was obsessed with being omniscient."

For those without a handy dictionary, "omniscience" is a word that means the capacity to know everything that can be known. It represents a quest for mental perfection, a state of absolute knowledge that is, of course, impossible for any human being to achieve.

"I not only read Nietzsche, I *lived* Nietzsche," said Czyz, who has an IQ of 135 and is a member of Mensa, an organization open to those with genius-level intelligence. "I think what he was looking for drove him nuts. I don't know how else to put it. My dad was a sociopath. He probably was insane."

24

But while the father, a district sales manager for the Yellow Pages, passed along some favorable genes to his kids, all of whom were advanced-placement students, his quest for perfection also extended into the physical. He was determined that his sons would not only be sharp of mind, but of body, even if he had to break them to do it.

"We were forced into boxing, plain and simple," Czyz said. "It was demanded of us. It wasn't as if we had a choice. I was 10, Vincent was nine and Tony was seven. We were told in no uncertain terms that we were going to the gym, and we would box until my father decided we didn't have to do it anymore.

"His rationale for that was fairly simply, at least in his mind. He likened young boys to malleable steel that needed be shaped and hammered to mold their character. He wanted us beaten into sharp blades. My father wanted us to come out of the chute as men. We weren't allowed to just be little boys."

Technically, the Czyz brothers didn't begin to be trained as boxers until they moved to Wanaque, New Jersey, in 1972, when Bobby was 10. But the pain began years earlier, as Bobby recalled. "My father began teaching me the basics of boxing when I was four," he said. "I have video of it. He was smacking me in the face. `Get your hands up, do this, do that.' It was crazy."

Although all three Czyz boys accomplished much at the amateur level, Bobby was the only one to stick with boxing after their father, somewhat inexplicably, decided in 1977 that they could quit if they wanted to. Then again, Bobby was the only one who had decided that there were places two hard fists and a good mind could take him that a good mind alone might not.

"East Orange was predominately black and Hispanic," Czyz said. "I was the tough white kid. There were 32 in my class when I was 10 years old, only four of whom were white. Guess who had to fight every day on his way to and from school? But that was no big deal. It was part of my life. I really didn't care. I actually kind of liked it. When my father told us we were moving to Wanaque, I didn't want to go.

"We probably never would have left East Orange, but the principal called my parents and told them my siblings and I were too advanced for the curriculum and that we needed to go into a better school system to maximize our potential."

But while Wanaque represented a new start for the family, some things remained constant for Bobby.

"Wanaque was a predominately white suburb, but I had the city in me," he said. "And I was the new guy. So guess what? I got into a lot of fights there, too. Within weeks, everybody knew that I could fight because I had beaten the crap out of everybody who mistakenly thought they could take me.

"You know how these things get started. My hair was a little longer than their's, my clothes were a little different. Somebody would say, `So you think you're a tough guy?' And I'd say `I know I'm a tough guy.' And the fight would be on."

Always the stern hand of his father was evident. The Czyz boys had to win, at whatever they attempted. Nothing less than total victory was acceptable in the father's eyes.

"I remember Vince getting beaten up by a kid the same age as him," Bobby said. "He came home with a busted lip, a black eye. My father said, `What happened?' Vince told him he had gotten into a fight with a kid named Jimmy, and he lost. I saw that fight but I was not allowed to jump in because they were the same age. That was the rule. If it had been a bigger, older kid, it would have been OK for me to get involved.

"My father trained Vince for two weeks, after which he told him to go to Jimmy's house, knock on the door and, no matter who answered it, say he wanted to see Jimmy outside because they were going to fight again. And if the answer was no, for Vince to go back every day and say the same thing.

"Jimmy's mother answers the door and Vince says, `I want to fight Jimmy.' She says OK. They went out on the lawn and, this time, Vince beat the crap out of Jimmy. And that was enough to satisfy my father."

He who has a why to live bear almost any how
*Nietzsche

Czyz still has difficult sorting out his myriad feelings toward his father. He said he and his brothers were "tortured, physically, mentally and emotionally," but, as is sometimes the case, much of the good things in life, including his boxing career, sprang from misery.

26

"My father taught me," Czyz said. "He taught me all the time. He'd say, 'Don't do what I do, do what I say. I'm not perfect. I have flaws. Take my good and keep it, take my bad and throw it away.' But if you pointed out his bad, he would beat the crap out of you.

"I had a fear of heights. Still do. But I don't let that fear stop me from doing what I need to do. I've jumped out of airplanes, on purpose, twice, parachuting in Arizona. I did it after my boxing career was over because I didn't want to risk hurting myself so that I couldn't fight anymore.

"How did I conquer my fear of heights, or at least control it? My father took me to the tallest tree in the neighborhood. It had to be 80 feet, higher than the tops of the surrounding buildings. He said, 'Climb the tree.' I said, 'How far up?' He said, 'Until I say so.'

"I'm 10 years old, and I'm holding onto that tree so tight I thought I'd break it. I was shaking and crying. Then my dad looked up and said, 'Who won, you or the tree?' I said, 'I did.' And he said, 'That's right, and it's because you were more afraid of taking a beating from me than falling out of the tree. Now come down.'"

The same do-or-die approach was used at the community swimming pool where a 12-year-old Bobby Czyz, who couldn't swim, was tossed into the deep end by his father.

"If you can't swim, there's a fear of drowning that comes over you and won't let go," Czyz said. "Why was my dad doing this to me? But I paddled, screamed and finally made it to the side of the pool where I could climb out. He said, 'Who won? You or the water?' I said, 'I did.' He asked me why that was. I said, 'Because I was afraid of dying.' And he said, 'Exactly.'"

Some of the elder Czyz's lessons, however, he didn't take unto himself. When he took his own life in an act of desperation or madness, his family was left with so many recriminations that it would take a platoon of psychiatrists to sort them all out.

"When he died, I felt a lot of guilt. I probably drank myself to sleep for four or five weeks," Czyz said. "For seven years I couldn't get rid of the nightmares, the horror that was going through my head. My heart would be racing. I'd wake up in a cold sweat. Sometimes it would be multiple times a week, sometimes only once or twice a month, but it always happened.

"I used self-hypnosis to finally get through it. Whenever my dad would show up in one of my nightmares, I programmed myself to subconsciously say, `Wake up, idiot. He's dead. He can't hurt you anymore.' Then I'd wake up, the nightmare would be over and I could get some peaceful sleep."

A Fistful of Kindness
Philadelphia Daily News, January 12, 2002

Wanda Little said it was "heart-wrenching" when her younger children talked about pooling their pocket change to buy her one of the nice, four-bedroom houses being built across the street in Sinking Spring, Pennsylvania, a Reading suburb.

"My babies, they saw that new development going up," said the widow of former WBA super middleweight champion Steve Little, who was 34 when he died of colon cancer on January 30, 2000. "They'd ask me, `Mommy, when are we going to move over there?' It hurt me to my heart …

"They're good kids. The younger ones, they just don't understand that things can't always be the way you want them to be. We never had much before, but when Steve died, our situation got much worse.

"We just try to make ends meet, but it's difficult. We live from month to month off $1,700 in Social Security. It's always a matter of robbing Peter to pay Paul."

The Littles' financial straits will be eased thanks to undisputed middleweight champion Bernard "The Executioner" Hopkins, who told the *Daily News* yesterday he would make a six-figure donation to the family from the purse for his title defense against Carl Daniels on February 2 at the Sovereign Center in Reading.

"You hope for a miracle, but miracles don't happen," Little said. "This thing that Bernard is doing is a miracle. It's a godsend. I'm just crying for joy now."

Hopkins wanted to go for a potential record 15th successful title defense in his hometown of Philadelphia, but all the major venues were booked, so promoter Don King chose Reading.

"When I found out the fight might be in Reading, the first thing I thought about was Steve Little," Hopkins said from his training camp in Miami. "Reading is Steve Little's town. Team Hopkins is going to make a substantial donation – six figures – to Steve's family.

28

"There wasn't anybody who didn't love Steve, who was just a genuinely good person. I never heard anybody say a bad word about him. He was a good fighter, but a better person. I always think of him as a hero, because he always did right by his wife and kids."

Wanda Little had been resigned to the fact her family would not be living in one of those new houses. She also understood they would have to move somewhere not as nice as the three-bedroom town house she shared with Steve and their six children, who range in age from seven to 14.

"This place is not big enough," she said of her tidy, but cramped rental unit. "The cheapest four-bedroom house to rent around here is, like, $800 a month, and I don't know how I was going to do it.

"Sure, you can rent a house for $400, but it's somewhere in the midst of drugs and what have you. I don't want that for my kids. I didn't know what I was going to do. All you can do is pray."

Hopkins (40-2-1, 29 KOs), who trained with Little at Champ's Gym in North Philadelphia, said he wants the focus for the fight with Daniels (47-3-1, 30 KOs) to be less about his bid to supplant Carlos Monzon in the record books for most successful middleweight title defenses and more about celebrating Little's life.

"I know what it's like to struggle to get what you're worth in this boxing business," said Hopkins, who earned a career-high $2.7 million in his electrifying, 12th-round technical knockout of Felix Trinidad at New York's Madison Square Garden on September 29 of last year. He will make approximately the same for the February 2 fight, which will be televised by HBO.

"Steve was a world champion who didn't benefit nearly enough from winning the title."

Little, who utilized every ounce of his boxing ability, compiled an unremarkable 25-17-3 record, with just six knockout victories, from 1983 to '98. For most of those years, he needed outside jobs to supplement his ring earnings.

"When he didn't have a match scheduled, he worked," Wanda Little said. "He was the breadwinner. Me, I knew nothing of being in the work force. I was here at home with the children.

"People thought Steve had a lot of money, because he carried himself like a champion, but when he'd get a fight, his purse would go to the bills from the times when he wasn't fighting. We were always trying to catch up. We never got to a point where we could say we were actually ahead."

Little's moment in the spotlight came February 26, 1994, when, as a 40-to-1 underdog, he scored a shockingly easy decision over Michael Nunn in London to capture the WBA super middleweight championship.

Little received a career-high $100,000 purse for his first defense, but was dethroned by Frankie Liles six months after winning the title and never again got a whiff at big money. He hoped to remain in boxing as a trainer, but was diagnosed with cancer in February 1999.

His many friends rallied to aid his family, but most of what was raised – such as $2,000 promoter Damon Feldman donated from a benefit card – helped stave off creditors for only a short time.

Hopkins' tribute to Steve Little will add to what figures to be a special night in Reading, which is not especially a hotbed of boxing.

The 9,000-seat Sovereign Center snagged the high-profile bout because the First Union Center and First Union Spectrum are hosting a Phantoms game and monster-truck show, respectively; the Liacouras is the site of a nationally televised Temple-Saint Joseph's basketball game, and the Pennsylvania Convention Center will be prepping for the NBA Jam Session as part of the following week's All-Star Game festivities.

"If I had a magic wand and could put the fight in Philly, I would," Hopkins said. "But sometimes circumstances are beyond your control. Anyway, things happen for a reason."

Epilogue: Bernard Hopkins was pitching a shutout on the judges' scorecards when he stopped the game but outclassed Daniels in the 10th round for his 15th successful defense of his 160-pound title, on his way to extending his division record to 20, since matched by Gennadiy Golovkin. Hopkins said he later heard that a "slick operator," promising to double, through investments, a large portion of the $200,000 he had presented to Wanda Little, had bilked her out of $100,000 in something B-Hop likened to a Ponzi scheme. In any case, Steve Little remains a beloved figure in his hometown, revered by many including his son, Steve Little Jr., who joined the Marine Corps and served with distinction.

Jimmy Lennon Jr., In His Father's Image
The Ring, June 2013 issue

Had Jimmy Lennon Jr. followed that well-worn other family path, he might now be singing for his supper or at least tickling the ivories for it. He is a cousin of the forever wholesome Lennon Sisters, who harmonized for years on *The Lawrence Welk Show,* and is also a blood relative of the Lennon Brothers, of whom his late father, Jimmy Lennon Sr., was a high-note-hitting Irish tenor. Some of his male cousins are members of a still-active pop band called Venice.

"The Lennon family is incredibly talented with singing," said Jimmy Jr., who, at 54, still appears to be as age-resistant as was America's Oldest Teenager, Dick Clark. "My father married someone (the former Doris Link) who also was gifted in that area. Mom studied vocal at Julliard, so there are very rich singing genes in my family.

"Maybe there was a little bit of intimidation with all the great singing that was around me as I was growing up. (He is the youngest of five children.) But the music gene didn't totally pass me up. I can play several instruments pretty well, especially keyboard. I was in a band in high school."

But Lennon Jr. – he always uses the "Junior" out of respect for his father – nonetheless makes his living, and a well-compensated one at that, with his vocal chords. Most people know him as one of the world's two most famous living ring announcers, the other being Michael Buffer, whose style is as different from Lennon's as Elvis Presley's would be from Bing Crosby's. Buffer is male-model handsome (one of his former occupations), dramatic of presentation and larger-than-life of personality. Lennon is the boy next door liked by everyone, with an announcing style that might be described as understated flair. At work, Lennon, the ring announcer for *Showtime Championship Boxing,* comfortably wears tuxedos, but it never seems as if he *lives* in them, which might be the case with Buffer, HBO's house announcer.

"Jimmy gives just enough flair to it," said a longtime family friend and occasional employer, Hall of Famer matchmaker/promoter Don Chargin. "He doesn't overdo it. He's such a terrific, humble kid, and I think that comes through."

31

John Beyrooty, the former boxing writer for the now-defunct *Los Angeles Herald-Examiner* and the former publicist for Forum Boxing, once described Lennon's style as "classy and simple."

Even Jimmy Jr. himself allows that, in transitioning from his rock-steady everyday persona, a certain metamorphosis is required to elevate his game. In an October 6, 1991, profile in the *Los Angeles Times*, the subject of the piece said, "To be a good announcer you have to be in charge. When I put on my tuxedo and walk from my car to the arena, I change. I've got to make a show of it."

It is a transformation that is eerily reminiscent of Jimmy Sr., the most recognizable ring announcer ever to step between the ropes in Los Angeles and throughout Southern California. There are numerous boxing fans in the region who insist that Jimmy Jr. is the living, breathing incarnation of his father, which the son considers to be the ultimate compliment. If there is a difference between them, it is that Jimmy Jr. will be enshrined in the International Boxing Hall of Fame in Canastota, New York, on June 9, an honor that was bestowed upon Buffer in 2012 but to date has yet to be granted the elder Lennon.

"It will be emotional," Jimmy Jr. said of his expected reaction to the day he officially joins a highly exclusive IBHOF club that includes only Buffer and the late Joe Humphreys, who was 73 when he died in 1936. Still waiting for a posthumous call to the hall are Lennon Sr. and celebrated New York-based ring announcers Johnny Addie and Harry Balogh.

"My father was so proud of me, I can't even put it into words," Jimmy Jr. continued. "When I got my first megafight, which was Mike Tyson-Buster Douglas in Tokyo in 1990, he literally had tears in his eyes when I told him.

"When he was in the hospital (Jimmy Sr. was 79 when he died of heart failure in April 1992) they didn't have cable TV, but he wanted to hear my announcing of that fight. My mother would call him at his hospital bed and hold the phone by the TV so he could hear my announcing. When I got back from Japan, he told me how thrilled he was. But he was always like that. When I was announcing fights at the Forum, when I came over afterwards, he'd be sleeping in his chair, wake up and he'd have these notes he wanted to go over with me about my announcing. They were always positive."

Now it is time for Jimmy Jr. to speak with moist eyes and the sort of unconditional love that exists between parent and child when their relationship is as strong as was the one between Jimmy Sr. and the son who followed in his large footsteps.

"He died before I became associated with Showtime, and the 'It's Showtime!' tag line," Jimmy Jr. said. "I think he would have been really happy with that. And now this (induction into the IBHOF). It's just the ultimate.

"So, yeah, (the induction) will be very emotional for me. It'll also be surreal. It's certainly not something I set out to achieve or made a goal. To look back on all the blessings I've received, it'll be a grateful moment, too. There are very few ring announcers who are in the International Boxing Hall of Fame, which brings me to a little bit of an awkward point. I really feel that my father should be in there. I would like to address that (in his acceptance remarks), but not in an inappropriate way.

"My dad was a great, great ring announcer who set the standard in so many ways, but there wasn't the sort of television coverage of the sport then as there is now. I travel all over the world, and my announcing is seen and heard in many countries. My dad's work was in and around Los Angeles, although he did some traveling, primarily to Las Vegas. My role is so much different."

Somewhat ironically, Jimmy Sr. never set out to become what he became. He expected to sing at a nightclub in 1943, but when he arrived at the venue, he discovered that the evening's entertainment had been switched from music to boxing. The management needed someone to serve as the ring announcer and, well, of such twists of fate is history sometimes made.

The slightly built Jimmy Sr. brought a distinctive flourish to the task, which opened the door to a long run as one of the few ring announcers who became as famous – and in some cases even more so – than the main-event fighters he introduced. He manned the microphone in dozens of movies and television shows with boxing themes, including *Raging Bull* and the remake of *Kid Galahad*, with Elvis. And Jimmy Jr. was along for most of the ride.

"His father was truly special," Chargin, then a matchmaker for promoter Aileen Eaton, said of Jimmy Sr.'s ring announcing at Los Angeles' famed Olympic Auditorium. "If there was a bad decision and crowd got unruly, he'd burst into a song and quiet everybody right down. I saw him do that I don't know how many times. I'll never forget the night fans were throwing coins and all kinds of stuff into the ring when Jimmy Sr. started singing a song in Spanish. The tension just lifted.

"When Jimmy Jr. – I still call him Jamie – was a young kid, he'd get in the ring with his dad and announce a few preliminary fights. Father and son were always real close. Jimmy Sr. was very, very proud of him. He'd say, 'There's my successor. He's going to be a great announcer someday.' He told me that a hundred times if he told me once. He really believed that would be the case."

But, deep as his love for his father and for boxing was, Jimmy Jr. had another vision of how his future would unfold. He graduated with a degree in psychology from UCLA and took a job as a teacher at a small private school, a laudable career in which he expected to spend his entire working life. Ring announcing, he now says, was more of a hobby then, something to pick up some extra cash while paying homage to his father's legacy.

"I never wanted to be so reliant on boxing and the whims of promoters and television stations that I might be stuck in a bad place," Jimmy Jr. said. "I wanted to have something I could always fall back on. Being a teacher, to be honest, was much more rewarding in some ways. It was something I considered to be of service to young people. I enjoyed it and I felt that I was doing something important. Announcing was a sidelight and I loved it, so I think it was a nice balance.

"I kept doing both things as long as I could, but it just became too difficult with all the travel in boxing. I just didn't feel it was fair to the school to be away so much."

So here Jimmy Jr. stands, at once the reincarnation of his legendary dad and yet his own man. He not only has filled those large shoes, but outgrown them to some extent.

"For many years I would hear, 'I remember your father,'" Jimmy Jr. said. "I just love that. It's a great compliment when people compare me to him, and it's something I never take for granted.

"But more and more now, which shocked me at first, there are people who come up to me and say, 'I heard that your dad announced, too.' That's such a funny thing to hear.

"As you get older, you begin to take pride in your own accomplishments. I don't know if my statistics, or whatever you'd call them, have surpassed his. Maybe they have. But to me, he'll always be the greatest announcer."

One thing is assured: Jimmy Jr. will never drop the suffix to his name. He made that pledge years ago, and he's kept it. He says he will always keep it.

"One time I was introduced on TV as Jimmy Lennon," Jimmy Jr. recalled. "My father was watching on TV and told me later, 'Boy, while I'm alive, I sure would like for them to have the 'Junior' on there.' So I've always made sure that that was the case, even after my dad died.

"But, you know, it is kind of strange. I really don't feel the need to constantly compare myself to him. I am my own man. I do feel like I learned my trade from the very best, and I happened to get some very good genes, but we are not exactly the same in every way."

One of the things for which both Lennons are known is the precise way in which they announce the names of fighters, referees, judges and boxing officials, especially those with Spanish surnames. It's a big reason the bilingual Jimmy Jr., like his father, is so beloved by Hispanic audiences.

Consider the tale of Jimmy Sr. emceeing a Greek-American awards dinner, with one of the trophies going to a man whose name was -- gulp – Anastasios Honchopathadurkomontorogiotopolous.

"I broke it down into syllables and then put it back together again," Jimmy Sr. told the *Times*, referring to one of his more challenging tasks. The recipient came to the podium after the introduction, kissed Jimmy Sr. on the cheek and said, "You are the only person to pronounce my name correctly since I come to America."

"To have an affinity for languages is important," Jimmy Jr. said. "That was instilled in me by my father. I take the time to talk to the fighters if I don't know them and find out the pronunciation of their names, their nicknames, what hometown they're from – everything that's important to them. They are, after all, the ones putting their lives on the line. There's nothing more sweet to a man's ear than to hear his name pronounced properly."

It is not beyond the realm of possibility that the Lennon legacy will continue well into the future. Jimmy Jr. and wife Christine have two sons, James III, 16, and Alexander, 13, and their father admits to dreaming that one or both will take up his craft as he once took up Jimmy Sr.'s.

"They both love boxing," Jimmy Jr. noted. "All sports, actually. I've thought about it, and how it would really be something for them to (announce) something very low-key, maybe some amateur tournaments. But it's not much on their minds at this point."

If James III and Alexander decide to follow their father into the ring, one can imagine strong but silky voices and perfect pronunciation of all words regardless of language. That's the family tradition.

Epilogue: Jimmy Lennon Jr.'s fond wish was answered when his ring-announcer dad, Jimmy Sr., also was inducted into the IBHOF in the Non-Participant category in 2017, to be followed a year later by Johnny Addie.

Marv Marinovich Had a Son, Not a Science Project
TheSweetScience.com, January 14, 2019

The father, now 79, has a memory being wiped slowly clean by the ravages of Alzheimer's disease, so perhaps he remains oblivious to the horrific damage done to his family by his selfish if perhaps well-intentioned plan for creating an athletically flawless son. Then again, human history should have alerted Marv Marinovich to the folly of conducting scientific experimentation in flesh and blood, an exercise in self-aggrandizement periodically repeated by tyrants and madmen who thought it was all right for them to attempt to play God.

The difference is that slaveholders intent on breeding their finest specimens like cattle, and Hitler's blueprint for creating a master race through a form of mass murder known as ethnic cleansing, did not involve the ongoing infliction of abuse and paralyzing pressure upon someone the obsessed experimenter purported to love more than anyone or anything.

Maybe Marv Marinovich really has loved his son Todd, now 49, whom the father was always intent, even before his wife's pregnancy, on making not just into a quarterback, but one crafted over time to someday represent perfection at the position. But it was not simply for Todd Marinovich's own sake that so much time, effort and money was poured into an ultimately failed project; the

36

companion goal all along was for Marv to be recognized and hailed as the genius he imagined himself to be.

The sad, tragic saga of the Marinoviches has been examined at length at various stages, through alternating moments of giddy highs and plunging lows. But the full extent of what went wrong has been laid bare in the current issue of *Sports Illustrated*, in a comprehensive article authored by Michael Rosenberg. Entitled *Learning to be Human*, it is a follow-up to a similar *SI* story, *Bred to be a Superstar*, that appeared in the magazine's February 22, 1998, issue. Twenty years ago some particulars of Todd's slide from grace, a downward spiral that saw him go from a first-round draft choice of the then-Los Angeles Raiders in 1991 (he was selected ahead of some guy named Brett Favre) and even deeper into drug addiction were mentioned, but so too were elements of the big lie that still persisted at that time. If Todd had not capitalized as much as he might have on the advantages afforded him by his tunnel-visioned and deep-pocketed father, then at least some of the blame had to be his own fault, right?

Genetically well-suited for the kind of success plotted by Marv (more on that later), and relentlessly poked and prodded by the 14 specialists employed by the father, including biochemists and psychologists, to help squeeze every ounce out of the kid's performance potential, Todd eventually was done in by a more gentle side of his nature. An introvert, he liked football well enough, but he found a more satisfying way of expressing himself through his fine arts studies at USC. Then again, Marv hadn't set out to create an improved version of Picasso or Monet, and try as he might no amount of parental bullying was going to instill into the son the same competitive fire that was forever raging inside Daddy Dearest's internal blast furnace. It therefore should not have come as a shock to the psychologists on Team Todd that the young man nicknamed "Robo QB" began self-medicating in high school with all manner of pharmaceuticals, eventually graduating from marijuana to cocaine, LSD and heroin while at USC.

As recently as eight years ago, an emotionally wrecked Todd still was delusional enough to parrot the key element of the big lie, that he had been a willing and even eager participant in a joint venture with his control-freak father that hadn't really been foisted upon him

37

since birth. "Someday people will realize what a genius you are," *Esquire* quoted him as telling Marv.

But now those segments of the big lie that haven't already been exposed as false are being revealed for what they were. The oft-repeated mantra that Todd had *never* consumed any unhealthy fast foods, carbonated beverages or desserts with refined sugar? The kid greedily gorged on Big Macs and Oreos slipped to him on the sly by his maternal grandparents, who wanted the boy to enjoy some small semblance of a "normal" childhood denied him by the son-in-law they also had come to fear. The whopper of a mendacity that Marv, under the guise of raising his only son with a brand of tough love that never crossed the line into brutality? The reality was that Marv smacked Todd around as if he were a sparring partner who was never allowed to strike back or even brook dissent. All it took to initiate a beating was for Marv to determine that Todd had not performed perfectly in that particular day's practice or game, and he never did, at least not to his demanding father's satisfaction.

As the father of two children that he fears he never will be able to raise as well as he knows he should, given that his own life is a perpetual morass of personal weaknesses and jagged scars upon his psyche, Todd at least has come to terms with the realization that continuing to repeat the big lie does no one any good. He now describes his father as a "raging beast" whose dictums he was powerless to reject or resist.

Only some of the facts of the Marinoviches' tortured relationship were available to me when I interviewed Marv, who was then training MMA superstar BJ Penn, in advance of Penn's main-event bout against Kenny Florian for UFC 101 on August 8, 2009, the first such event to be held in the Wachovia (now Wells Fargo) Center in Philadelphia. Penn – who forced Florian to tap out on a rear-naked choke hold in the third round – was effusive in his praise of Marv's somewhat unorthodox techniques.

"Everything happens the way it should. If I had won my last fight (a fourth-round stoppage loss to Georges St. Pierre in UFC 94 on January 31, 2009), I probably wouldn't have wound up with Marv," Penn said. "But being that I did lose, I started thinking about going in another direction. I was frustrated; some people were beginning to question my desire.

"Then some buddies of mine introduced me to Marv, and it's like losing my last fight was a blessing in disguise. I've always trained hard, but I trained like everyone else trained. Marv has opened my eyes to a different way, a better way."

The Marv I interviewed then – by phone, as he had not traveled to Philadelphia with Penn – did not come across as a raging beast. Then again, Penn was merely his client, not the son whom he was doggedly determined to make over into his own image.

"BJ had some definite physical weaknesses," Marv pointed out. "If you compete with weak links, you have to compensate and maybe even overcompensate for those problem areas. It can lead to injuries and stamina issues. Without question it can and does affect overall efficiency.

"They say athletic training in the past was prehistoric. I think it's still prehistoric. Coaches in all sports – basketball, football, baseball, whatever – still believe the ability to lift heavy weights slowly is going to make you explosive and fast and increase limb speed. Nothing can be further from the truth. That's why you don't see boxers do traditional weightlifting. All that does is slow down the rate of muscular contraction. Bench-pressing, squatting and dead-lifting not only puts your body out of balance, it destroys limb speed. If you want to jump high and run fast, lifting heavy weights is not the answer. But people over here (in America) still think that it does. You've got strength-and-conditioning coaches all over the country who cling to the old methods."

The training methods espoused by Marv Marinovich leaned heavily toward those devised by his counterparts in Soviet Bloc countries, which is hardly surprising. His over-the-top, obsessive-compulsive personality might owe in large part to genetic makeup; his Croatian grandfather, J.G. Marinovich, is said to have been in the Russian Army and overseen the battlefield amputation of his own arm. Marv thus was raised to believe that he was from a line that was tougher than tough, so therefore his mission in life was to perpetuate the family tradition of absolute dedication to whichever task its members sought to undertake. And for Marv, the path to the higher purpose that defined his existence was on the football field. He was a starting guard on the USC Trojans' undefeated national championship squad of 1962, a relentlessly driven and vocal leader so intense that his teammates voted him "most inspirational."

It hardly mattered to Marv that his own NFL career with the Oakland Raiders lasted only three disappointing seasons and was marked by frequent injuries stemming from overtraining. He simply would funnel all the hopes and ambitions he once reserved for himself into the son he knew would be special, having specifically selected a USC swimmer, Trudi Fertig, as his bride not only because of her athletic makeup but because she was the sister of his Trojans teammate, quarterback Craig Fertig. How could Marv's yet-unborn son be anything but great with all that going for him, and especially with the expert technical assistance Marv planned to introduce into the child's upbringing?

"It's very sick," Marv's other child, a daughter, Traci, whom he shamefully neglected while solely focusing on Todd, said of a dysfunctional family dynamic that saw the father's volcanic temper erupt with disconcerting regularity. It was one thing for Marv to lash out at strangers with balled fists, quite another when he took out his frustrations on Todd and Trudi, whom he once picked up and threw across a room onto a dining room table. The couple divorced in 1985.

So immersed in the notion of athletic dominance within his family circle was Marv that, when Traci got married in 1988, he refused to give her away and almost skipped the ceremony. His objection: Traci's fiancé, Rick Grove, was not athletic enough. Marv even refused to shake his new son-in-law's hand, or to be there for the births of the three children that Traci bore him.

Imitation being the most common form of flattery, you have to wonder what might have been the result had an undamaged Todd blossomed into the superstar quarterback he was supposed to become instead of the drug-addled head case that now stands as a cautionary tale to all fathers who might otherwise be inclined to follow the Marv Marinovich playbook in the raising of their children. Even as Todd was refining his footwork and arm-angle release of his passes under the watchful eye of the experts brought in by Marv, the Robo QB was emotionally coming apart at the seams, an inevitable dissolution which must have been apparent to everyone but the father. Todd played only eight unspectacular games over two seasons with the Raiders prior to his release, and in 2004 the editors of ESPN.com placed him fourth on their list of all-time sports flops. One ESPN columnist absolved Todd of at least some of the blame, chastising Marv, with ample justification, as one of the worst sports dads ever.

While the road to ruin by the Marinoviches – forget football stardom, Todd may never become a fully functional human being and the Alzheimer's-stricken Marv no longer can bathe himself without assistance or control his bodily functions – represents something of a worst-case scenario, theirs is a story that was, is and again will be played out by others, more than a few of whom have ties to boxing. It is a fine line that separates necessary commitment to the achieving of a goal and borderline insanity, and examples of those who tight-rope walk along that border are legion.

The pitched battles between International Boxing Hall of Fame inductee Wilfred Benitez and his trainer-father, Gregorio, are the stuff of legend and caused Teddy Brenner, the late, great matchmaker at Madison Square Garden, to weigh in on a topic of eternal interest. Just who does or should run the show once a son, so used to acquiescing to his father's unyielding discipline, decides he must live his own life?

"I've noticed it since (Wilfred) won the title and people began to pat him on the back and he realized he was an individual," Brenner said. "Rebellion sets in. It happens all the time in the boxing business between father and son. Never fails."

Former heavyweight contender Gerry Cooney, now 62, had an ironworker father, Tony, whose implementation of parental authority was nearly as stern as Marv Marinovich's, minus the bloated crew of technical advisers. Author Charles Euchner, in an article entitled *The Rise, Fall and Redemption of Gerry Cooney*, examined the conflict faced daily by young Gerry, a gregarious sort who long sought the love of his dad, who either chose not to acknowledge his son's needs or didn't know how to.

"Sons with troubled relationships with fathers struggle to develop their own identity," Euchner wrote. "They desperately want attention and approval, but they also want separation and independence. When they get too far away, they veer back toward their dads, no matter how much pain they get for the effort."

Said Cooney, of his subsequent battles with depression, alcoholism and drugs, twisted relationships and squandered possibilities: "(Tony) would belt me with his hands, his belt. How do you do that to your kids? He drank and was very physical. He kept us under control. He kept us (Gerry is one of Tony's eight kids, including three brothers) separated. We all had different hiding places. Mine was in the basement."

It is a terrible thing when a bond that should have been based in love takes on the trappings of hatred, even if the end result is not always totally negative. Rosalio Pacquiao, father of Manny, took his son's dog away from him, cooked it and ate it in front of him, inciting a traumatized Manny years later to run away on a ship headed to Manila where he turned to boxing. Fernando Vargas and James Toney so detested their absentee fathers that they imagined every opponent to be the man who had abandoned them, further fueling their desire to inflict beatdowns; and Shane Mosley, Roy Jones Jr. and Floyd Mayweather Jr. all fired their trainer-dads.

Nor is Marv Marinovich's smothering obsession a detrimental trait exclusive to fathers who were absent the day patience, understanding and compassion were handed out. Masha Godkin, now a psychologist specializing in counseling performers, remembers what it was like to be constantly dragged to auditions by a stage mother who wanted to live out her dreams through a daughter who simply wanted a regular childhood.

"I felt if I didn't get roles, I wasn't good enough," Godkin said. "Everything revolved around pleasing my mother. She wanted to be an actress. She assumed I did, too."

Few if any magazine articles about sports are as significant as the one about the Marinoviches. After all, what is the most important job any man can have? President of the United States? Well, maybe. But with the possible exception of confirmed bachelors with playboy tendencies, for most adult males it is the linked responsibilities of being a husband and father. As the former for 50 years, and the father of four children (two sons and two daughters), I know I have not fulfilled those duties as well as I might have, but I hope to God I have met at least an acceptable standard in each instance. Both my sons are around Todd Marinovich's age. I count myself fortunate that they sought and found their own path, and not one I attempted to force upon them.

Epilogue: Now 80 and still in the firm grasp of the Alzheimer's that has made him a virtual prisoner in his own mind and body, Marv could not be involved, even if he wanted to,   in the athletic development of a second son, Mikhail Marinovich, whom he had with his second wife, Jan Crawford. There are signs, however, that Todd, now 51, is going about repairing the damaged pieces of himself. He currently is living in Orange County, California, and has an online art gallery, which features original works of impressionist-style paintings.

One Joe's Helping Hand to Another
TheSweetScience.com, March 8, 2011

The passage of 40 years can dim the recollections of even the sharpest minds, and Joe Hand Sr., now 74, admits to being a bit fuzzy about some details of his everyday life in 1971.

But there is one charmed evening from that year that is forever branded into Hand's memory, like a hot iron applied to the backside of a steer. That is an appropriate analogy given the former occupation of another determined guy named Joe, the one who came north from Beaufort, South Carolina, to Philadelphia a dozen years earlier and for a time worked in a slaughterhouse until he found a more profitable way to earn a living.

It was exactly 40 years ago today, on March 8 1971, that Smokin' Joe Frazier floored Muhammad Ali with his trademark left hook in the 15th and final round of what arguably was the most anticipated boxing match of all time. A tuxedoed Joe Hand Sr. was there at ringside in Madison Square Garden, beaming with pride in anticipation of the monumental victory his friend soon would be accorded by unanimous decision. It was that single punch, one of the most memorable in boxing history, which served as an exclamation point to a night that even now, so many years later, remains as indelible a moment as the sweet science has known.

"Yank Durham's wife was with us, and she passed out," Hand said of the sequence in which Frazier's thunderous hook sent Ali crashing to the canvas as if he'd been poleaxed. "She actually fainted when Ali went down. Me, I was shocked that Ali could even get up.

"Joe's feet were probably three inches off the ground when he connected with that hook. I have a picture of it in my office. It wasn't as if his feet were planted or anything like that; it was a leaping punch. Joe hurled himself at Ali and down he went."

Less than seven years earlier, Joe Hand Sr. was a Philadelphia police officer whose interest in boxing was negligible almost to the point of being non-existent. He'd never seen a fight in person and felt no particular need to rectify the situation. But when patriotism, civic pride and a desire to rub shoulders with some of the city's social elite merged, Hand took steps to become one of the original investors in Cloverlay, the consortium of Philly businessmen that financially backed Frazier, who had won the heavyweight gold medal at the 1964 Tokyo Olympics.

In its own way, the $250 that Hand plunked down, much of which he had to borrow, served as an entry into a sport that ultimately would yield nearly as much to him as it did to Joe Frazier, the 13th and final child of Rubin and Dolly Frazier. The future heavyweight champion's early life was as a child laborer whose work ethic was baked and hardened under an unforgiving Southern sun.

"If it wasn't for Joe, I might still be in the subway," Hand, now the prosperous president of Joe Hand Promotions and the proprietor of the Joe Hand Boxing Gym, said in recalling his days stationed on a Philly subway platform. "I would give whatever I have to him if he needed it. I love the guy."

Hand is one of the few surviving members of Cloverlay, and the last one who was so active in its operation that he was involved in nearly every detail from its start-up to its dissolution in 1973, after Frazier lost his title on a second-round stoppage by George Foreman in Kingston, Jamaica. It is a remarkable tale of fortuitous developments, both for the fighter and his backers, that came together in such a manner that almost defies description. Certainly, given the economics of boxing today, in which premier performers like Manny Pacquiao and Floyd Mayweather Jr. can earn upwards of $20 million for a single evening's work, there is no chance a reigning Olympic gold medalist could return home without a megabucks offer to turn pro under a well-connected promoter.

Frazier's Cinderella fitting of his figurative glass slipper came even before he defeated Germany's Hans Huber to become America's only gold medalist in boxing in Tokyo. Were it not for an injury sustained by Buster Mathis, who would have represented the United States in the heavyweight division, Frazier, an alternate, wouldn't even have made the Olympic team.

But instead of returning home to a hero's welcome, Frazier arrived in Philadelphia alone and seemingly unappreciated. He also had a broken thumb, which clouded his possibility of even pursuing a professional career in the ring.

"He couldn't even work at a regular job," said Hand, noting that Frazier still was bothered by the injury some months later, as the Christmas season approached.

"Joe had children – I don't recall how many it was then, maybe just Jacqui and Marvis – and he couldn't afford to buy them presents. There was a politician in Philadelphia named Thatcher Longstreth who came up with the idea of getting people together and forming a company to support Joe. Thatcher went to some of his rich friends and asked them to donate something to Joe for his kids for Christmas."

From such humble origins did Cloverlay – the name was an amalgamation of "clover," meaning good luck, and "overlay," a British term for a good deed – came into existence. But even Longstreth, a tall, bespectacled patrician known for his elegant manners and ever-present bow tie, had no inkling that the enterprise would advance as far as it did.

"Most of the original 14 members of Cloverlay were members of the exclusive Union League of Philadelphia," Hand noted. "Dr. Bruce Baldwin as named the president of the corporation. The stock issued was called `cocktail' stock, because those gentlemen, all of whom had a lot of money, would go to cocktail parties and say, `Oh, I own a fighter.' It was kind of a prestige thing.

"The only stipulation for becoming a member of Cloverlay was that you had to be a Pennsylvanian to own stock. You were ineligible to buy in even if you lived in South Jersey."

That was a stroke of luck for Hand, and even more so that he resided on Jackson Street.

"A couple of guys bought two shares at $250 a share," Hand said. "Really, nobody thought they would ever make any money. And the $250 I put in was a pretty steep buy-in, considering that police officers were making something like $3,500 a year at the time. That was nothing to some of the investors, but it was a lot to me.

"Like a lot of people, I read about this local kid coming out of the Olympics who had won a gold medal for his country. I was not a boxing fan. But when I found out about some of the people who were backing Joe, I recognized that they were among the city's foremost movers and shakers. There was Harold Wessel, who was a senior vice president for Ernst & Ernst, which is now Ernst & Young, a large national accounting firm. Bob Wilder was the president of Lewis & Gilman, probably the largest public-relation company in Philadelphia. One of the fellows who bought stock was Jack Kelly, Grace Kelly's brother."

So, how did a cop on a budget join the rich-guys Cloverlay club?

"I wrote a letter to Dr. Baldwin and let him know I wanted to buy a share of Cloverlay stock, if I could," Hand recalled. "As it turned out, I lived on Jackson Street, where Dr. Baldwin had lived as a kid. He wrote me back and told me he'd be glad to see me a share of his stock. I guess he had two shares at the time. He said, `If I can't help a Jackson Streeter, I can't help anybody.'"

So Hand was in, and it turned out to be one helluva ride to the top with Frazier. It was an interesting trip for other Cloverlay investors, too, one of whom – Larry Merchant, then the sports editor of the *Philadelphia Daily News*, now the veteran boxing color analyst for HBO – was obliged to sell his share because his bosses deemed it to be a conflict of interest.

"Joe got 70% of his purses and the investors got 30%," Hand said. "He didn't have a regular contract filed with the Pennsylvania State Athletic Commission, but a personal-services contract with Cloverlay. We were responsible for seeing that he arrived for his fights at a designated time and date."

Hand said he first believed Smokin' Joe was destined for great things when, after a tough start, he rallied to beat rawhide-tough Canadian George Chuvalo, a victory that brought him increasing national attention.

But the highlight of Frazier's career came on March 8 1971, when he and Ali squared off in a showdown of undefeated champions, the biggest boxing match since the Joe Louis-Max Schmeling rematch.

"That was, and still is, the biggest sporting event of all time," Joe said. "There's nothing that compares to the drama and the excitement of that night. The *Philadelphia Daily News* had at least a column, and sometimes an entire page, on the fight beginning 21 days out. Burt Lancaster, the movie star, was a color announcer for the telecast. Frank Sinatra was taking photos for *Time-Life*. To get a ringside seat – and there were no exceptions – you had to wear formal attire, a tuxedo or an evening gown.

"The day of the fight I ran the train from Philadelphia to New York. We had eight cars and sold them out (500 tickets at $25 each). There also were some very wealthy people who had private cars that were attached to our train. We had two policemen who collected the tickets and provided security."

And while Ali had many supporters in the Garden, throughout the nation and around the world, the Cloverlay people were convinced "The Greatest" was in for a smoking.

"There was never a doubt in any of our minds that Joe would win," Hand said. "For him to lose, you'd have had to stab him or shoot him … all that anger he'd built up from Ali's insults. Ali might have been the best fighter, but Joe had the biggest heart."

That heart, as much or more as that sledgehammer left hook, carried Frazier to the greatest victory of his career. Using the archaic scoring system then in place in New York, judges Bill Richt and Artie Aidala had Frazier winning 11 rounds to four and 9-6, respectively, with referee Arthur Mercante Sr. submitting a card that had the Philadelphian ahead 8-6-1.

"When it was over, back in Joe's dressing room, two guys came in and took everything Joe had worn, the green-and-gold robe, the boxing trunks, the gloves," Hand said. "Left him with a jockstrap and socks. I don't know what happened to all that gear."

What Hand does know is that both winner and loser that night paid a high price for taking each other to the limit in the first fight of their magnificent trilogy, against which all other boxing rivalries are measured.

"Joe went home, checked into St. Luke's hospital," Hand said. "His blood pressure was sky-high. If it got any higher, they said it would cause a stroke.

"I stayed with him through the night. Yank Durham (Frazier's manager-trainer) went off on a trip to Europe. Bruce Wright, the attorney, he had someplace to go. I was the only one. He was my friend. It hurt me to see him so beat up.

"Both fighters were never the same after that night."

Hand said the then-record $2.5 million purse paid to each fighter could have been larger, had they accepted an offer from Sonny Werblin, then the owner of the New York Jets.

"Madison Square Garden wasn't the only venue we considered," Hand said. "There was a guy hooked up with Sonny Werblin. We – meaning the Cloverlay guys – went up there to meet with Werblin, in his penthouse overlooking the East River. It was around the same time the World's Fair was being held. There was an open-air building called Schaefer Center. They were going to put an inflatable roof on it. We could have gotten maybe another $2 million for the fight if we had put it in there, but we were so afraid the roof wouldn't stay up, so we declined the bid. This past football season, when I saw that the inflatable roof collapsed under the weight of snow in Minneapolis, I thought, 'Holy cow, that could have happened to us.'"

Fortunately for Hand, Ali-Frazier I was televised via closed-circuit and someone with Cloverlay needed to learn the whys and wherefores of the new technology. Hand volunteered for the assignment.

"Bruce Wright, the attorney, said, 'Find out everything you can about it.' I did. And when Cloverlay dissolved, there was a question as to who was going to wind up with that part of it. Nobody else wanted it, so I said I'd take it. That's how Joe Hand Promotions came to be."

After Frazier defeated Ali, Hand traveled to Smokin' Joe's birth city of Beaufort to represent Cloverlay, which wanted to build a playground there to honor Joe. But the city fathers were only willing to go so far to recognize the signal accomplishments of a native son.

"I talked to the mayor, told him what we had in mind, flew down there," Hand said. "I call the mayor, they tell me he'll meet me at Howard Johnson's. He walks in, walks out. I was sitting there with two of Joe's sisters and I figure out later he did not want to sit in a restaurant with two black people.

"The playground never got built."

Fast-forward 39 years and the landscape had changed, in its own way as dramatically as the moment that Smokin' Joe uncorked that spectacular left hook that, for a time, changed the face of boxing. On September 25, 2010, the then-66-year-old Frazier returned to Beaufort to receive the Palmetto Award, the highest distinction a South Carolinian can receive, from Governor Mark Sanford. Frazier's lone surviving sibling, sister Maizie, could not attend because of age and infirmity, nor could she be there later that evening when her famous brother was feted in Columbia, the state capital.

Times had changed in Philadelphia, too. Joe Frazier's Gym closed in 2010, as had his restaurant, the site of a triple killing, years earlier. Bit by bit, his fortune melted away. His primary source of income now is paid appearances at card shows and the like, where he cashes in on, well, being Joe Frazier.

"I talk to his family," Hand said. "Joe, I don't speak to. There's not a reason for it. There's no animosity, certainly not on my part. I call Joe every year on his birthday and leave a message on his voice mail. I say, 'Joe, happy birthday. I'm thinking of you. Why don't we get together and have lunch or dinner? You know how to get a hold of me. Give me a call.' But I don't hear from him."

Hand tries to pay homage to that other Joe whenever and however he can. He has his gym in the Northern Liberties section, where Bernard Hopkins trains when he's in town, and he has a promotional interest in rising welterweight contender Mike Jones. He's hosted a number of Philadelphia Golden Gloves tournaments.

"Boxing has been very good to me and my family, and we try to give back to it," Hand said. "But none of it could have happened without Cloverlay and Joe Frazier."

Ringling Brothers Throws in the Towel; Boxing's Ringmasters Next?
TheSweetScience.com, January 15, 2017

Two definitions of "tradition," as listed in the Merriam-Webster dictionary, describe it as "cultural continuity in social attitudes, customs and institutions, " as well as "an inherited, established or customary pattern of thought, action or behavior."

At 69 years of age, I consider myself a staunch proponent of tradition, at least those customs that can be traced back to my impressionable youth and have somehow survived in a constantly evolving society. But perhaps I have not clung to all the old ways as tenaciously as I would like to think. I last attended a circus performance 30 or so years ago, accompanied by the two youngest of my four children, and even that marked the first time for me to take in the so-called "Greatest Show on Earth" in the 25 years that preceded it.

Nonetheless, I couldn't help but feel a pang of remorse to find out that the Ringling Brothers and Barnum & Bailey Circus will close forever in May, ending a tradition of providing wholesome family fun that goes back 146 years. But they say nothing is forever, and 21st century kids apparently prefer to keep playing video games than to head off to a big-top tent or arena and watch clowns with bulbous noses, grease-painted faces and oversized shoes scramble out of a tiny car and do silly stuff.

"The competitor in many ways is time," said Kenneth Feld, chairman and CEO of Feld Entertainment, which bought the circus in 1967. "It's a different model that we can't see how it works in today's world."

It did occur to me that one difference between Ringling and the ring is four little letters, and that the parallels between the two forms of tradition-encrusted entertainment are numerous and so obvious as to be undeniable. If the lords of boxing do not take care to mind their troubled store and make necessary changes, who's to say they won't eventually be obliged to close up shop as the flying trapeze artists, lion tamers and high-wire walkers must soon do?

Circuses have existed in one form or another for centuries, but the inventor of what might be described as the version we know today was an unapologetically shameless huckster and showman named Phineas T. Barnum, who was 80 when he died on April 7, 1891. Although he is erroneously credited with coining the phrase "there's a sucker born every minute," Barnum was only too happy to describe himself as the "Prince of Humbugs" whose mind conceived an endless stream of oddities, authentic or not, to separate a willingly gullible public from some of its money. "The people like to be humbugged," he reasoned.

Among the non-authentic come-ons invented by Barnum was Joyce Heth, a blind slave touted as being the 161-year-old former nurse to toddler George Washington, who enthralled paying customers with her totally fictitious remembrances of "dear little George." When she died in 1836, an autopsy revealed that Heth was most likely no older than 80.

Some of Barnum's more notable humbugs included the "Feejee Mermaid," which was hyped as a creature unlike any ever seen, but was actually the upper half of a stuffed monkey sewn to the bottom of a similarly preserved fish, and "General Tom Thumb," a child dwarf who was then four years of age but was stated to be 11. A natural mimic, by five the little boy – later presented at court to England's Queen Victoria – was drinking wine and smoking cigars for audiences' amusement.

The most obvious boxing equivalent of Barnum is, of course, electric-haired octogenarian Don King, but another master of trickeration with Barnumesque flourishes is King's contemporary, Bob Arum, by virtue of his propensity for overstatement. He once predicted that a matchup of Oscar De La Hoya and Dana Rosenblatt would be the biggest attraction in boxing history, and that a Top Rank fighter, super welterweight prospect Anthony Thompson, who was 11-0 with eight KOs at the time, "has the chance to become the best fighter ever to come out of Philadelphia."

Where Barnum trotted out General Tom Thumb, Arum helped fill out the undercards of De La Hoya-headlined fight cards in the mid- to late 1990s with novelty acts Eric "Butterbean" Esch and Latina lovely Mia St. John, who in tandem became known as "Beauty and The Bean." Esch was a bald, obese former Toughman contestant (the erstwhile "King of the Four-Rounders" weighed 426 ½ pounds for his final pro bout) while St. John was a smokin' hot babe featured in the pages of *Playboy*. "I know how they were marketing me," St. John once said. "I don't blame them. I was what you'd call a willing victim."

Stealing a page from Arum's playbook for the Butterbean/St. John pugilistic sideshow, Fox-TV's second installment of its short-lived *Celebrity* Boxing series paired 7'7", ultra-skinny former NBA center Manute Bol and ultra-wide former Chicago Bears defensive lineman William "The Refrigerator" Perry, who tipped the scales in Butterbean territory somewhere north of 400 pounds. 'Nute won because he landed a few boarding-house-reach jabs and a gasping Fridge ran out of gas moments after he waddled from his corner following the opening bell.

You like clowns? Sad-faced Emmett Kelly Sr. was the most famous graduate of The Ringling Brothers' "College of Clowns," but boxing had spectators rolling in the aisle, one way or another, because of the frequently outrageous antics and garb of such fighters as the late Hector "Macho" Camacho Sr. (who, it should be noted, was good enough at the serious business at hand to be a 2015 inductee into the International Boxing Hall of Fame) and Jorge Paez.

Animal acts are, or at least used to be, highly popular staples of the circus. Of particular interest were the trained elephants, a reality that dates back to Barnum's purchase of a gargantuan, six-ton African elephant named Jumbo from the London Zoological Society in 1882. So popular was Jumbo, who died after accidentally being hit by a freight train in 1885, that he helped birth the now-familiar adage of an "elephant in the room" that no one can ignore or look away from

But PETA (an acronym for People for the Ethical Treatment of Animals) fought a long and ultimately successful battle to remove elephants from circuses on the premise that the stress of performing, as well as the cramped conditions on the trains used for travel, made them skittish. PETA's argument was bolstered by several instances of elephants going on rampages, perhaps most notably one on August 20, 1974, in Honolulu, when an African elephant named Tyke killed her trainer and badly injured her groomer before running through the Kakaako central business district for more than 30 minutes. Police had no choice but to fire 86 shots at the enraged animal, which according to PETA, had been involved in three previous incidents before it collapsed and died.

Juliette Feld, Kenneth Feld's daughter and the Chief Operating Officer of Feld Entertainment, noted that circus attendance has been dropping for 10 years and the removal of the company's elephants in May 2016 to a conservation farm in central Florida has caused an even more precipitous decline in ticket sales. She said it is paradoxical that so many people say they don't want big animals to perform in circuses, while many others refuse to attend a circus without them.

Boxing's most massive elephants during my lifetime were the late, great Muhammad Ali and Mike Tyson, who commanded so much global attention that they were bigger draws than a veritable herd of Jumbos. But Ali, who was 74 when he died on June 3, hadn't fought since dropping a 10-round decision to Trevor Berbick on December 11, 1981, and Tyson, who is 50, last stepped inside the ropes for a bout that counted on June 11, 2005, when the rusted remains of what once had been Iron Mike fell in six rounds to the very ordinary Kevin McBride in Washington, D.C.

With no elephants to happily stampede through our consciousness, fight fans are left to wait on Floyd Mayweather Jr.'s possible return against MMA standout Conor McGregor, a humbug event if ever there was one. Oh, sure, Gennadiy Golovkin-Daniel Jacobs and Danny Garcia-Keith Thurman are nice coming attractions, but we ain't talking Ali-Frazier I. Mayweather-Manny Pacquiao in 2015 had a chance to throw a few logs onto the embers, but blew it.

Boxing's movers and shakers need to look at the imminent shuttering of the Greatest Show on Earth and acknowledge the clear and present danger to all traditional enterprises that don't adjust to new realities. The fight game's tent hasn't folded, and is in no real danger of doing so, but steps must be taken to ensure that all that is still good is made better.

Because extinction is never as far away as you might think.

The Fonz in Bronze
MaxBoxing.com, January 31, 2008

Regular guys are hoisting beers in Milwaukee, and more cultured types are spitting out their white wine spritzers in outrage, at the announcement that the city will soon have a statue of the fictional Arthur Fonzarelli, aka "The Fonz," the leather-jacketed biker on TV's *Happy Days*, which ran from 1974 to '84. The popular series was set in Milwaukee.

Two booster groups, VISIT Milwaukee and Spirit Milwaukee, raised the $85,000 needed to fund the project, with TV Land (reruns forever!) among the major donors. TV Land has sponsored similar statues in other cities, such as the ones of Bob Newhart in Chicago and Mary Tyler Moore in Minneapolis.

"It's not often you have a dream when you're seven, lying in your bed, you get to live your dream and then someone is going to erect a life-sized statue of your creation," actor-director Henry Winkler, who played Fonzie, told *The Associated Press* last week.

I'm having a little difficulty accepting the notion that a seven-year-old Henry Winkler actually dreamed of one day having his own statue, but let us continue along the winding trail where this tale ultimately will take us.

Serious art lovers are less enthusiastic about the statue of some faux '50s greaser adorning public space along the Milwaukee River. Mike Brenner, founder of the Hotcakes Gallery, called the statue a "publicity stunt" that perpetuates lowbrow stereotypes about Wisconsin.

I, of course, would never suggest that many Americans' prevailing image of Wisconsin is of guys wearing cheesehead hats at Green Bay Packers games. Nor would I point out that someone heading up an art gallery apparently named after breakfast hasn't much of a platform for being snooty. Besides, I'm pretty sure the 62-year-old Winkler, who holds a masters degree from the Yale School of Drama as well as two honorary doctorates, can go highbrow-to-highbrow with Brenner any time.

This sort of civic furor has arisen before, in my town, Philadelphia, where the "Rocky" statue that was cast as a prop for *Rocky III* for a time was as homeless as a shopping-cart-pushing bag lady. Star Sylvester Stallone wanted the statue in a place of honor, atop the steps of the Philadelphia Art Museum, where it appeared in the movie; our local Mike Brenner equivalents wanted it somewhere else, like in a far-away town and maybe warehoused.

For years, the "Rocky" statue was stashed, so to speak, in front of the Wachovia Spectrum, which had been replaced as Philly's principal sports arena by the newer, spiffier Wachovia Center across the parking lot. The Wachovia Center is the home of the 76ers and Flyers; the 40-year-old Wachovia Spectrum, which likely would be razed if plans for a multimillion-dollar entertainment complex finally are implemented, hosts games of such minor-league franchises as the Kixx, Phantoms and Soul.

(Personal note: I was deeply saddened when our arenas' corporate sponsorship changed from First Union to Wachovia. There is absolutely nothing that captured the feisty spirit of Philadelphia better than having visiting teams play in the "F.U. Center.")

But Art Museum officials grudgingly came to accept the fact that thousands of tourists have continued to run up the steps and jump around, their arms upraised, as Rocky Balboa had done, so they gave in and agreed to welcome back the "Rocky" statue in 2006, the 30th anniversary of the release of the original, Academy Award-winning film. It's now displayed near the foot of the steps.

All of which leads me to ask: In a town where we have bronze likenesses of Richie Ashburn, Mike Schmidt, Steve Carlton, Bobby Clarke, Julius Erving and even Kate Smith, who used to belt out *God Bless America* before Flyers games during their "Broad Street

Bullies" heyday, why is there no statue of former heavyweight champion Joe Frazier?

Somebody please call TV Land, or at least ESPN Classic.

Epilogue: Much has happened in Philly on the statuary front since this story first appeared. The Wachovia Spectrum was imploded on November 23, 2010, a massive sports restaurant/bar, XFINITY Live!, rising in its place. That prime location in the Philadelphia Sports Complex is now fronted by a 12-foot statue of Joe Frazier, the result of a $200,000 fund-raising drive, which was unveiled on September 12, 2015. The Smokin' Joe statue, the creation of sculptor Stephen Layne, joins one of former middleweight titlist Joey Giardello, the handiwork of sculptor Carl LeVotch, which was unveiled in Giardello's old South Philadelphia neighborhood on May 21, 2011. Joining the aforementioned statues of non-boxing sports heroes at the First Union Center (its most recent name) is one of basketball legend Wilt Chamberlain, but the statue of Kate Smith, deemed by some to be racially insensitive, has been removed.

Section B
The Heavyweights

Remembering the Mike Tyson Rape Trial
Sherdog.com, February 8, 2016

The United States' most-publicized jury trial of a professional athlete has an undisputed champion. The February 2 debut of the FX miniseries, *The People v. O.J. Simpson: American Crime Story*, drew an audience of five million-plus viewers, a record for the cable network, and again brought attention to the double-homocide of Simpson's former wife, Nicole Brown Simpson, and her friend, Ron Goldman. It also reintroduced us to a cast of characters that became as familiar to many Americans as any tabloid celebrity: prosecutor Marcia Clark (played by Sarah Paulson), defense attorneys Robert Shapiro (John Travolta) and Johnnie Cochran (Courtney B. Vance), surfer-boy house guest Kato Katelin (Billy Magnussen) and, of course, Simpson himself, with Academy Award winner Cuba Gooding Jr. as the celebrated former football star/actor accused of a horrific, violent crime. A nation stood transfixed from the infamous slow-speed police chase after Simpson's white Ford Bronco through the eight-month trial, which ended with Simpson's acquittal on October 3, 1995.

What the Simpson trial indirectly accomplished was to surpass, at least as far as the level of public attention, another high-visibility trial which had concluded in Indianapolis three years earlier and involved the former heavyweight champion of the world, a ferocious fighter who, to his devoted legion of fans, still was hailed as the "Baddest Man on the Planet." Maybe that's because the courtroom proceedings in the Simpson trial were nationally televised and the trial of Mike Tyson was not, or maybe it was the Simpson trial involved a grisly double-murder and Tyson was being tried on lesser but still-sordid charges of rape and deviant sexual conduct. Mostly, the difference was that Simpson ultimately heard a verdict of "not guilty" while Tyson, so used to winning by devastating knockout, was determined by an Indiana jury to have committed the crimes he was accused of against an 18-year-old beauty pageant contestant.

As it turned out, no one died in Indianapolis during Tyson's disastrous 1991 visit to the Miss Black America contest except, maybe, "Iron" Mike's reputation as the most feared individual ever to have stepped inside the ring – a human force of nature no less frightening than a tornado, earthquake, volcanic eruption or Category 5 hurricane making landfall. Separated from the sport he had for most part utterly dominated by a 10-year sentence (four years suspended) given him by presiding judge Patricia Gifford, he served a little more than three years. After his release, Tyson – whose aura of invincibility had previously been cracked by his 10th-round stoppage by 42-to-1 underdog James "Buster" Douglas on February 11, 1990, in Tokyo – was clearly a diminished fighter. His skills had atrophied, his focus on boxing had blurred and the intimidation factor he had generated like a nuclear reactor was dialed way down.

Although a freed Tyson still managed to win a couple of other versions of the heavyweight title, he was emphatically dethroned against Evander Holyfield. That loss accelerated a slide that ended with defeats in three of his last four bouts – to fellow future Hall of Famer Lennox Lewis, which was hardly a surprise, and to Danny Williams and Kevin McBride, which nonetheless qualified as shockers.

At 49, Tyson remains one of the most recognizable fighters ever, like 74-year-old Muhammad Ali much better known to boxing fans and non-fans alike than the three men who presently hold versions of the championship Tyson possessed during his pre-Douglas reign of terror -- Tyson Fury (who actually was named in "Iron" Mike's honor), Deontay Wilder and Charles Martin. While his devotees are adamant that Tyson was and is among the greatest of heavyweight champions, there are others who, while appreciating all that he had been in a professional sense, regret that his reckless lifestyle prevented him from becoming all that he *should* have been. The post-rape-trial Tyson became as much of a punchline as a puncher, with critics dismissing him as (Behind) Iron (Bars) Mike and Rusted Iron Mike. Somehow, the $300 million fortune he had amassed dissipated through profligate spending and his misplaced trust in members of his inner circle who treated him as their personal ATM.

Perhaps it all would turned out differently – which is to say better – for Tyson had he decided not to accept that invitation to attend the Miss Black America pageant. Perhaps his fate would have been the same in any case. Any conclusion reached now is purely speculative. Despite the jury verdict, the fact remains that only two people, Tyson and Desiree Washington, absolutely know what happened in that Indianapolis hotel room in the early-morning hours of July 19, 1991. Their versions of the story were and are markedly different, and what is true or not true came down to the perceptions of 12 human beings who bore the grave responsibility of determining the guilt or innocence of another – and a famous and controversial athlete at that. What we know of the case is compelling stuff nonetheless, some of which bears re-telling.

It was viewed by some as a miscalculation when Tyson's defense was handled by Vincent J. Fuller, a prominent Washington, D.C., attorney who had successfully defended Tyson's promoter, Don King, on a tax-evasion rap. It was King who hired Fuller to represent Tyson. Fuller, who was 74 when he died of lung cancer in 2006, argued not only that the sex between his client and Washington was consensual, but that Tyson's reputation as a ruffian and indiscriminate womanizer was such that Washington should have known better than to go out with him if she was not prepared for his advances.

There were several prosecution witnesses who testified about Tyson's callous attitude toward women, with Fuller countering by detailing the circumstances of the fighter's rise to prominence and the insular environment that might have contributed to that attitude.

"He lived in an all-male world," Fuller said. "He had no people skills with girls his age. He did not grow up appreciative of how he should conduct himself."

One of the pageant contestants, Parquita Nassau, said Tyson had told a group of the young women, "I want to f--- you and you and you – and bring your roommates because I'm a celebrity and we do that kind of thing." Nassau said she was offended by such talk and added that when she rebuffed Tyson's crude come-on, he said, "Doesn't matter. I could have any of you bitches here."

Nassau's damaging testimony was countered by another contestant, Madelyn Whittington, who recounted a conversation she had with Washington in a restroom following a pageant rehearsal. Washington was primping, putting on lipstick, and allegedly told Whittington she had been asked out on a late date by Tyson.

"Are you going to go?" Whittington asked.

"Of course I'm going," she claimed Washington replied. "This is Mike Tyson. He's got a lot of money. He's dumb. Did you see what Robin Givens (Tyson's first wife) got out of him?"

As Fuller and prosecutor Gregory Garrison made their cases in a courtroom in which television cameras were not allowed, the scene outside and around the country was a chaotic circus, with Tyson's supporters and detractors jostling for TV face time and loudly offering thoughts and opinions that the sequestered jury wasn't going to hear anyway.

Billionaire Donald Trump had brought Tyson to Atlantic City for five title defenses funded in no small part by the hefty site fees put up by Trump. He proposed that Tyson be allowed to give "millions and millions" of dollars to rape and domestic abuse victims rather than to be incarcerated in the medium- to high-security Indiana Youth Center, where he would be paid $1.25 a day to perform standard menial duties as a prisoner. Claude Lewis, a prominent black Philadelphia newspaper columnist whose position was that Tyson finally had been forced to face up to his litany of misdeeds, took exception to Trump's offer, writing that "the public should ignore the irrational ravings of Trump, who apparently possesses a selective outrage and an attachment to 'checkbook justice.'"

When Tyson was convicted, about a dozen protestors who had been bused in from Chicago – as reported by the *Chicago Tribune* – stood in front of the courthouse, chanting "Free Mike Tyson" and waving small Mike Tyson flags with the insignia of King's company on the back.

During the sentencing phase on March 26, 1992, Tyson made a rambling, 12-minute statement, continued to proclaim his innocence of the charges. However, his words were chilling and more than a little scary. "I'm not guilty of this crime. It's something that occurred, but I didn't hurt anybody. No black eyes. No broken ribs. When I'm in the ring, I break their ribs. I break their jaws. To me, that's hurting someone."

In addition to the 10-year sentence, Gifford maintained that Tyson – who had faced a maximum of 60 years imprisonment – be placed on four years' probation after the jail term, as well as mandatory psychotherapy and 100 hours of community service with delinquent youths. He also was ordered to pay $30,000 in fines and $113 in court costs. A request to pay the $150,000 cost of staging the trial was denied.

Even in prison, Tyson continued to command headlines. It was revealed that Gifford had disallowed testimony from two potential defense witnesses who claimed they saw a couple resembling Tyson and Washington acting in a "highly affectionate" manner in the lobby of the hotel where Washington was staying. The fact that Washington had hired an attorney, Ed Gerstein, to handle a planned civil suit against Tyson on a contingency basis was not revealed to the jury. Washington did in fact file a civil suit in which she alleged that Tyson had infected her with not one but two venereal diseases. That suit was settled out of court for an undisclosed sum in June 1995.

In an attempt to gain early release, which was denied, Tyson wrote a letter to Gifford in July 1994. In it he stated, "I want you to know, and I want the Washingtons to know, that my conduct was inexcusable. I should not have expected a woman to come to my room late at night, not knowing her, and to expect her to have sex with me."

It was the closest thing to a conciliatory gesture ever offered by Tyson, but Michael Weisman, another attorney representing Washington, contended the letter to Gifford was self-serving and that the boxer had not demonstrated "even a glimmer of remorse" for "the trauma inflicted on Ms. Washington."

Once free, however, Tyson renewed his verbal attacks on Washington, who had withdrawn from public view. During an appearance on Fox in May 2003, Tyson reiterated to interviewer Greta Van Susteren that he was innocent of the crime for which he was convicted, describing Washington as "slimy," "lying" and "reptilian." He also said that, although he had not raped Washington, he now "really (did) want to rape her and her mother." In Philadelphia, Curtis Douglas, a former assistant district attorney in the Family Violence and Sexual Assault Unit, reacted with revulsion to Tyson's venomous spiel. "The victim could take this as a terroristic threat," Douglas said. "It indicates a coldness of heart. Obviously, the experience hasn't taught him anything."

Tyson – whose boxing license had been suspended and revoked in 1997 for biting Holyfield's ears in their rematch – later had a return engagement behind bars. In February 1999, he was sentenced to two years (one suspended) for a road-rage attack on two motorists in Maryland. The conviction might have been considered a breach of his parole on the rape conviction and resulted in his being returned to Indiana to compete the unserved three years of that conviction. Tyson's lawyers had paid substantial amounts – reportedly $250,000 apiece – to Richard Haddick and Bimelic Saucedo in return for their requests for clemency, which Judge Stephen Johnson declined.

"Imagine what you must feel to have an agitated Mike Tyson coming toward you," assistant district attorney Carol Crawford told the jury. "Mr. Tyson has said in the past that he is a time bomb waiting to blow. The bomb exploded that day."

Johnson expressed concern with Tyson's apparent pattern of behavior. "The defendant repeatedly reacts compulsively and violently," he said. "He is almost predictable in this way."

The lyrics to a Linda Ronstadt song tells us that "time washes clean, life's wounds unseen." Maybe that is at least partly true. If Washington had indeed been violated, one can only hope that in the intervening years she has found some measure of peace. Tyson, married for a third time, has known agony beyond that which he felt in the ring and in prison; his four-year-old daughter, Exodus, died in a freak treadmill accident in May 2009. His inner demons presumably under control, Tyson claims to have kicked his cocaine habit, and he has pared down from 300-plus pounds to a weight within reasonable proximity of his onetime fighting prime of 220 or so.

Meanwhile, Simpson is back in jail, sentenced to 33 years for his part in the theft, at gunpoint, of sports memorabilia he claimed was his in 2007. He is eligible for parole in May 2017, when he will be 69 years old. The wheel, as always, goes round and round.

Gridiron Greatness No Sure Path to Gloved Glory
TheSweetScience.com, January 31, 2013

Try to imagine Mike Tyson or Joe Frazier as Pro Bowl football players, or even holding end-of-the-bench roster spots with an NFL team.

Isn't easy, is it?

Now try to imagine actual All-Pro defensive ends Ed "Too Tall" Jones and Mark Gastineau as heavyweight champions of the world.

That's even a more difficult concept to accept, yet there are dreamers – past, present and probably future – who dare to believe that superior athletic ability in one sport is easily transferable to another. It is a fallacy that has been proven wrong any number of times with football players trying to make the extremely difficult crossover into boxing, but there is always someone who thinks he'll be the one to cash that lottery ticket.

Perhaps the exception to the rule will be former Michigan State University linebacker Seth Mitchell. Decide for yourself whether Mitchell's second-round stoppage at the hands of Johnathon Banks on November 17 – a devastating defeat that either exposed the ex-Spartan as another overhyped gridiron-to-ring wannabe or, in his words, as a "learning experience" that ultimately will make him a better fighter – will be reversed or reprised in a February 16 rematch in Atlantic City's Boardwalk Hall.

"It was a tough defeat for me," said Mitchell (25-1-1, 19 KOs) of his come-uppance from Banks (29-1-1, 19 KOs), a longtime disciple of the late Hall of Fame trainer, Emanuel Steward, who now doubles as an active boxer and chief second for heavyweight champion Wladimir Klitschko. "Just experiencing that first loss was a tough pill to swallow, but I tell people it's a gift.

"(January 12) actually was six years altogether in boxing for me, amateur and pro, so I'm learning on the job. But I'm a quick learner and I definitely learned a lot from that fight. This is the classroom I want to be in, and I understand that I'm young in the game and learning. But I've got to learn and win at the same time."

Mitchell, in truth, isn't as young as he'd like the public to believe. He's 30, clearly unschooled in the subtle nuances that Banks, also 30, picked up during his many years of instruction from Steward, and another loss could forever delete his vision of multimillion-dollar purses and a bejeweled world title belt cinched around his waist. If the confused Mitchell who was floored three times by Banks in the second round three months ago shows up again, the likelihood is that people will be lumping him with the inept Gastineau more than with the heavyweight legends he aspires to join.

"He never saw my left hook," Banks said after his first meeting with the spectacularly muscled Mitchell, which also was staged in Boardwalk Hall. "He was not experienced enough to know what to do when he got in trouble, to hold on or grab me. I was able to keep punching him. He's a big, tough guy, but he couldn't handle me."

The decision to immediately enforce a rematch clause that was included in the contract for the original fight constitutes something of a gamble for Golden Boy Promotions, which sees Mitchell as a potential high-reward entry into the heavyweight division, and for HBO, which has been yearning for a genuinely skilled and marketable American big man since Tyson, Evander Holyfield and Riddick Bowe retired or became too old to continue trading on past glories. But going all in on a relative neophyte like Mitchell calls to mind one of the more memorable sayings of Spanish-born philosopher George Santayana: "Those who do not learn from history are doomed to repeat it."

The suits at HBO especially should be aware of the potential pitfalls of the football-to-fisticuffs path the premium-cable giant has traveled in the past. Cases in point: Jimmy Ellis (no, not the former WBA heavyweight champ and Muhammad Ali stablemate) and Michael Grant. On December 7, 1991, in Reno, Nevada, HBO paid former (and future) heavyweight champion George Foreman $4.95 million for a bout with the other Jimmy Ellis, who had been a player with the Los Angeles Raiders' replacement team during the 1987 strike-shortened season. The 228-pound Ellis wasn't appreciably better than some of the cupcakes the then-42-year-old Foreman had been beating up for $40,000 paydays since resuming his career in the spring of 1987, but George's bouts again were becoming must-see events and HBO promos played up Ellis' football background as proof that he somehow was not just another designated victim.

Foreman relentlessly battered the game but woefully overmatched Ellis until referee Richard Steele mercifully halted the slaughter in the third round.

"This was not a fight to be proud of," then-HBO Sports executive Ross Greenburg said of Foreman's obliteration of Ellis. "HBO should have taken more time checking out Ellis' background."

To a lesser degree, the same might be said of HBO's temporary fascination with Grant, whose imposing 6'7", 250-pound physique cause the imagination of many to run wild.

"He has the potential to be the greatest heavyweight of all time," Grant's veteran trainer, Don Turner, gushed in May 1998.

Lou DiBella, then a senior vice president of HBO Sports, chimed in around the same time with the opinion that "Michael Grant, without question, is the best of the young heavyweights. He's the guy who's going to lead the way into the next millennium."

But Grant, a former defensive end at two California junior colleges who had bragged that he "could have been a Pro Bowl football player," was taken to hell and back in rallying for a 10th-round stoppage of Andrew Golota on November 20, 1999, after he twice had been floored in the first round. Grant rightly was hailed for his tenacity and heart, and the HBO-televised victory earned him a shot at champion Lennox Lewis five months later. But not everyone was quite so eager to climb onto the Grant bandwagon.

"Grant has stamina and a good right hand, but beyond that I don't see much," said Steward, Lewis' trainer, who was at ringside that night. "He's not a real solid fighter. He's just fortunate to be here now, when the heavyweight division is weak. He's an athlete who treats boxing like it's another sport."

Those comments eerily sound like what some skeptics are saying about Mitchell right now. Hey, what goes around eventually comes around, right?

Despite his failure to fulfill the most optimistic projections for him, Grant (48-4, 36 KOs) – who was knocked out in two one-sided rounds by Lewis and in one round by Jameel McCline in the bout after that – just might be one of the most accomplished former football players to dive into the shark-infested waters of professional boxing, the other being Charlie Powell.

Powell's record (25-11-3, 17 KOs) might not look all that impressive these days, but the NFL veteran – five seasons with the San Francisco 49ers, two with the Oakland Raiders – was the No. 2-ranked heavyweight in the world at one point in the late 1950s. Although Powell never played college football, he was a superb athlete in high school who once ran a 9.6-second 100-yard dash and posted a 57'9¼" toss in the shotput. He matched punches with some of the best fighters on the planet, losing to Muhammad Ali, Floyd Patterson and someone named John Riggins, who is not to be confused with the former Super Bowl-winning running back for the Washington Redskins.

It is almost understandable why some football players, and those willing to back them, cling to the notion that someone who excels while wearing a helmet and shoulder pads can do so when stripped down to a pair of satin trunks. After his retirement from the ring, the legendary Rocky Marciano and his pal, Lou Duva, decided they would hang around NFL camps in the hope of identifying the next great heavyweight. The person or persons of their choosing would, of course, be big, strong, fast and susceptible to the notion of a career change. But Marciano died in a tragic plane crash and the plan was never put into effect. Then again, perhaps it was doomed from the outset.

Which is not to say the Marciano/Duva blueprint periodically hasn't risen again, like Count Dracula at sunset. One of the more ambitious such undertakings was launched by Michael King, who made his fortune as CEO of King World Productions. An avid boxing buff, King founded All-American Heavyweights in 2008 with the goal of producing Olympic medalists who, presumably, would use that platform to go on to professional stardom.

"A great athlete in any sport can pick up another sport faster than most people," King reasoned. "It really all stems from a lack of talent and lack of apprenticeship for trainers. The pipeline is dead ... (Boxing is) not an NCAA sport, so it's typically dependent on the Olympic program, and that NGB (USA Boxing is its national governing board) does not have a lot of resources.

"Instead of getting some thug off the street, why not tap into the greatest talent pool in the United States? You're talking about elite athletes who are in great shape, who are really big, who are unbelievably coordinated, and they are articulate college graduates."

America's super-heavyweight representative to the 2012 London Olympics was Dominic Brezeale, a 6'6", 260-pound former quarterback at Northern Colorado University. Despite his obvious physical tools, Brezeale lost a 19-8, electronically scored decision to Russia's Magomed Omarov in the first round and was quickly

65

eliminated from medal consideration. "It's like night and day, man," Brezeale said of being in there with an opponent with vastly more ring experience. "With football you get an off-season, in boxing you don't. In football, you can play it. In boxing, you've got to live it. And when you're in the ring, there's no blaming anyone else."

Angelo Dundee, the late, great trainer of 15 world champions, including Ali and Sugar Ray Leonard, warned against the notion that accomplishments on the football field were a natural precursor to similar success inside the ropes. Responding to a question from a *Los Angeles Times* reporter in 1989 about the feasibility of the Green Bay Packers' No. 1 draft choice, tackle Tony Mandarich, fighting Mike Tyson for the heavyweight championship of the world despite never having boxed before, Dundee said the idea was beyond preposterous.

"Athletically, boxing is the toughest profession in the world," Dundee said. "Just because you're big and strong and great in football or basketball shape has nothing to do with it. I've seen it many times over the years, football players walking into gyms, asking me to turn them into boxers. It never works.

"I always try to talk them out of it, but they never take 'no' for an answer. About 15 years ago a lineman from the University of Miami, a 6'4", 250-pound guy, wanted me to turn him into a pro. I tried to talk him out of it, to get him to start in the amateurs, but he wouldn't listen. In a few weeks, I got him in decent boxing shape and put him in the ring against a very ordinary guy, who tapped him on the noggin and knocked him cold.

"The qualities that a boxer has to have to be really good are different than in any other sport. It's a special kind of balance, a special feeling in there."

Exhibits A and B in the argument that boxing is no more difficult to master than football are Jones and Gastineau, who soon discovered otherwise. Although their records have a glittery veneer – Jones' one-year sabbatical from the Dallas Cowboys yielded six victories, five of which were inside the distance, while Gastineau was 15-2 with 15 knockout wins – they were fed a steady stream of cupcakes, fall-down guys selected solely for their likelihood to make the NFL stars look more formidable than they really were.

Jones, who boxed a bit as a kid, might have become something legitimate had he taken up the sport exclusively and stuck with it.

But he was 28 when he tried his ring thing, far too late to make up ground on short notice. "'Too Tall' was a very good athlete, an exceptionally strong guy, and he gave it a real shot," Dundee said. "He went to the gym with real trainers and really worked hard. And he still couldn't do it. Now if he had gone into boxing when he was a teenager, in the amateurs, instead of football, maybe that would've turned out OK."

Armed with a CBS contract and a spotlight on him that made it impossible to develop at his own pace, Jones could not live up to all those wildly inflated expectations. In his pro debut on November 3, 1979, a six-round majority decision over journeyman Abraham Yaqui Meneses, Jones was floored in the sixth round and was the beneficiary of what seemingly was the world's longest standing-eight count. His final bout, in that boxing hotbed, Jackson, Mississippi, is more notable for the fact that Jones was in the main event and a lightweight you might have heard of, Ray "Boom Boom" Mancini, on the undercard. The guy Jones blew out in the first round, a flabby Rocky Gonzalez, fought just that one time and looked like someone randomly picked out of the audience.

It was Gastineau, however, that gave boxers who had been football players a bad name. Gastineau had 51 sacks between 1981 and '84, terrorizing quarterbacks throughout the NFL. Facing guys not protected by blockers, flak jackets and facemasks, he was less frightening. After beating a steady stream of setups, he was 11-0 and reportedly in line for a million-dollar purse to fight George Foreman were he to get past a competent trial horse, Tim "Doc" Anderson, on June 9, 1992. But Anderson outpointed Gastineau and the proposed Foreman fight went up in flames, no doubt in part because the folks at HBO did not want a repeat of Foreman-Ellis.

Gastineau did "avenge" that loss by knocking out Anderson in six rounds on December 3, 1992, but Anderson later claimed he had been drugged after he refused to go into the tank, making him a defenseless target for Gastineau's ponderous bombs. Anderson later was convicted of murdering his corrupt manager, Rick "Elvis" Parker, the alleged architect of the proposed dive.

Subtract the records of Anderson (27-16-1, 13 KOs) and another former NFL player, Alonzo Highsmith (27-1-2, 23 KOs), who stopped Gastineau in one round in his final fight, on November 3,

1996, in Tokyo, and the cumulative record of Gastineau's opponents is horrible: 5-91-3 with two knockout victories and 77 losses by KO.

There is a current NFL player, Indianapolis Colts safety Tommy Zbikowski, who might have amounted to something as a professional boxer had he chosen what he describes as his "first love" in sports. Zbikowski, a former Chicago Golden Gloves fighter who posted a 75-15 record, is 4-0 with three KOs as a pro, those bouts taking place as a Notre Dame undergraduate and during NFL off-seasons and work stoppages.

"I think eventually I'll be judged as a fighter, not as someone trying to fight who played football at Notre Dame or in the NFL," Zbikowski said after his pro debut, a one-round TKO of Robert Bell on June 10, 2006, in Madison Square Garden. "It's not going to happen right away, but it will. I'll make sure of that. To tell the truth, I never thought I'd go as far as I have in football. I thought I'd be in boxing a long time ago.

"Growing up, whatever sport I was doing, I loved. But I always missed what I wasn't doing. When I was boxing, I missed football. Once you get to college and the NFL, though, football takes up so much of your time you have to choose."

Even Steward, so critical of most football players' boxing designs, praised what Zbikowski, a cruiserweight, could have been had he not become an All-America at Notre Dame, for whom he intercepted five passes, returning two for touchdowns, and scored two more TDs on punt returns in helping the Fighting Irish to the Fiesta Bowl that capped the 2006 season.

"He has such beautiful balance," Manny said of Zbikowski. "He has great natural rhythm, and he's always in position when he is punching. He doesn't box like a football player. He boxes like a boxer."

Mitchell, alas, boxed too much like a football player in his first matchup with Banks. It remains to be seen whether he can correct his flaws and do what no former football player of any consequence has done: become a world champion. It wasn't his first goal as an athlete, or even the second, but it what he is striving to become now because, well, what other choice does he have?

"I never put myself in that category," Mitchell, when advised of the abysmal history of football players trying their hand at boxing, said before his third-round stoppage of Chazz Witherspoon on April

28, 2012. "I always wanted to be a basketball player. I wear a size 16 shoe. I thought I'd be 6'6", 6'7" (he is 6'2"). When I played basketball, I didn't judge myself on the college aspect. I was thinking NBA.

"And when I played football, my mindset was making it to the NFL. But I had seven surgeries on my left knee. Other than to take some Motrin and to ice it down, I'm good to go in boxing, whereas in football I had 100 cc's drained out of the knee at one time. I've had cortisone shots until football wasn't fun anymore.

"But listen, I'm not saying football is harder than boxing. Boxing is a tough, lonely sport. You can be a beast on the football field and a pussycat in the ring."

Epilogue: After he evened the score against Banks with a 12-round unanimous decision that revealed he still had much to learn, Mitchell fought just once more, a first-round knockout loss to veteran contender Chris Arreola that apparently convinced him that to keep chasing his boxing dream was pointless. Zbikowski continued to show some promise, but he also hung up the gloves in 2017, with an 8-0 record and five KOs.

Riddick Bowe: Really Good, But Could've Been Even Better
The Ring, August 2015 issue

As a young amateur boxer, Riddick Bowe aspired to become the second coming of Muhammad Ali. He didn't quite make it, as is the case with any number of Ali imitators who attempted to duplicate the original. Instead, the two-time former heavyweight champion became the first coming of Riddick Bowe, which in some people's eyes is very much like the second coming of Ingemar Johansson. That's why "Big Daddy's" election to the International Boxing Hall of Fame's Class of 2015 has sparked such spirited debate.

Enshrinees into any sport's hall of fame can be divided into two categories. There are slam-dunk selections whose credentials are so impeccable that nary a voice is ever raised in dissent. But sports halls are not universally populated with Babe Ruths, Johnny Unitases, Bill Russells and, in the case of the IBHOF, Alis and Sugar Ray Robinsons. Thus the age-old question: Is a particular nominee to boxing's highest individual honor indisputably worthy of such a designation?

Bowe, former lightweight champion Ray "Boom Boom" Mancini and former featherweight titlist "Prince" Naseem Hamed comprise the first IBHOF class in the Modern category since the adjustment of the eligibility period. Each will be inducted on June 14 in Canastota, New York, with question marks attached. But, perhaps even more so than those other newly minted Hall of Famers, Bowe has sparked the kind of barstool and media-fueled objections not raised for any heavyweight candidate since the late Johansson gained admittance to the club in 2002.

Like Johansson, who won a silver medal in the 1952 Helsinki Olympics, Bowe has an Olympic pedigree, having taken silver in the super heavyweight division in Seoul in 1988. Like Johansson, best known for his three-fight series with Floyd Patterson, Bowe's primary distinction as a professional is his epic trilogy with Evander Holyfield. The difference between them in that respect is Johansson was 1-2 against Patterson while Bowe won two of three against Holyfield.

Like Johansson, whose 26-2 pro career (with 17 knockout victories) includes few big-name opponents with the exception of Patterson and Eddie Machen, Bowe's 43-1 (33 KOs) mark is somewhat bereft of matchups with the finest heavyweights of his era. Yes, he did go to hell and back with Holyfield three times, but his other title bouts during his two championship reigns hardly reads like a Who's Who of the division: Jorge Luis Gonzalez, Herbie Hide, Jesse Ferguson and Michael Dokes. Yes, Bowe did face credible opponents in non-title matchups – Andrew Golota (twice), Bruce Seldon, Pierre Coetzer, Buster Mathis Jr., Larry Donald, Tony Tubbs, Tyrell Biggs and Bert Cooper – but, considering the talent-enriched period in which he competed, where is the name Lennox Lewis? Mike Tyson? Not to mention Michael Moorer, George Foreman, Larry Holmes, Ray Mercer, Buster Douglas, Tommy Morrison, Razor Ruddock and David Tua.

Bowe, now 47, acknowledges that his enshrinement into the IBHOF has met with some resistance. But he said it isn't his fault that his path to Canastota detoured around some of the more dangerous intersections. He said he "desperately" wanted to test himself as a pro against Lewis, who, representing Canada, stopped

70

him in two rounds in the gold-medal bout in Seoul. Bowe insists he was just as eager to mix it up with homeboy Tyson, who came from the same gritty, crime-infested Brownsville neighborhood in Brooklyn, New York, that he did but was steered away from those and other potential career-defining bouts by his manager, Rock Newman. Newman, according to Bowe, was in "total control" of any and all decisions regarding who and when he fought.

"I really don't have any regrets," Bowe said. "The fact I fought Evander three times pretty much made up for everything else. I think those other guys (Lewis and Tyson) realize that they couldn't have done anything better than I did when I fought Holyfield. They couldn't even have done it as good. When they saw what I did with Holyfield, they had to know they couldn't have beaten me anyhow."

So if Bowe is confident that he would have had success against the two most obvious omissions from his resume, why didn't he just go ahead and fight those guys? Bouts with Lewis and Tyson, perhaps even multiple times, would have significantly added to his net career earnings of $30 million, a tidy sum nonetheless that has all but vanished due to profligate spending and a raft of legal problems that also served to drain his bank account.

"If I could change anything, the No. 1 thing is that I wouldn't have Rock Newman as my manager," Bowe said. "I wish I had people around me who had my best interests at heart, like (Floyd) Mayweather has. I wish I was more into the financial part of the game, that I had paid more attention to what was going on around me. There were meetings and stuff where I needed to be there. I really thought that (Newman) had my back. He didn't. That made all the difference."

Newman, who was sued by Bowe and whose relationship with him has turned so frosty as to be non-existent, has contended that some of the signature fights that Bowe might have had didn't get made because, well, doing business in boxing can be difficult and closing multimillion-dollar deals at the negotiating table isn't always as easy as an elite fighter hooking off the jab.

"Bowe wanted fame and fortune," Newman told the *Washington Post* in 2010, describing his oversight of Bowe's career as one might the difficulty of dealing with a petulant child. "He wanted to be Muhammad Ali. But he didn't want to pay the price for it. He could not internalize the process. He hated the process."

That might explain why Bowe constantly had problems maintaining an optimal fighting weight and so disliked the rigors of training camp. But that should not have been an obstacle to arranging fights that the public wanted to see and that Bowe insists he wanted to participate in.

"When it comes to making big fights, nothing is automatic," Newman said, comparing Bowe's circumstances with the long delay in finalizing Mayweather-Manny Pacquiao. "The bridge between wanting to see something and actually seeing it can be steep and long. Sometimes it's a bridge that leads nowhere."

That bridge that never reaches the other side, Bowe said, began with the injudicious decision to toss his WBC championship belt into a trash can in London (he retained his WBA and IBF titles) after Lewis had won a WBC elimination bout by stopping Ruddock in two rounds in that city on October 31, 1992. The prevailing impression then, and now, is that it was Bowe ducking Lewis, not the other way around.

"That was Rock Newman's idea," Bowe said of the trash-can deposit that so impacted his career and how so many have come to perceive that career. "I wish I never would have done that. I really wanted to fight Lennox. I wanted to fight him so bad I could taste it. I wanted to fight him more than anyone."

Opinions, of course, will have to suffice when hard evidence is lacking. If there is anyone who has a reasonable claim to knowing what might have happened had Bowe and Lewis ever squared off, it is Holyfield, who spent a lot of time trading leather with both. And the "Real Deal" – past and present – casts his ballot for Bowe.

Prior to his first scrap with Lewis on March 13, 1999, Holyfield, his three wars with Bowe already in the books, suggested that "Lennox Lewis can't show me anything that I haven't already seen from Bowe. Bowe is a bigger, more complete fighter than Lewis. He can fight on the inside and from the outside. Lewis is kind of one-dimensional by comparison."

Sixteen years later, has Holyfield reversed course on that somewhat daring suggestion? No, he has not. He also believes that Bowe – at least a fit, motivated Bowe – would have been too much for Tyson to handle.

"It's still the same," Holyfield said when asked to confirm or deny his original projection of the Lewis-Bowe fight that never happened.

"Lennox Lewis is a very strong guy, but he just held you when he got on the inside. That's it. Riddick Bowe, he'd punch you when you got in tight. Lennox would try to hit you with one shot and if he hit you with shot, he'd try to hit you with another one. But if he missed, he'd grab a hold of you and put all his weight on you. Bowe, to me, was a more complete fighter.

"I also think Bowe would have been too much for Tyson. Lewis, I don't believe, wanted to fight Tyson when he was younger. I know Lennox was scared of that Tyson."

Controversial opinions, to be sure, and not shared by everyone. But Kathy Duva, whose Main Events was Lewis' American promotional company, agrees with the notion that a Bowe-Lewis fight never came to be primarily because of interference from Newman.

"I can't speak for what Riddick thought, but we definitely wanted the (Bowe-Lewis) fight," she said. "Everybody knew that. We tried and tried and tried to make it happen. Lennox wanted to unify all the titles but Rock just didn't want to do it, and Bowe literally threw the (WBC) belt in the garbage. I'm sure that was Rock's idea.

"Rock was impossible. The way we get frustrated now with Richard Schaefer and Al Haymon, that was Rock back then. You couldn't deal with him."

Fight fans thus are left to sift through the whys and wherefores of the enigmatic Riddick Bowe. Is the real Bowe the steadfast guy who refused to yield to the lure of drugs and crime in Brownsville, who walked his mother home from her bus stop to protect her from any possible harm, and who earned Holyfield's undying respect where it counted, inside the ropes? Or is the real Bowe the clownish figure who routinely gained 30 or 40 pounds between fights, who lacked the discipline to have the kind of staying power that would have prolonged his prime and who washed out of Marine boot camp after just a week?

He likely is a little bit of both, just as Johansson was an assemblage of seemingly mismatched parts comprising an intriguing whole. But sometimes it is an individual's inconsistencies that set him apart and form the basis of his legacy, for better or worse.

Renowned strength and conditioning coach Mackie Shilstone, whose celebrity client list also included such fighters as Michael

Spinks, Roy Jones Jr. and Bernard Hopkins, said he can never forget the time he spent with Bowe.

"Getting Riddick into the condition he needed to be in just became a battle," Shilstone said. "It almost burned me out. But he also was the funniest guy I ever worked with. When he fought Holyfield the first time, Evander and Tim Hallmark (Holyfield's conditioning coach) were floored by Bowe's mobility. They thought he'd be slow and ponderous, but he outpunched Holyfield 2-to-1. After the fight, Holyfield even said he thought Bowe wouldn't have anything left after the eighth round.

"I just hope Riddick finds whatever it is he's looking for. It always seemed to me he was looking for some alter ego. I think that's what happened when he went into the Marines. You know that was a form of escapism. He was always trying to escape from, or to, something."

Shavers Rates Himself – Who Else? – Hardest-Hitting Heavyweight
RingTV.com, October 1, 2013

It is human nature, one supposes, to compile lists for anything and everything. A cornerstone of late-night television host David Letterman's popularity is his whimsical "Top 10 List" segment. Recalcitrant husbands receive "Honey-do" lists of household chores to perform when they aren't slipping off to the golf course or the neighborhood tavern for a cold one.

Boxing analysts, and just plain fans, are no different when it comes to an obsessive need to arrange things in some kind of order. It's why there are so many pound-for-pound lists, HBO Sports' Jim Lampley's "Gatti List" (for fighters whose bouts are always exciting) and, of course, lists for the most devastating punchers. All sports fans are enthralled by demonstrations of power, whether it comes in the form of tape-measure home runs, rim-rattling slam-dunks or turn-out-the-lights knockouts.

There were two sudden endings in Bethlehem, Pennsylvania, last Thursday night, during a seven-bout professional fight card at the Sands Bethlehem Events Center. Junior welterweight Jason Sosa (10-1-3, 6 KOs) deposited the very unlucky Tyrone Luckey (5-4-1, 5 KOs) on the canvas with a crushing left hook to the midsection in the second round of a scheduled eight-rounder, and Luckey remained

74

on his hands and knees, gasping for breath, for over two full minutes. Then, in the main event, welterweight Ronald Cruz (19-2, 14 KOs) roused himself from a bout-long stupor to starch Alberto Morales (11-3-1, 8 KOs) with two knockdowns in the 10th and final round, much to the relief of Cruz's anxious promoter, J Russell Peltz.

But the really big hitters were the four aging men who were seated at ringside, watching fighters 30 or 40 years their junior attempting to summon some of the quick-strike power they so routinely delivered during their remarkable ring careers. Five-division former world champion Thomas "Hitman" Hearns was there for what was billed as "Legends of Boxing" night, as were stellar heavyweights Larry Holmes (from nearby Easton, Pennsylvania), Gerry Cooney and Earnie Shavers. Collectively, that quartet of graybeards – Shavers, at 68, is the oldest and Hearns, at 54, the youngest – compiled a record of 232-28-2 with 184 victories inside the distance. It's little wonder that quite a few of the paying customers ponied up a bit more of their disposable income to attend an earlier meet-and-greet with the legends, their tickets providing them the privilege of having the Fab Four sign autographs and pose for photos.

As first-ballot inductees into the International Boxing Hall of Fame, local hero Holmes and Hearns were the most accomplished of the legends in attendance. But much of the buzz, as always, centered around the shaved-skull and still-menacing Shavers, who isn't enshrined in the IBHOF, never won even an alphabet-soup version of the heavyweight title and was stopped himself in seven of his 14 defeats.

That's what happens when there are a whole lot of boxing folks who will swear that Shavers was, and to this day remains, the biggest bopper ever among the sport's big men. To hear some tell it, "The Acorn" – the nickname Muhammad Ali gave him, and which has stuck to him like lint on Velcro – could send an opponent to lullaby land with a single shot more emphatically than anyone, including such dependable power sources as Jack Dempsey, Joe Louis, Max Baer, Rocky Marciano, Sonny Liston, George Foreman, Mike Tyson and Wladimir Klitschko.

"You think some puffed-up cruiserweight is gonna scare me?" fringe heavyweight contender James "Quick" Tillis said in July 1988, a few days before he was to be the guy across the ring for the heavyweight debut of undisputed cruiserweight king Evander Holyfield in Stateline, Nevada. "Man, I been in there with the best. I fought a bald-headed guy named Earnie Shavers, who was the baddest dude in the world. He hit so hard, he could turn goat milk into gasoline."

It should be noted that Tillis *beat* Shavers, on a 10-round unanimous decision on June 10, 1982. If fighters who bested him felt that way, what about those who Shavers put down for the count with that overhand right delivered with the force of a runaway locomotive?

Not surprisingly, Shavers has considered the question of listing the heavyweight division's premier knockout artists and he casts his vote for himself.

"Number One," he responded when asked where he should land on any such list. "No one can outpunch me, except God."

Holmes, who held the title for 7¾ years and made 20 successful defenses, second only to Louis' 25, knows what it was like to be on the receiving end of one of Shavers' explosive rights. In fact, there is a widespread belief that the "Easton Assassin" never stood taller than he did when he arose, on wobbly legs, after Shavers dropped him in the seventh round of their September 28, 1979, title bout at Caesars Palace in Las Vegas. But Holmes, who had previously outpointed Shavers on March 25, 1978, staved off the challenger's desperate attempt to close the show and went on to win on an 11th-round TKO.

"I always tell Earnie that he hit me *too* hard," Holmes said with a skewed reasoning that apparently makes sense only to him. "If he hadn't hit me quite so damn hard, he would have knocked me out for sure. That punch actually kind of woke me up when I hit the floor.

"Man, I still got knots in my head where he hit me. Earnie could punch very hard, incredibly hard. I hear people say, 'Aw, man, he couldn't possibly have hit as hard as everybody says.' They think that the stories about Earnie's power are exaggerated. It's no exaggeration. That power was real."

Shavers, born in Garland, Alabama, raised in Warren, Ohio, came by that awesome power naturally, with some help from his upbringing on a farm. You spend a lifetime doing what farm kids are obliged to do every day, you can't help but develop an impressive set of muscles that are adaptable to what fighters do.

"My back and legs got built up from toting bales of hay, from chopping trees for a wood-burning furnace," Shavers recalled. "That's where your punching power comes from – your legs and your back."

But while there is a distinction between baseball players who not only can produce tape-measure shots when they connect just so, but become Hall of Famers because their skill set includes the ability to hit for average, run, throw and field on an exceptionally high level, so it is for one-trick ponies with padded gloves on their fists. The knock against Shavers is that, although his big punch made him special in an obvious way, he lacked stamina and the overall abilities of some of his contemporaries. The 1970s to early '80s represented a golden age of heavyweights whose ranks were populated by the likes of Ali, Foreman, Holmes, Cooney, Joe Frazier, Ken Norton, Michael Spinks, Ron Lyle, Jimmy Ellis, Jerry Quarry, Jimmy Young, George Chuvalo, Oscar Bonavena and even cross-generational Floyd Patterson, who won the title vacated by Marciano in 1956.

Shavers stood apart because of the freakish power that carried him to quick knockouts of Norton, Ellis and Young, but his limited gas tank and own relative inability to shake off a crushing blow cost him in losses via stoppage against Quarry, Lyle, Bernardo Mercado and Randall "Tex" Cobb. His final record of 74-14-1, with 68 KOs, is a hodgepodge of exhilarating highs and plunging lows.

"I used to tense up," Shavers said when asked about his reputation for being at his most dangerous only through the first four or five rounds, and not so much afterward. "That burned my energy out real quick. I went out there trying to kill everybody."

Lists, of course, are like noses; everybody has one and not all are alike. In 2003 Shavers was listed as the 10th-greatest puncher of all time by *The Ring*, which is understandable considering that Ali, Joe Bugner, Holmes, Cobb, Lyle and Norton all tabbed him as the hardest puncher they ever faced. But that list, which encompassed all divisions, had heavyweights Louis (No. 1), Dempsey (7) and Foreman (9) ahead of him, although Marciano (14), Sonny Liston (15) and Tyson (16) were rated lower.

Another list, of the "hardest hitters in heavyweight history," was posted by ESPN.com's Graham Houston on December 27, 2007, and had Tyson at No. 1, ahead of Liston (I2), Louis (3), Foreman (4), Marciano (5) and Shavers (6).

In the end, it's always a matter of opinion, which is the basis of every debate. Earnie puts himself in the top slot, and he figures his take on the matter is as worthy as anyone else's.

"If I had one fight, one moment, I could do over, it'd be in the second fight with Larry Holmes," Shavers recalled. "I had him hurt. I had him hurt *bad.* But he got up I was surprised he got up, and he probably was, too. Most guys I hit like that, they'd still be out today."

Another regret of Shavers' is that, when Sylvester Stallone was casting the part of Clubber Lang for *Rocky III*, he got passed over in favor of Mr. T. The story – which, apparently, is true – is that Shavers' audition took a wrong turn after he hit Stallone too hard while practicing some in-ring choreography.

"We were circling; I was pulling my punches" Shavers said during a 2001 interview with ESPN.com's Ralph Wiley, who was doing a piece on the 25th anniversary of the 1976 release of the original *Rocky*. "(Stallone) said, 'Don't hold back, Earnie. Hit me.' I said, 'I can't do that, Mr. Stallone.' I could've, but I wanted that job, and I didn't think that would help me get it.

"But he kept pushing me, saying, 'C'mon, show me something,' and sort of hitting me. Finally, I said, 'OK,' and a give him a little one under the ribs, where the livers of boxers are. Don't know about actors, but if they got livers, they probably are in the same place. Anyway, Mr. Stallone called time – he didn't say nothing, just kinda doubled over a little bit and sort of waved his hand – and then somebody helped him out of the ring and to this bathroom or somewhere, and he sent word out that they couldn't use me. I guess I blew it."

It was Wiley's belief that Shavers wasn't going to snag the role in any case, because he was so clearly better at delivering punches than lines of badass dialogue.

"Earnie didn't sound like a killer," Wiley, who died in 2004, wrote of Shavers' brush with Hollywood. "He had a voice so light it made Mike Tyson's Tweety Bird pipes sound like Darth Vader's. Earnie's voice would've stopped him from being Clubber Lang in *Rocky III*, even if a sparring session with Stallone hadn't."

But Tyson's Tweety Bird pipes didn't stop him from appearing in *The Hangover* movies, or in that one-man stage show that toured the country recently. So maybe there's hope for Shavers yet to make it onto the big screen.

Anyone up for *The Hangover IV*? If there's anyone as familiar as Tyson with inducing day-after headaches in opponents, you have to figure that "The Acorn" is that guy.

Tyson Fury Gets Offensive for Rematch with Wilder
TheSweetScience.com, February 13, 2020

It has been said that a kangaroo is a horse designed by a committee, but nature tends to work best when a horse doesn't try to be anything but a horse and a kangaroo happily remains a kangaroo. But that doesn't stop the experimenters among us, always looking to modify what was or is, from fiddling with the status quo in an effort to produce a new and hopefully superior version of something.

When lineal heavyweight champion Tyson Fury (29-0-1, 20 KOs) enters the ring for his rematch with WBC titlist Deontay Wilder (42-0-1, 41 KOs) on February 22 at Las Vegas' MGM Grand, he won't exactly be a patchwork kangaroo with a few residual equine traits. Nor will he have three trainers, all of whom have had their turn constructing the "Gypsy King" to their preferred specifications, working his corner that night. The last of that trio of chief seconds is recently hired Javan "Sugar" Hill, nephew of the late, great overseer of Detroit's legendary Kronk Gym, Emanuel Steward. Manny, a 1996 inductee into the International Boxing Hall of Fame who was 68 when he died in 2012, was like a pass-happy offensive coordinator in football, as are his disciples, all partial to high-scoring contests in which their guy wins by making more splashy big plays (think knockdowns and impressive displays of power-punching) than whomever is working the other sideline and playing D.

There are two ways, and two ways only, to win any athletic contest or boxing match. One is to score more than the other side; the other is to allow the other side to score less than you do. Those objectives might sound the same, but they are fundamentally worlds apart. Rare is the team or fighter equally adept at mastering both strategies and employing them interchangeably.

Hill takes the place of the more defense-oriented Ben Davison, jettisoned after his most recent outing as Fury's coach *du jour,* a unanimous but nonetheless worrisome decision over Sweden's Otto

Wallin on September 14, 2019, at the MGM Grand, a bout in which Fury incurred an ugly gash over his right eye that required 47 total stitches to close. It would not have been a travesty of justice had referee Tony Weeks or the ring physician stopped the fight at some point in the later rounds and awarded the underdog Scandanavian southpaw a shocking upset victory.

"I had a good defensive coach in Ben Davison," Fury, who also will have a new cut man, "Stitch" Duran, noted of the young trainer who took the place of his original trainer and uncle, Peter Fury, who also was determined to be lacking in some way. "We worked a lot on defense every single day for two years. It was defense, defense, defense.

"But I needed an aggressive trainer. I worked with Sugar Hill in the past. I knew he was a good guy. I knew we got on well, which was very important. Communication is key to any relationship. That's why I brought him in. It was one of the best decisions I ever made."

Now that he is better acquainted with the attacking Kronk methods passed on by Steward to Hill and some of his other assistants, it is little wonder that the 31-year-old Fury is uncharacteristically predicting a second-round knockout of Wilder, whose *modus operandi* is always the same: throw right-hand bombs until one connects and the dude laying on the canvas has been counted out. If you want to call the "Bronze Bomber" from Tuscaloosa, Alabama, a one-trick pony, that's all right. He knows who and what he is, and he makes no apologies for firmly adhering to the singular principle that has made him one of the hardest-hitting heavyweights of all time, and arguably the biggest bopper ever, according to Top Rank founder and CEO Bob Arum, who promotes Fury. You wouldn't think Arum would approve of Fury, a clearly more polished boxer, choosing to slug it out with Wilder in the center of the ring, but, as always, there are different paths to victory. The best fight plan indisputably is whichever one that works.

"I have confidence in Tyson," Arum said of his new-look heavyweight headliner. "There are guys who say they're going to knock out their opponent, but it's like a baseball player getting up to the plate and trying to hit a home run. Anybody who knows baseball will say that the guy who looks to make contact has a better chance to hit a home run than the guy that's swinging from his heels."

A let-'er-fly guy like Wilder, in other words.

"Tyson is a great boxer, but he has the determination to knock out Wilder," Arum continued. "He's not going to force it, but the knockout will come. Unlike the first fight, when he got Wilder into trouble – and Wilder was in trouble a couple of times – he's not going to let him off the hook."

To Fury's way of thinking, the huge Briton – when you're 6-foot-9 and 254½ pounds, as the badly bleeding Gypsy King was for his excursion into the danger zone against Wallin – the only certainty of outcome is when the winner snatches the pencils out of the judges' hands. In their first clash, on December 1, 2018, in Los Angeles' Staples Center, Fury was floored twice, a flash knockdown in the ninth round and something much more perilous in the 12th and final round, but he barely beat referee Jack Reiss' count and somehow managed to stay upright for more than two minutes until the final bell. The outcome – a split draw – satisfied neither Wilder, who figured two knockdowns should have given him the edge, or Fury, who seemingly stockpiled most of the non-knockdown rounds as a squirrel might horde acorns for the winter. The tabulations read 115-111 for Wilder on Alejandro Rochin's scorecard, 114-112 for Fury on Robert Tapper's, and 113-113 on the one submitted by swing judge Phil Edwards.

"I didn't get the decision because I didn't keep working on my boxing," Fury said. "I believe I can outbox Deontay Wilder very comfortable like the last time. But it's no good me believing it; the judges have to believe it. To guarantee victory, I've got to get the knockout. I don't want another controversial decision.

"Look, I'm not a judge. They see what they see. That's what they get paid to do. This time my destiny lies in my own two fists."

But what of the presumed imbalance of power? What if Wilder really does wield the biggest hammer in heavyweight history? Won't going toe-to-toe with him be like engaging Babe Ruth in home run derby or Michael Jordan in a slam-dunk competition?

"That was one of my easiest fights," Fury said of his first go at Wilder. "Other than the two knockdowns it was pretty much a one-sided fight. I've had fights much harder than that. My toughest opponent was Steve Cunningham, the former cruiserweight champion (who decked Fury in the second round of their April 20, 2013, bout in New York before finally succumbing on a seventh-round stoppage). It was my first step up to anybody with that type of ability. He was slick and hard to hit, awkward but a very good boxer."

It is Fury's contention that his various trainers have supplied him with the versatility to enter the lion's den and emerge relatively unscathed, while Wilder lacks the imagination and ability to go to a Plan B, if indeed he has one.

"I think there's nothing to worry about," Fury said of what he expects from Wilder. "He's got a big right hand and that's it. He's a one-dimensional fighter. The one who should be concerned is Deontay Wilder. He had me down twice, but he couldn't finish me. He landed the two best punches any heavyweight in the world could ever land on somebody else and the Gypsy King rose, like a phoenix, from the ashes.

"I'm match-fit, I'm ready, I'm confident, I'm injury-free. I'm ready for a war, one round or 12. And when I get him hurt, I'll throw everything but the kitchen sink at him. He won't know what hit him."

Maybe. But if another stylistic makeover on short notice doesn't yield the desired result, Tyson Fury could wind up looking like the horse that tried to be a kangaroo.

Epilogue: For Hill and Fury, the strategic makeover plotted by the former and executed by the latter proved to be a smash hit. Fury did exactly what he had imagined himself doing, flooring Wilder in rounds three and five before referee Kenny Bayless stepped in and awarded Fury, who was well ahead on points, a TKO victory in the seventh round.

Foreman-Holmes Would Have Been One for the Aged
TheSweetScience.com, January 22, 2015

On January 15, 1990, heavyweights George Foreman and Gerry Cooney squared off in Atlantic City's Boardwalk Hall. Some clever punster had dubbed it "the Geezers at Caesars," a backhanded swipe to an event which, to some people's way of thinking, paired a couple of over-the-hill, used-up fighters who should have been content to sit on their rocking chairs and sip their Geritol.

Cooney was 33 at the time and was fighting for just the third time in six years; Foreman was 41, having celebrated his birthday just five days earlier.

Geezers? In retrospect, it now seems obvious that Cooney and that reasonably fresh version of Big George, who won on a second-round stoppage, were just a couple of kids going at it in the schoolyard.

Last week, the boxing world celebrated the 50th birthday of an actual geezer, Bernard Hopkins, who took the occasion to tell everyone he believed he had one more fight in him, and that it would come against a younger (of course), highly credible opponent. But even "The Alien" against anyone might not seem so age-defying when stacked against a matchup of Jurassic Park heavyweights that had been scheduled to take place on January 23, 1999, in Houston's Astrodome.

Had that pay-per-view bout (suggested purchase price: $39.95) gone off as scheduled, the combatants would have been a 50-year-old Foreman (then 76-5, 68 KOs) and 49-year-old Larry Holmes (66-6, 42 KOs). Oh, sure, smarmy critics would have sneered at it and someone surely would have come up with a derogatory phrase, maybe "Old Folks Home at the Dome." But here's the truth: Hundreds of thousands of fight fans would have bought it, maybe because it would have finally pitted two of the better big men in boxing history, even if they were grandfathers, or maybe because it came with an element of morbid curiosity.

"There was interest, a whole lot of interest," Foreman said when I asked about his recollections of a bout that would have been a real-life enactment of *Grudge Match*, a bad 2013 movie whose premise was a 30-years-in-the-making rematch between sixtysomething antagonists played by Sylvester Stallone and Robert De Niro. But the notion of a "Rocky Balboa" and "Raging Bull" somehow getting together to make box-office magic fizzled.

Might the same thing have happened with Foreman-Holmes?

"Larry and I were really in the mood to do it," Foreman recalled. "When we met at the press conference in New York, we started selling woof tickets, the whole deal. And it would have sold, I'm sure of that. There was so much name recognition there. That's what made it more important on the later end.

"I left boxing in 1977 (the start of Foreman's 10-year retirement from the ring). At that time, it wouldn't have meant much for me to box Larry Holmes; he was just making a name for himself at that point. Then, by me going off the scene, Don King went all-in on promoting Larry. When I made my comeback, can you believe that Larry was retired then? So the timing never was right for us to fight, for one reason or another."

For his part, Holmes was just as anxious to throw down with Foreman, and not just because, had the bout come off, Big George would have been paid $10 million and Holmes $4 million.

"When it didn't happen, I was very disappointed," the "Easton Assassin" said. "That was my dream, man, to fight George Foreman. I got tired of people saying, 'What about George Foreman? Why don't you fight George Foreman?' All I could say was, 'It ain't me that won't fight George, it's George that won't fight me. I'm ready when he's ready.' But he was never ready.

"But you know what? Looking back at it now, I don't blame him. I wouldn't have fought me either. I could still fight then, man, and George did not want to lose. But winning or losing didn't matter as much to me. I wasn't fighting for a championship. I was fighting to pay the rent, and I would give my all to do that."

Debate if you must the possible outcome of the fight-that-never-was – and Teddy Atlas and renowned journalist Jerry Izenberg will do just that, a little later in this piece – but know this: Foreman-Holmes wasn't just a fantasy. The legendary figures had collected a non-refundable 10% of their contracted purses ($1 million to George, $400,000 to Larry), the Astrodome was booked and a press conference held. All that remained was for the promoter, an Englishman named Roger Levitt, to produce letters of credit that would have ensured that the fighters receive their full purses.

"On the date that letters of credit were supposed to be posted, the guy missed it," Foreman, who pulled the plug on the fight, said in early January 1999. "My instincts were to say, 'That's it.' My attorneys were a little lenient with him. They gave him a week's extension. He just couldn't come up with a letter of credit. A fight just couldn't be made without a letter of credit."

Sixteen years later, Foreman stands by that statement. He was a fighter, to be sure, and a proud one, but he also is a businessman and he wasn't about to give himself away at a discounted rate.

"I think (Levitt) thought that since he put that first million dollars up, I would blindly follow him along," Foreman said. "But I'd dealt with Don King and all those guys. I knew you must have the money in the bank to proceed. I wasn't going down that trail, not knowing where it would lead, as some guys have done.

"It probably was one of those situations that was just not meant to be. Larry and I kept missing each other."

At the time, Levitt insisted he had arranged for a $9 million insurance bond, which he said was "almost as good" as a letter of credit. But additional financing dried up when a younger heavyweight, and a superstar at that, scheduled a pay-for-view fight just one week before Foreman-Holmes was to take place. If a financial knockout blow was dealt to George and Larry, it came in the form of the January 16, 1999, PPV scrap between Mike Tyson and Frans Botha at the MGM Grand in Las Vegas. Tyson, as expected, battered Botha into submission in five rounds.

It was Levitt's contention that a key financial backer for Foreman-Holmes got cold feet in fear of going against Tyson for fans' PPV dollars.

"We had an Arab business who I've known for some time, who was putting up $12.6 million," Levitt said of the time of the cancellation. "He pulled out because of the timing of the Tyson fight. His advisers told him we were going to get killed on the pay-per-view." Tyson-Botha, by the way, came with a PPV tariff of $49.95.

Interestingly, it wasn't the first time that Tyson had torpedoed a possible Foreman-Holmes scrap.

"When I fought Evander Holyfield in Atlantic City (Holyfield defended his WBC, WBA and IBF titles on a unanimous decision on April 19, 1991), we did real well," Foreman recalled. "Holmes had come back and (promoter Bob) Arum had a lot to do with Larry's fight with Holyfield (which Holyfield also won, on a unanimous decision, on June 19, 1992). Arum was thinking about doing something with Larry and me, and he even printed up a poster that had us fighting for the heavyweight championship. He wanted to promote that fight if Larry beat Holyfield. But Larry didn't win."

Perhaps Foreman is right. Can there really be something to astrology? Could it be that the stars never properly aligned themselves to make Foreman-Holmes doable?

Atlas and Izenberg each is of the opinion that had they fought in the late 1970s, boxing master Holmes, with that laser-accurate jab, ability to pace himself and superior ring skills, might have been too savvy for the young George, whose stock in trade then was to throw as many loaded-up haymakers as he could, and as quickly as he could, until he flattened his opponent or ran out of gas.

But the 1999 version of George vs. the 1999 version of Larry? That likely would have been another matter. That George fought more under control and had – gasp! – learned some of the finer points of boxing. Atlas and Izenberg each see him as being too much for Holmes to have handled.

"The old George Foreman, the reincarnated George Foreman that came back after a 10-year hiatus, was tougher than the young George Foreman," Atlas offered. "He was smarter in a lot of ways, he was just better. He wasn't better physically, having gotten older and fatter, but he was better in the most important areas. He understood the difference between truth and lies.

"He bought into a lie in Zaire (against Muhammad Ali). He was a bigger, stronger guy than Ali, but Ali made him feel that that didn't matter. George couldn't make the decisions he needed to make. He couldn't endure what he needed to endure. He wasn't tough enough to handle the things that Ali represented that night. But of course he could have; thinking he couldn't was the lie he bought into. He didn't have to cave in.

"George had to live with that for 10 years, and living with it was a helluva lot harder than the punches he would have had to take for a few more rounds. So when he came back, he came back tougher. I think the older George Foreman would have beat the crap out of the younger George Foreman, and I think the older George would have beat the older Larry. But I would have taken the young Larry over the young George. That George didn't have as many dimensions as Larry. When his power didn't work, like it didn't work in Zaire, he didn't have anything else to back it up."

Izenberg pretty much sees it the same way as Atlas.

"The Foreman who fought Ali in Zaire would not have beaten Larry, I don't think," said Izenberg, the sports columnist emeritus for the *Newark Star-Ledger*. "George became a far, far better fighter, a far, far smarter fighter, in the second phase of his career.

"When Big George first came back, I laughed. We all did. But the more he fought, the more he got into a groove. I think he proved to everyone how much he had learned as a fighter when he was doing television (commentary)."

Which is not to say Izenberg is convinced Foreman-Holmes would have been PPV gold in 1999.

"Forget about Tyson (fighting Botha the week before)," he said. "Who would have put up 40 bucks to see those guys fight at that stage, 15 years past their prime? I personally believe that it should not have been allowed to take place."

Holmes, of course, sees himself as the winner against the young George and the old George.

"The way I would have fought George (in the late 1970s) is the way I would have fought him in 1999, or now," Holmes said. "I'd move side-to-side, use the jab, sneak in the right hand, put some combinations together, get in there a little bit and box him inside. Just tire him out. That's it.

"George was good for four or five rounds. If you hurt George, he'd fight you harder. But when he did that, he'd either take you out or empty his gas tank. He didn't have good stamina. Take him into the sixth and seventh rounds or later and he couldn't go."

You'd think Foreman would offer a stern rebuttal, but it isn't necessarily so. He thinks some of the points Holmes makes are valid.

"I was smarter the second time around," he agreed. "I learned how to pace myself. I'd wait around for a few rounds, then try for a seventh- or eighth-round knockout. I didn't want to burn myself out like I did in the early part of my career. But that would have played into Larry's box of tricks because he was a guy who always knew how to pace himself.

"If I was a betting man, I'd give the edge to Larry in a 12-round fight. I'm just being honest. Larry always made sure he had something left in the tank in the 10th, 11th, 12th rounds. But if a fight between him and me ended early, I'd have to give it to myself."

Foreman said he understands why Holmes always seems to carry a chip on his shoulder, and why he wanted a fight with him so badly.

"Larry became heavyweight champion after Muhammad Ali, and he might have thought, 'Now I'll be as big as Ali.' But what's that old saying? Beating The Man or succeeding The Man doesn't make you The Man. Nobody could supplant Ali in terms of recognition. Realizing that probably kept Larry angry for a while. A lot of us went through that, but I think Larry struggled with that more than anyone."

Butterbean Turns 50: Pass the Cake (and a Slab of Ribs)
TheSweetScience.com, August 3, 2016

Perhaps it was just a coincidence, but there was a late-night showing on cable TV on August 1 of one of my favorite movies, *Forrest Gump*, which I watched in its entirety for what must have been the 10th time. It's the Academy Award-winning 1994 film (Tom Hanks received his second Oscar in the lead role) about a slow-witted, kind-hearted and athletically gifted Alabama country boy who, by chance or fate, happened to be a participant in or witness to many of the most notable events of a 30-year span in the 20th century.

In many ways, the real-life story of retired heavyweight boxer Eric "Butterbean" Esch mirrors the fictional tale of Forrest Gump, the main exception being that the erstwhile "King of the Four-Rounders" is uncommonly bright for someone not blessed with the advantage of an extensive formal education. Where Gump's most obvious trait was his below-average IQ, that shortcoming failed to hinder him throughout a remarkable life's journey which proved, as if there ever was any doubt, that first impressions aren't always the most accurate gauge of who and what any human being is, or can become.

For Eric Esch, bullied as a pudgy child growing up in Jasper, Alabama, the first thing that is noticeable is his massive girth. He is, and always has been, fat. But, like Gump, who rose to renown in the fictional town of Greenbow, Alabama, a remarkable set of circumstances enabled the really large kid who came to be known as Butterbean to tap into a hidden talent that would make him moderately rich and even more famous. That talent was the ability to knock a succession of other large men (although not nearly as much so) cockeyed, and so what if most of his victims were third- and fourth-tier types who were fed to The Bean as if they were so many barbecued ribs?

August 3 marks the estimable Mr. Esch's 50th birthday and, although it has been a little more than three years since his final bout, a loss to Kirk Lawson in New South Wales, Australia, that saw The Bean retire after the second round with shoulder pain, he waddled into well-fed retirement from the ring with a 77-10-4 record that included 58 victories by knockout. That number is all the more impressive when you consider that of his 91 pro fights, all but one were scheduled for four rounds, meaning his demolition work had to be done in a hurry. Including late-career dalliances in kickboxing and mixed martial arts, Butterbean's overall combat-sports record stands at 97-24-5, with 66 wins inside the distance.

And while it is easy for skeptics to dismiss Butterbean as a freak show, a carnival act promoted by Top Rank impresario Bob Arum in much the same manner that legendary 19th-century huckster P.T. Barnum made major attractions of a dwarf he renamed General Tom Thumb, an immense African elephant called Jumbo, and opera singer Jenny Lind, "the Swedish Nightingale," it is difficult to sell the sizzle unless there is at least a bit of meat attached.

The most notable entry on The Bean's resume as a professional pugilist came in his one and only scheduled 10-rounder, on July 27, 2002, in which he was paired against long-reigning heavyweight champion Larry Holmes. And while the "Easton Assassin" – in what proved to be his final bout – might have been 51 years old and, at 254, a good 25 or 30 pounds over his prime fighting weight, the fact he was unable to put away his 334-pound opponent was shocking to boxing purists. Although he lost a unanimous decision, Butterbean managed to win some rounds and even registered a dubious knockdown in the closing seconds of round 10.

Eric Esch was a 400-pouns-plus itinerant installer of flooring in prefabricated homes in Addison, Alabama, when several co-workers challenged him to enter a local Toughman contest. He did so, on a lark, but the 5'11¾" youngster was obliged to pare 20 or so pounds to get down to the weight limit of 400. He did so, primarily subsisting on a diet of skinless chicken and butterbeans ("which I hated," he later admitted), and, to his surprise, and that of his buddies who urged him on with cries of "Butterbean! Butterbean!" the nickname stuck.

With his shaved head and considerable corpulence, Butterbean became a bit of a sensation, compiling a 56-5 record, with 36 KOs, on the Toughman circuit, albeit against assorted civilians who had once beaten up a classmate in fifth grade and figured they could somehow summon their inner Sonny Liston. Arum figured – with some justification – that a novelty act, if sufficiently distinctive, would be as valuable an addition to an undercard as a legitimately talented pro who wouldn't add much to a promotion's bottom line and would cost more to pay, anyhow.

Thus began the era of "Beauty and The Bean," in which Butterbean often found himself on undercards with lovely Latina fighter Mia St. John, a bit of eye candy who was once featured in a *Playboy* magazine pictorial. Butterbean and St. John quickly gained prominence as lead-ins to some of Oscar De La Hoya's pay-per-view bouts in the mid- to late 1990s.

"I knew how they were marketing me," St. John said years later, after her association with Top Rank had ended, as had Butterbean's. "I don't blame them. I was what you'd call a willing victim."

After winning his first 15 pro fights, including 10 knockouts, The Bean – who it should be noted, had even gotten down to a career-low 300 pounds for back-to-back fights, against Louis Monaco and Mitchell Rose, in 1995 -- was surprised in losing on a second-round stoppage to Rose on December 15 in Madison Square Garden, on the undercard of a Top Rank show headlined by De La Hoya's two-round quickie over Jesse James Leija.

Considering it was his Garden debut, Butterbean was devastated to lose to the likes of Rose, who, despite being a New York Golden Gloves champion as an amateur, had gone in with a nondescript 1-7-1 pro record, with just one KO victory. So incensed was Arum by the damage done to the Butterbean brand that he soon severed his relationship with matchmaker Ron Katz, whose job it was to find fighters unskilled and crystal-chinned enough to be added to the corpulent crusher's roll call of the doomed.

"Beating Butterbean at the Garden was my version of the 'Thrilla in Manila,'" Rose said in 2005. "I still get a lot of respect for that fight. I surprised a lot of people. It was fun to piss a lot of people off and spoil the show."

Not one to stay down in the dumps for long, Butterbean consoled himself with bigger servings of his favorite comfort foods, and the notion that, at a relatively svelte 300 pounds, he was too undernourished to wreak the kind of damage he was accustomed to dishing out. So his weight began to creep upward, slowly at first, then on an express elevator straight to clogged-arteries country. For that final fight, the loss to Lawton, he came in at a career-high 426½ pounds. But by then he was 46, and acknowledging of the fact that there can indeed be too much of a good thing.

Was Eric "Butterbean" Esch a total fraud, or was there some legitimate skill encased in that ponderous body? Making it to the end of 10 rounds against Holmes suggests the latter, but The Bean admits to feeling insulted by the *Miami Herald* which, in its October 31, 1999, editions, claimed to have evidence that more than 30 Top Rank fights over a 12-year period had predetermined outcomes. A formal investigation, however, failed to prove any of the supposedly tainted fights were fixed.

"I was in damn good company in that investigation," Butterbean said in January 2009. "They had George Foreman's name on it, and other big-name fighters, too. In my opinion, Top Rank never rigged fights. But did they overmatch fights? Yes, many times. They do it in MMA and in every sport."

While there are those who refuse to believe that Butterbean had even the tiniest trace of talent, be advised that more than a few of those who felt his power said he was as strong a puncher as they had faced. Remember Louis Monaco, the guy he whacked out in one round? Well, Monaco had wins over Peter McNeeley, Michael Dokes and Kevin McBride, and he also squared off against Vitali Klitschko, Buster Douglas, Michael Grant, Trevor Berbick, Lamon Brewster, Kirk Johnson, Monte Barrett and Fres Oquendo. If Monaco says The Bean had sledgehammers for fists, consider it so.

Is there another wide-bodied version of Butterbean around at present? And if not, might there be one to come along in the future? Doubtful, although some would say "Bronco" Billy Wright – 51 years old, with a 52-4 record (43 KOs) – is an improved version. Bronco Billy, though, is 6'4", has never fought above 325½ pounds and has had only two scheduled four-rounders in his entire pro career. The Las Vegas-based Wright, who currently holds the FECAR Box and WBC Latino heavyweight titles (he fights mostly out of Bolivia), grunts in dismay when anyone dares to compare him to The Bean.

"If you think I'm a bum or a joke, say it to my face," Wright, whose mood is decidedly less jovial than Butterbean's, told me in November 2015. "I guarantee you won't be laughing long. I can knock out anybody on the planet, with either hand. I can knock them cold. I train to break people's ribs. I train to make their heads rattle so much that they don't wake up for three minutes.

"OK, so I have a belly. So what? I don't kid nobody about that. I like my sweets. Look, I know the public wants to see Calvin Klein underwear models that can punch like King Kong. But you don't have to be an Adonis to be a heavyweight boxer."

If there is any athlete whose disproportionate proportions and amiable nature approximate those of The Bean, it would have to be former Chicago Bears defensive tackle William "The Refrigerator" Perry, recently profiled in a "Where are they now?" story in *Sports Illustrated.* The 6'2" Fridge, who was in the 330-pound range when he was a member of the 1985 Bears' Super Bowl championship team, is still livin' large in his hometown of Aiken, South Carolina . Now reportedly 450 pounds, he is an alcoholic and diabetic whose NFL wealth is gone.

During his heyday, Butterbean was pulling down $50,000 a fight, and he fought frequently. How much of his ring nest egg remains is uncertain, but his restaurant, Mr. Bean's Barbecue and Steak, is still serving up heaping portions of stick-to-your-ribs fare. Here's hoping that he is happy, healthy and able to enjoy the fruits of a life that, by all accounts, was Gumpian in most respects, which should be taken as the compliment it was meant to be.

A Salute to the Razor Ruddock That Might Have Been
TheSweetScience.com, October 29, 2016

Donovan "Razor" Ruddock was, nearly everyone agreed, destined for greatness. Twenty-four years ago there was a spreading belief that he was the best heavyweight in the world not named Mike Tyson, whom he already had fought twice, losing both times. But that Tyson, circa 1991, was still viewed by many, despite a knockout loss to Buster Douglas (Tyson's legion of supporters were insistent that their hero had lost because he had hardly trained for what he had presumed would be another ho-hum blowout victory), as an almost superhuman wrecking machine, and Ruddock had acquitted himself better than most of Tyson's previous victims in their two matchups.

With Tyson convicted of rape and out of the picture for who knew how long, Ruddock was seen by more than a few knowledgeable observers as the candidate most likely to emerge as the last man standing in an unofficial four-man scrum to determine the true post-Tyson king of the division. The other entrants were Evander Holyfield, who had starched Douglas to claim the WBA, WBC and IBF belts, but still was considered in some quarters as a place-holder until Tyson's return from the slammer, Lennox Lewis and Riddick Bowe. The "semi-finals," if you will, were to be Lewis-Ruddock on October 31, 1992, in London's Earls Court Exhibition Hall and, two weeks later, a defense by Holyfield of his undisputed championship against Bowe in Las Vegas' Thomas & Mack Center.

The *Philadelphia Daily News*, my employer at the time, ran a story in its August 13, 1992, editions that listed the result of a poll I had conducted of nine notable boxing figures as to the identity of the presumed "tournament" victor. The balloting, now viewed through the prism of history, might seem surprising: former heavyweight champions Larry Holmes, Tim Witherspoon and Ernie Terrell voted for Ruddock, as did future WBO heavyweight titlist Tommy Morrison and longtime contender Earnie Shavers; former heavyweight contender Marvis Frazier and legendary trainer Angelo Dundee went with Bowe, while Holyfield, amazingly, failed to garner a single vote. Another former (and future) heavyweight champ, George Foreman, abstained from picking the ultimate survivor on the basis that he hoped to fight that person himself, but his comments suggest that he was leaning toward Lewis.

"Nobody can take Ruddock's punches," opined Terrell, who picked the Jamaican-born Canadian citizen to knock out Lewis before doing the same to Holyfield in the tourney finale.

Added Shavers, who also envisioned Ruddock whackings of Lewis and Holyfield: "Ruddock is a real big puncher, and you know I'm partial to big punchers. You can never count a puncher out. He's got a chance to end things with one good shot right up to the last bell."

But the more optimistic projections of Ruddock's celebrity boosters came crashing down in London, where Lewis, the 1988 Olympic super heavyweight gold medalist, stamped himself as a superstar-in-the-making with an emphatic, second-round stoppage.

I was there not only to chronicle Lewis-Ruddock, but what, in retrospect, also proved to be a sad look at how far a Philly guy, WBA welterweight ruler Meldrick Taylor, had slipped in the aftermath of his heart-rending, talent- and spirit-sapping 12th-round

TKO loss to Julio Cesar Chavez on March 17, 1990. Taylor was floored in the third, sixth, seventh and eighth rounds in losing by eighth-round TKO to No. 1 contender Crisanto Espana, a Venezuelan based in Belfast, Northern Ireland. No disrespect to Espana, but I could not, and still can't, imagine him doing anything close to the pre-Chavez Taylor what he did that night.

In retrospect, perhaps the way in which Ruddock went down against Lewis was nearly on a par with the shocking way in which Taylor was so easily dismissed by Espana. Ruddock, still 51 days from his 29th birthday, should have been in his prime when he was chopped down by the 1988 Olympic super heavyweight gold medalist. Had Razor – so nicknamed during his amateur days for his penchant for slicing up opponents with his strong and accurate jab – been irreversibly damaged in his two slugfests with Tyson? In their first meeting, on March 18, 1991, Ruddock was floored in the second and third rounds, but he rocked Tyson with a big left hand late in round six. Tyson came right back firing in the seventh, prompting referee Richard Steele – who also worked Chavez-Taylor I – to award "Iron Mike" a controversial TKO despite the fact that Ruddock appeared to be capable of still fighting back.

"No," Steele insisted when asked. "I saved a life. The guy was hurt. There was no need in counting him out. It is my job to stop him from being seriously hurt and the next punch would have done that." Steele also indicated he had "seen surrender" on Ruddock's face.

The rematch, on June 28, 1991, was just as brutal, and that one went the distance. Ruddock again went down twice and suffered a broken jaw, while Tyson came away with a perforated eardrum.

"Man, that guy was tough," Tyson said in praise of Ruddock. "He'll be champion of the world one day if he stays dedicated and doesn't slip up."

Ruddock followed his twin trips into Tyson hell with perfunctory stoppages of a faded Greg Page and fringe contender Phil Jackson before the setback against Lewis, from which he never truly recovered. He rebounded somewhat with a 10-round unanimous decision over Anthony Wade, but fell off the big-time radar when he was taken out in six rounds by Tommy Morrison on June 10, 1995, which precipitated a three-year retirement, the first of two times he voluntarily stepped away from the ring wars.

When last we saw Ruddock with padded gloves on his hands, he was a plump 51-year-old savagely knocked out by 29-year-old Dillon "Big Country" Carman in three rounds on September 11, 2015. He has not fought since, and it is doubtful that he will ever again step inside the ropes in quest of the heavyweight title he once seemed so close to attaining.

As for that poll conducted by the *Philadelphia Daily News* in 1992 ... well, four-time former heavyweight champ Evander Holyfield is a shoo-in for induction into the International Boxing Hall of Fame in June 2017. Lewis was a first-ballot inductee in 2009, Bowe in 2015. Ruddock has yet to appear on the IBHOF ballot, and if he ever does he'd be a longshot to receive enough votes to get a call to the hall.

But when he was at the top of his game, Ruddock inspired near-Tysonesque fear in opponents with his signature punch, which he called "The Smash," a left-hand bomb that was part hook, part uppercut and completely devastating. Fans that were in Madison Square Garden the night of April 4, 1990, saw him devastate former titlist Michael Dokes in what many still cite as the most chilling knockout they've ever witnessed. In the fourth round, "The Smash" clearly hurt Dokes, who stumbled backward into the ropes where Ruddock followed up with an overhand right and another "Smash," which seemingly left an unconscious Dokes frozen in place. And when referee Arthur Mercante Jr. did not step in to end a fight that by all rights was already over, Ruddock figured what the hell and delivered another "Smash" for good measure.

Dokes pitched forward onto his face where he remained out cold and motionless for 4½ minutes.

"I knew he was hurt," Ruddock said of Dokes, "but I had to do my job."

At 6'3" and 228 carved-from-granite pounds, Ruddock was one of the finest physical specimens ever to grace the heavyweight division. No, he was never a champion, but a case can be made for his being better than some of the former titlists he defeated, a list that includes not only Dokes and Page but Mike "Hercules" Weaver and James "Bonecrusher" Smith. It would have been interesting to see what he might have done had he ever been paired with Bowe and Holyfield, or, for that matter, Foreman.

95

If, as it now appears, Ruddock never fights again, his final record stands at 40-6-1, with 30 KOs and a nod toward 19th century American poet John Greenleaf Whittier, who was writing about a horse, but just as easily could have been summing up Ruddock's boxing career when he noted:

For of all sad words of tongue or pen,
The saddest are these: "It might have been."

Section C
2016 Olympic Boxing Redux

When Will the Corruption End?
TheSweetScience.com, August 25, 2016

Truth be told, a shadow has been enveloping the Olympic movement for at least 50 years. The pall might have begun to descend even earlier than that; one of history's most evil men, German chancellor Adolf Hitler, sought and procured the 1936 Berlin Olympics with the goal of using it as a showcase for the Aryan "master race" he believed his nation was in the process of creating. That fallacy was disproved by a black American sprinter and long jumper, Jesse Owens, who won four gold medals during that Olympiad and again, on June 22, 1938, by a black American heavyweight champion, Joe Louis, who knocked out Germany's Max Schmeling in one round in Yankee Stadium to avenge a shocking, 12th-round KO loss to Schmeling two years earlier.

The Olympic Charter, last revised on September 9, 2013, is a five-chapter, 61-article codification of the goals and bylaws of the International Olympic Committee. It defines Olympism as a "philosophy of life, exalting and combining in a balanced whole the qualities of body, will and mind. Blending sport with culture and education, Olympism seeks to create a way of life based on the joy of effort, the educational value of good example, social responsibility and respect for universal fundamental ethical principles."

Every four years – or every two years, given the time now separating the Summer and Winter Olympics – the world at large allows itself to believe, for 16 days of athletic competition, that those noble ideals are still the primary reason that the imperious IOC continues to exist. But like the Wizard of Oz, operating behind a curtain of secrecy, the organization headquartered in Lausanne, Switzerland, frequently does not rise to the level of the spectacular feats of such Olympic heroes as Owens and, in the Rio de Janeiro Olympics which ended on August 21, Jamaican sprinter Usain Bolt, U.S. gymnast Simone Biles and American swimmers Michael Phelps and Katie Ledecky. The Olympic movement as presently constituted is increasingly about power, privilege and, perhaps most of all, money. Lots and lots of money.

"As long as there's a cheery picture to present to millions of people, especially in America, it'll continue," Teddy Atlas, the analyst for NBC's coverage of Olympic boxing for four Olympiads (2000 in Sydney, 2004 in Athens, 2008 in Beijing and 2012 in London) told me when asked if the day might come when there no longer will be an acceptable reason to stage Olympiads. "People love good stories and happy endings. As long as you have a Michael Phelps and the (U.S. women's) gymnasts with gold medals around their necks – and those are good stories – a lot can be and is overlooked. A blind eye is turned. But it's getting harder and harder to forget about the bad stuff, the corruption and the manipulation and the politics. The Olympics are supposed to be an escape from that. We have enough of that in government.

"When the Olympics are no longer an escape, enough to continue to blind us to what the Olympic movement is meant to be but isn't, then there will be no more Olympics."

Atlas' harsh view might be described as that of an embittered former employee whose withering criticism of what he saw from ringside during those four Olympic fortnights eventually put him at loggerheads with the IOC, AIBA (the International Boxing Association, governing body for Olympic boxing) and, perhaps most significantly, his bosses at NBCUniversal. It is not unreasonable to infer that the Peacock network's multibillion-dollar investment in Olympic programming might result in directives to on-air personnel to tilt more toward accentuation of the positive at the expense of objective reporting.

Boxing, of course, is a subset of a subset, just one of 28 Olympic sports which were contested in Rio. For those who might not totally buy into what Atlas – who, as always, is unapologetically blunt – is pitching, consider a respected voice from beyond the grave who foresaw the direction the sport, as least as it pertained to the United States' involvement in the Olympics, was headed.

Hall of Fame trainer Emanuel Steward, who was 68 when he passed away on October 25, 2012, was named USA Boxing's director of coaching in 2002. He served only one year in that mostly ornamental capacity, resigning in disillusionment by what he perceived to be the subversion of a dream he and so many others once held dear.

"There are a lot of us who are not digging the system at all," Steward said in April 2002, shortly after he stepped down. "Before he left office, Gary (Toney, the former USA Boxing president) told me he was prepared to pull America out of the f------ Olympics.

"Are we prepared to just walk away? I don't know. I do know that Olympic boxing is not what it used to be, and nobody in America is in agreement on what they want to do. To me, it's been steadily declining since 1988. I don't even have my amateur kids today pointing toward the Olympics. When I started coaching in 1961, that was everyone's dream. It was my dream to make the Olympic team in 1964. Your first thought was trying to go to the Olympics, then you worried about turning pro afterward."

Given current realities, the concept of "simon-pure amateurism," as espoused by Pierre de Coubertin, is as rapidly disappearing from the Olympic movement as the number of, say, endangered tigers in the wild. An aristocratic French educator and historian who was the founder of the IOC in the late 19th century, de Coubertin is widely considered the "father" of the modern Olympics, first held in Paris in 1896. He believed that the Olympics periodically staged in ancient Greece encouraged competition among amateur rather than professional athletes, and that the Games could play a role in promoting peace. Toward that end, he was unwavering in his perhaps naïve position that the competition itself, the struggle to overcome opponents of different nationalities and cultures, was more important than winning. "The essential thing," he wrote, "is not to have conquered, but to have fought well."

De Coubertin was 74 when he died in 1937, old enough to have witnessed, sadly, Hitler employ those 1936 Berlin Olympics as a metaphor for war, and a precursor of the second global conflict the Nazi dictator would soon instigate. And if that alone weren't enough to keep de Courbetin forever spinning in his grave, then the widespread boycotting of two Olympiads (Moscow in 1980 by the U.S. and several of its allies in protest of the Soviet Union's invasion of Afghanistan, and Los Angeles in 1984 by the USSR, Cuba and a number of Eastern Bloc nations in retaliation for the U.S.-led boycott four years earlier), hate-inspired murder (of 11 Israeli athletes by Black September terrorists in Munich in 1972), proliferation of performance-enhancing drugs among participants and official endorsement of pro involvement by profit-aware IOC officials surely would.

As exemplified in Rio – and, really, there can be no turning back now – the Olympics are increasingly about the boosting of nationalistic pride brought about by high medal counts (the U.S. again blitzed the field, with 121 medals [46 gold] to 70 for runner-up China) and the influence that can be purchased by countries amenable to feathering the IOC's well-appointed nest. The dye was permanently cast in 1992 with the incredible popularity of the NBA-superstar-laden American "Dream Team" that crushed all comers in winning the men's basketball gold medal in Barcelona. Just like that, Michael Jordan, Magic Johnson and friends nudged de Courbetin's quaint notion of fraternity and brotherhood through unsullied amateur sport into the dusty annals of what used to be but ain't no more. If the 1980 Lake Placid Winter Olympics were to be held in the post-"Dream Team" era, there could be no "Miracle on Ice" triumph by a group of U.S. collegiate players, on the way to one of the most stunning gold medals in Olympic history, over a veteran and seemingly invincible Soviet squad; the American team would instead be stocked with NHL standouts.

Oh, sure, the notion of would-be Olympians training on their own time and dime, driven by a desire to represent their country for altruistic reasons and not necessarily for personal profit, hasn't died out completely. There are still college kids and budget-conscious plain folk who receive few if any subsidies to pursue their Olympic dreams, but there is and always will be a divide between competitors in lower-interest events such as badminton, archery, fencing and trapshooting and those competing in big-ticket sports such as basketball, golf, tennis, soccer, ice hockey, swimming and track and field. What, you say that swimming, which commands a sizable chunk of prime-time exposure on NBC, doesn't have a professional league? True, but the United States Olympic Committee provides its finest hopefuls with generous stipends, and endorsements can bring in millions of dollars more to the best of the best. Phelps, he of the

28 Olympic medals, including 23 golds, plunked down $2.5 million the day after the Rio Olympics ended to take title to the palatial house he will share with his fiancée and infant son. Given the 31-year-old's incredible body of work in the five Olympiads in which he participated, few would object to his rewarding himself with digs spacious enough to showcase his medal collection.

The roughly 90 members of the IOC's international hierarchy, more than a few of whom are titled royalty and have had their place at the Olympic table passed on by their forebears, are acutely aware of the benefits attendant to the selective wielding of influence. After being rejected four times on previous bids to host the Winter Olympics, Salt Lake City in 1995 was tapped as the site of the 2002 Games. It was later proven that, to seal the deal, bribes were offered to and accepted by several IOC voters to cast favorable ballots for the Utah city.

Although such obvious malfeasance cannot be substantiated in other instances, eyebrows were raised when Sochi, Russia, was chosen to host the 2014 Winter Olympics, even though Sochi, located along the shores of the Black Sea, is a resort town with a subtropical climate and mild winters (meaning a lack of natural snow). But Russian president Vladimir Putin wanted those Games, perhaps to bolster his image with his countrymen, and he was willing to put up the rubles to make it happen. The Sochi Olympics cost a staggering $51 billion, making it far and away the most expensive Olympiad ever, with a not insignificant part of that going for equipment to produce vast amounts of artificial snow.

Amazingly, all things considered, the 2018 Winter Olympics were awarded to PyeongChang, South Korea, which also has minimal snow in mid-February. The projected cost for those Games has been optimistically pegged at $13 billion, but expect major budgetary overruns, and the use of the same fake-snow-producing machines that gave Sochi that white, winter-wonderland sheen.

Almost without exception, since the red-ink-drenched 1976 Montreal Olympics, host cities have been bankrupted for the privilege of shining on the world stage for those two weeks. And when the Games end, costly Olympic Villages, stadiums and venues, some never to be used again, are left abandoned, decaying with the passage of time like the bleached bones of long-extinct dinosaurs.

The familiar tale was again played out in Rio, which erupted with civic pride at the 2009 announcement that, seven years later, the Brazilian city would become the first South American host of the Olympics. The IOC brass promised that Rio would emerge from the process better in every way, but thousands of people in local *favelas*, or slums, were forcibly evicted to make way for the gleaming edifices that would house the various Olympic events. There also was a guarantee that Rio's water problem, which literally involved raw sewage emptying into waterways that would serve as venues for several aquatic competitions, would be cleaned up to near-pristine levels. It didn't happen.

But, despite mounting evidence that still another Olympics had produced as many nagging question marks as exhilarating exclamation points, other cities are lining up to bid for the right to be branded with the familiar and incredibly expensive five-ring symbol. Paris, Rome, Budapest and Los Angeles all had representatives in Rio to curry favor with IOC bigwigs responsible for selecting the host site for the 2024 Summer Olympics, which will be awarded next year. If there's one certainty, it's that at least some of those bigwigs will be fawned over and lavishly complimented by the aforementioned suitors, willingly cast in the role of bespectacled math geeks asking the prettiest and most demanding girl in school to be their date for the prom.

Back to boxing. For AIBA, which has its own soiled past, the tearing down of traditional barriers to allow pros into the Olympic ring in Rio was a long time coming, and probably inevitable. The former president of AIBA, the late Dr. Anwar Chowdhry of Pakistan, had floated the idea of welcoming pros during his tumultuous 25-year reign, but it never gained the necessary traction, and it still hadn't when he finally was voted out of office in 2006 and replaced by Dr. Ching-Kuo Wu of Chinese Taipei, who promised sweeping reforms. Chowdhry had all but winked at AIBA's rumored sale of gold medals, which during his tenure hung in the air like toxic smog. Prior to the 2006 AIBA election in which Chowdhry was ousted, a pro-Chowdhry Russian delegate is said to have brought in outsiders who were members of the "Russian Mafia" to intimidate delegates into voting for the incumbent. Perhaps it is just coincidence, but one pro-change delegate was found murdered. If that didn't scare the hell out of the electorate, nothing could.

"If I had lost, boxing is out of the 2012 Olympics, maybe even out of the 2008 Olympics," Wu, who edged Chowdhry in that 2006 election by an 83-79 margin, told me during the November 2014 AIBA Congress in Jehu, South Korea. Confirming that possible gloom-and-doom scenario was USA Boxing interim executive director Mike Martino, who, at that same AIBA Congress, noted that "I've been hearing for the last three Olympics that we (boxing) might be on the chopping block."

Wu at least succeeded in one area where Chowdhry had failed; he also championed the introduction of pros into Olympic boxing, and toward that end he initiated the World Series of Boxing and AIBA Pro Boxing, in which elite fighters could maintain their Olympic eligibility and also get paid. It was a concept embraced by numerous nations, with the chief pocket of resistance predictably coming from powerhouse American promotional companies that objected to certain restrictions of movement placed upon AIBA-signed fighters.

The fear in some quarters in the U.S. was that experienced pros, possibly competing against American amateurs still in their teens or early 20s, would overmatch our kids. It was a legitimate concern; after the 1984 U.S. Olympic boxing team scored a record haul of 11 medals (nine golds, a silver and a bronze) against a boycott-thinned field, it has been a case of diminishing returns for the country which introduced such future greats as Muhammad Ali (still known then as Cassius Clay), Joe Frazier, George Foreman, Sugar Ray Leonard and Oscar De La Hoya to the world with their gold-medal performances. U.S. men managed just two medals (one gold, for Andre Ward) in 2004, one (a bronze, for Deontay Wilder) in 2008 and none at all in 2012, something that had never happened before. Another embarrassing shutout for American men was predicted by *Sports Illustrated* in its pre-Olympic issue.

But not all went as anticipated. For one thing, the three pros that competed in Rio – Cameroon's Hassan N'Dam N'Jikam, Thailand's Amnat Ruenroeng and Italy's Carmine Tommasone, all of whom are at least 30 years of age and who arrived with a combined record of 66-3 (29 KOs) – failed to even make it to the medal rounds. For another, Shakur Stevenson, the 19-year-old bantamweight from Newark, New Jersey, impressed by taking a silver medal in a 2-1, split-decision loss to defending Olympic champion Robeisy Ramirez of Cuba, while 20-year-old lightweight Nico Hernandez, of Wichita,

Kansas, went home with a bronze. It might seem like a skimpy haul compared to Uzbekistan, which garnered seven medals (three golds) and Cuba (six medals, three golds), but at least it provided something to build on. Oh, and 21-year-old Claressa Shields, of Flint, Michigan, lived up to her status as the defending champion and favorite in the women's middleweight division by taking a second straight gold medal.

Still, you have to wonder if with the burgeoning number of pros that figure to be involved in the 2020 Tokyo Olympics, USA Boxing will be able to continue pinning its hopes on talented but relatively inexperienced amateurs. Change did come to Olympic boxing in Rio, which not only included those cameo appearances by pros but also the removal of headgear on the men's side and addition of computer-generated selection of the three judges (of five at ringside) scoring on a pro-style 10-point-must system, which replaced the widely despised electronic scoring which turned bouts into Xbox video games. Other things, however, disturbingly remained the same, namely several head-scratching decisions that raised standard questions as to whether those outcomes were more the result of bias or incompetence than to what actually transpired inside the ropes.

Foremost among the dubious verdicts was the gold-medal heavyweight bout, in which Kazakhstan's Vassiliy Levit appeared to be the clear winner over Russia's No. 1 seed and reigning world amateur champion Evgeny Tischenko. When the decision for Tischenko was met with loud booing from spectators in *Riocentro Pavilion 6*, some noted the presence at ringside of IOC president Thomas Bach of Germany alongside someone he has described as his "good friend," the $51 billion architect of the Sochi Winter Olympics, Russian president Vladimir Putin. Neither appeared distressed at the apparent injustice. Make of that what you will, along with the fact that, of the original entry list of 389 Russian athletes for Rio, 271, including all 11 boxers, were cleared to compete by World Anti-Doping Agency (WADA). Despite the fact that the entire Russian track and field team (68 athletes), 17 rowers and eight weightlifters were banned from competing, there was more than a little grumbling in other countries that 70% of the Russian delegation passing performance-enhancing-drugs muster was overly generous, given incontrovertible proof that virtually every Russian athlete competing in Sochi had benefited from the administering of state-sanctioned PEDs.

A smidgeon less egregious than the shafting of Levit was the hotly disputed, medal-eliminating points loss of top-seeded bantamweight Michael Conlan of Ireland to eventual bronze medalist Vladimir Tikitin of Russia, which came the morning after Levit graciously accepted his Olympic heartbreak. All three scoring judges went for Nikitin, which prompted an irate Conlan to rip off his shirt in the ring and flash a pair of obscene one-finger salutes to the offending officials. During a post-fight press conference with an Irish broadcaster, RTE Sport, Conlan spewed expletives and accusations, calling everyone involved with AIBA "cheating bastards. They're paying everybody. They've always been cheats. It's a shambles, to be honest. Today just showed how corrupt the organization is."

On August 17, AIBA, in what was widely seen to be in damage-control mode, acknowledged the raft of wacko decisions (two of which involved U.S. boxers, light welterweight Gary Antuanne Russell and women's lightweight Mikaela Mayer) by removing four referees and judges and, a day later, reassigning executive director Karim Bouzidi and replacing him with Italy's Franco Falcinelli, president of the European Boxing Confederation and the most senior vice president of AIBA's executive board.

"The Olympic Games, of which boxing has been a part since 1904, represent the pinnacle of all sports," a statement issued by AIBA read. "Since the beginning of Rio, 2016, AIBA has conducted over 250 bouts and remains fully committed to fair play in boxing, always seeking to act in the boxers' best interests. The decisions taken emphasize that AIBA will not shy away from its responsibilities and will continue to ensure a level playing field and a fair and transparent sport. It is of paramount importance to protect our sport and its R&J (referees and judges) community whose integrity has been put into question."

ESPN reporter Steve Bunce opined that Levit was the victim of the most outrageous call since Roy Jones Jr. beat the hell out of his South Korean opponent, Park Si-Hun, in the 156-pound gold medal bout in Seoul in 1988, only to be stunned when a 3-2 verdict was announced for the home-country fighter. But was justice truly served by the suspension of the Rio Five? Although the U.S., with ample justification, filed a protest on Jones' behalf 28 years ago, it was not upheld and the three officials who voted for Si-Hun, although suspended, were quietly reinstated six months later. And despite AIBA's preemptive strike to quell the furor in Rio, its official stance was that its officials had done nothing unethical. In any case, a rule had been instituted beforehand that no protests could be filed and thus no seemingly unjust outcomes overturned.

"With regard to corruption, we would like to strongly restate that unless tangible proof is put forward, not rumors, we will continue to use any means, including legal or disciplinary actions, to protect our sport and its R&J community, whose integrity is constantly put into question," the statement continued. "The organization will not be deterred by subjective judgments made by discontented parties."

Translation: the banished officials will be back in AIBA's good graces sometime in the not-too-distant future, and likely without a public announcement to that effect.

Atlas, Olympic boxing's most persistent and vocal critic, admits to not having watched a single round of the action from Rio. Then again, he said he didn't have to. Reports of the latest mess requiring cleanup were as predictable to him as morning sunrise. He also foresees the day when the IOC, weary of the never-ending drama involving boxing, simply decides to excise that area of malignancy.

"They are going to surgically remove certain sports," Atlas predicted. "They will get rid of boxing, to stop all the noise. I really believe that."

Atlas noted that he and NBC broadcast partner Bob Papa (who was reassigned to rugby in Rio) became aware prior to the London Olympics of a British Broadcasting Company report the previous September that alleged someone from Azerbaijan, an oil- and mineral-rich former satellite country of the old Soviet Union, was prepared to pay millions of dollars to "buy" two Olympic gold medals in boxing.

The BBC report found documents showing a $9 million bank transfer, funneled through Switzerland, to a boxing organization owned by AIBA. Talk about your smoking gun …

"The story was never properly refuted," Atlas explained. "There were a lot of lingering questions. What that told me was that Bob and I had to be alert. Our first night, I mentioned the story in a journalistically responsible fashion. A lot of people would have stayed away from it, I know that, but I thought it would be irresponsible to stay away from it. So I said, 'Look, this is out there. I'm not pointing fingers. All I'm saying is I'm aware and now you're aware. Let the Games begin.' And the Games began."

They began with what Atlas said were "bad decisions. I mean, really bad decisions. I watched this guy from Japan (Satoshi Shimizu) knock down a guy from Azerbaijan (Magomed Abdulhamidev) *seven* times and the Azerbaijan guy's point total kept going up! Bob and I were, like, 'Can they really be this arrogant? This cold, this uncaring? Don't these people have any sense of right and wrong, that they can do this in front of the whole world?'"

The outcry over the 22-17 computer-scored decision for Abdulhamidev was so intense that, in a rarity that can't be repeated given the no-protest rule now in place, AIBA reversed itself and upheld Japan's protest, giving Shimizu the victory he so obviously deserved. Curiously, less than two years after USA Boxing hired acclaimed former Cuba Olympic coach Pedro Roque Otano – he of the 36 Olympic medals, including 11 golds – in September 2012, he resigned to accept a better-paying position (drum roll, please) as the coach of Azerbaijan's national team. Roque Otano's team departed Rio with one silver and one bronze, the same as the U.S.

Atlas was not surprised to learn that no Olympic boxing was televised on over-the-air NBC, which accounts for around 90% of its total Olympic viewership. All the fights, including the gold-medal ones involving Shields and Stevenson, were on secondary outlets. He said NBC was attempting to "hide" Olympic boxing, and that "(AIBA is) the most corrupt organization I've ever seen, and that's a very powerful statement coming from me because I've been in this business 40 years and I've seen a lot of bad stuff."

All of which begs a question: Why did Atlas remain as NBC's color analyst through four Olympiads if what he had to wade through each time, as many as 278 bouts in a two-week period, was so objectionable?

"I got paid very well, but the honeymoon wore off," he responded. "The first one (in Sydney, Australia), I was, like, 'Wow. They must think I'm very good at this.' If you get asked to do the Olympics, it's supposed to be a big honor. So I was glad to do it. Then I saw what it was. It's a marathon. By the time I got to the fourth one, I was done. I only did it because of Ebersol."

That would be Dick Ebersol, the former head of the NBC Sports Group and a man Atlas trusts implicitly, which is a club with few members. But Ebersol was gone, replaced for London by Mark Lazarus, which was the Olympics when Atlas saw what he saw and expressed it with no-doubt-about-it indignation, so much so that Wu called for Papa and him to be removed from ringside for the medal round bouts. They were given the choice of returning home immediately or calling those last few fights from a cramped studio Atlas described as "a closet."

"The new guy said (NBC) was standing behind me and that I was right to say what I had been saying," Atlas said. "I said, 'OK, I'll finish the job. But I want something in return. Dick Ebersol hired me in 2000. We have a good relationship and I trust him. I have no idea if I can trust you.'

"He was a little taken aback by me saying that. I said, 'But I know how to find out if I can trust you. I want your word, if I go into the studio and finish calling the fights, that before NBC ever broadcasts another Olympic boxing match that you will help me do something about the corruption. We can actually help these fighters that are being robbed one after another. They're falling on the canvas crying when their dreams are crushed. I'm tired of seeing it.

"'This is what I want. I want you to go to the IOC – you pay a lot of money to them and they'll listen to you – and demand that they conduct a full investigation of AIBA before you ever do another Olympic boxing match. If you give me your word that you will do that, then you can march me into that tiny closet for the last two days and I'll call those fights.' He put his hand out, we shook and he said, 'You have my word.'"

A month or so later, Atlas said he received a telephone call from someone "pretty high up" at NBC and was confidentially told, "He's not going to keep his word."

"I wasn't shocked," Atlas said, "but I was disappointed."

Lazarus was not available for comment, but Christopher McCloskey, vice president of Communications for the NBC Sports Group, responded to Atlas' charges with an email that read, in part, "We met with AIBA and the IOC in Lausanne after London and reviewed the London tournament. AIBA took us through their plans to reform."

Now, about all that money that NBC pays to remain the network of the Olympics: in May, NBCUniversal shelled out $7.75 billion for the exclusive U.S. broadcast rights to the six Olympiads from 2022 to 2032. That is a continuation of an association that began in 1992 in Barcelona, Spain, with two other Olympic rights packages prior to the most recent deal totaling $7.88 billion.

In an August 13 conference call with reporters about Olympic TV viewership, Lazarus dismissed double-digit ratings drops from London by saying, "This will be our most economically successful Games in history," and he defended the network's decision to "create our storytelling and our narrative," even if it mean holding events that could have been shown on live TV in the afternoon for delayed prime-time slots.

But despite the Olympics' warts and blemishes, including those of the Quasimodo that is AIBA, Atlas is indisputably right about one thing. The wondrous feats of a Phelps, a Ledecky, a Bolt, a Biles, the powerhouse U.S. men's and women's basketball teams, and even the occasional epic failures of those who for whatever reason are blinded by the glare of a global spotlight, can't help but hold our attention. The Olympics are like a bacon double cheeseburger and ice cream sundae to dieters who can't resist gorging on a quadrennial treat that is irresistible if solely for the fact that it comes along only so often. That, or we simply are suckers for unvarnished sentiment serve up with a side order of patriotic pride.

"If I could re-live anything, I would want to re-live that moment when I was on the medal stand," Sugar Ray Leonard, one of five gold medalists from the legendary 1976 U.S. Olympic boxing team in Montreal, said prior to a 40-year reunion with his surviving teammates in June, at the International Boxing Hall of Fame induction weekend in Canastota, New York. "Those Olympics were the best time of my life. I was young and everything seemed so exciting."

A lot of us aren't so young anymore, but far more cynical. Once we sought perfection in an imperfect world, hoping to glimpse it in an Olympic swimming pool, on the track or in the ring. Maybe it was never there in its entirety, only bits and pieces to fill in the gaps of our wildest imagination of what human beings are capable of doing.

Until something better or fairer comes along, that just might have to suffice.

Section D
The Non-Heavyweights

Oscar & Felix: Boxing's Odd Couple
Philadelphia Daily News, September 16, 1999

LAS VEGAS

Sugar Ray Leonard grew up poor in Palmer Park, Maryland.

Oscar De La Hoya's economic circumstances were no better during a childhood spent in the East Los Angeles barrio.

But Leonard and De La Hoya won Olympic gold medals in boxing – Leonard in Montreal in 1976, De La Hoya in Barcelona in 1992 – and they had smiles and personalities with enough wattage to match the shine of their hardware.

The Olympic successes helped Leonard and De La Hoya barge into the select circle of The Chosen, superstars whose fame and wealth extends beyond their considerable athletic talent. Members of The Chosen have legions of fans that may not normally follow their particular sport, but are enthralled with them because they have style, class or some luminescent quality that transcends the sweaty endeavors of their less charismatic counterparts.

Those counterparts, for purposes of identification, shall henceforth be known as The Outsiders, and they tend to see The Chosen as spoiled brats who pick the roses and leave the thorns. They are preconditioned to despise The Chosen, and supporters of The Outsiders also come to detest those fortunate few who seemingly have to work less to achieve more. Contests between The Chosen and The Outsiders thus boil down to the most basic of conflicts: class struggle in a world forever divided by caste systems of one sort or another.

At first glance, Saturday night's welterweight unification showdown here at the Mandalay Bay Events Center between De La Hoya (31-0, 25 KOs), the World Boxing Council champion, and Puerto Rico's Felix Trinidad (35-0, 30 KOs), the International

110

Boxing Federation titlist, appears to be different because it is the first eagerly anticipated megabout pitting two fighters of Hispanic heritage. But, upon further inspection, this Latin-flavored matchup is no different than John L. Sullivan vs. "Gentleman" Jim Corbett, Jack Johnson vs. James Jeffries, Muhammad Ali vs. Joe Frazier.

Leonard, even in retirement a lifetime member of The Chosen, understands the sociological forces that are in play here.

"For personal reasons, I like Oscar," Leonard said from his home in Pacific Palisades, California. "Quite frankly, he reminds me of me. Strictly from a boxing perspective, we are very similar.

"Another thing we have in common: all of Oscar's opponents believe he was born with a silver spoon in his mouth. It's a misconception, but it exists. (Marvin) Hagler resented me because of it, Tommy (Hearns) resented me because of it, (Roberto) Duran resented me because of it. I'm sure Trinidad looks at Oscar pretty much the same way those guys looked at me.

"The funny thing is, Oscar has worked hard for everything he's achieved. It wasn't as if anything was handed to him that he didn't deserve. He's earned his status. I think I earned mine, too."

Promoter Bob Arum, who is paying premium prices to the fighters – De La Hoya is guaranteed $15 million and Trinidad $8.5 million, although those figures could rise substantially if pay-per-view subscriptions meet Arum's most optimistic expectations – obviously knows what buttons to push with the public. He has likened De La Hoya-Trinidad to the cataclysmic first pairing of Leonard and Hearns, on September 16, 1981, also a welterweight unification with strong societal undertones. As is now the case with De La Hoya, Leonard was cast in the role of the had-it-too-easy pretty boy; as is the case with Trinidad, Hearns was depicted as the working-class Everyman who had to pull himself up by his bootstraps.

What happened that night 18 years ago, of course, was pure magic. Leonard, behind on the scorecards through 12 rounds and with his left eye swollen shut, launched a 13th-round rally (title bouts were still 15 rounds then) that left Hearns hurt and vulnerable. Leonard, his face no longer pretty and showing a determination that was more blue-collar than blue blood, then closed the show in the 14th round with a TKO that, perhaps most notably, gained him grudging converts from the ranks of The Outsiders.

111

For the sake of boxing, a sport in desperate need of an electric moment, it can only be hoped that De La Hoya and Trinidad can generate the same excitement that Leonard and Hearns did that glorious fall evening in 1981. Too often, the most obvious of boxing matchups never are made (Riddick Bowe-Lennox Lewis, Bowe-Mike Tyson) because of political squabbles, and, when marquee pairings do occur, too often the outcome is marred by controversy (Julio Cesar Chavez-Meldrick Taylor I, Lewis-Evander Holyfield I).

De La Hoya, who has boasted of "carrying boxing on my shoulders," thus finds himself in the pressure-packed but somewhat enviable position of having to deliver, in conjunction with ideological-opposite Trinidad, a fight that will remind a jaded and shrinking fan base just what it is that can make this sport so special when all the pieces fall just right.

The fact that the outcome is not a foregone conclusion – De La Hoya is a narrow 6-5 wagering choice after Nevada oddsmakers made the fight an opening-line pick 'em – only contributes to the feeling that history is about to be made, or at least revisited.

"I don't think this fight can miss," said Hall of Fame trainer Angelo Dundee, who was in Leonard's corner for his watershed first bout with Hearns. "It's been building to a climax for years. Everybody knew these two guys were going to fight someday, and it's picked up to a point where the public is getting really excited.

"It's big for the same reason Ray's fight with Hearns was big. That fight, if you recall, came along at a time when the heavyweight division was getting a little quiet. Well, it just so happens that the heavyweight division is a little quiet right now. So here come a couple of quality welterweights, riding to the rescue."

Joe Hand Sr. has been the Philadelphia-area contractor for major closed-circuit fights for three decades. He, too, sees De La Hoya-Trinidad as the sort of attraction that boxing needs to reestablish itself in a sports spectrum that in recent years has had less space for the sweet science.

"This is the hottest fight we have handled in a long time – maybe since Hagler-Leonard (in 1987)," Hand said. "By that I mean, the hottest fight not involving Mike Tyson. You have to put Tyson's fights in a different category.

"Not all hot fights live up to the hype, as we all know. But De La Hoya-Trinidad, I honestly believe, is going to be a great fight. These two guys can be what Ali and Frazier were. Every great fighter needs a great rival. De La Hoya needs Trinidad, and Trinidad needs De La Hoya. They're going to bring out the best in each other."

De La Hoya, the "Golden Boy," has the endorsements, matinee-idol looks and the devotion of female fans that see him as boxing's answer to Leonardo DiCaprio and Ricky Martin. There is no greater testament to his popularity than the 45,000 spectators, many of them women, who packed the Sun Bowl in El Paso, Texas, on June 13, 1998, to see his systematic, third-round destruction of no-chance French challenger Patrick Charpentier. It was less a title bout than a concert by boxing's only Beatle.

But De La Hoya doesn't only want to be seen on billboards wearing a milk mustache, or to be characterized as a champion who only appeals to groupies, network suits and the well-connected. He desperately wants to convince fans of The Outsiders that there is steel and grit behind that pretty façade.

"When he fought (Ike) Quartey, he showed me more in that last round, when he knew he was (losing), then he'd shown me in his whole career put together," two-time former world champion and current Showtime analyst Bobby Czyz said of De La Hoya's most recent bout, a disputed, split-decision escape. "He showed me right there he won't go gently into that good night. He'll fight back. But Trinidad is going to be much too much for him."

If De La Hoya can sway Czyz, and others of like persuasion, that he has the same stern stuff inside him as the best of The Outsiders, he truly can consider himself a crossover sensation.

For Trinidad, the challenge is no less daunting. "Tito" doesn't speak English, doesn't have an Olympic medal, isn't prepping for a singing and/or acting career and doesn't have Oscar's key to the executive washroom. Despite 14 winning defenses of the IBF title he claimed on June 19, 1993, with a two-round wipeout of Maurice Blocker, Trinidad remains a splendid fighter whose appeal has been limited to boxing purists. He knows, unlike De La Hoya, what it is to perform on undercards for short money.

That makes for powerful incentive to break through to the other side, if he can.

"I kind of feel for Trinidad," Czyz said. "He's never going to be as big as De La Hoya, even if he wins. Oh, he'll be as big – bigger – in boxing circles, but he doesn't have that across-the-board appeal that De La Hoya has, that Leonard had. Those guys came right off the front of Wheaties boxes."

Right analogy, wrong brand of cereal. See, it really doesn't matter whether more fans have a taste for The Chosen or The Outsider. As long as this fight produces two-way snap, crackle and pop, one thing is certain.

Boxing wins.

Epilogue: As it turned out, De La Hoya-Trinidad did not turn out to be an instant classic as was Leonard-Hearns I. Perhaps it was unfair to expect that same sort of magic to be made. Perhaps out of respect for Trinidad's reputation as a lights-out puncher, De La Hoya, utilizing his boxing skills instead of engaging the Puerto Rican knockout artist at close quarters, seemingly had built a comfortable lead heading into the 10th round, whereupon the presumed frontrunner went into safety-first mode, dancing away and virtually conceding the last three rounds to his pursuer. The majority decision for Trinidad – who came out ahead by two points and one point, respectively, on two judges' cards – was widely seen as at least somewhat controversial. It also proved to be a one-and-done, as the two superstars never fought again.

Mayweather's Lifestyle of the Rich and Famous
TheSweetScience.com, September 1, 2015

Making history by matching Rocky Marciano's 49-0 record? Forget it. Mere boxing considerations no longer are what drives the public to follow the aptly nicknamed Floyd "Money" Mayweather Jr. (48-0, 26 KOs) as the sport's most ostentatious cash cow collects another $32 million or so of chump change for cuffing around doomed challenger Andre Berto (30-3, 23 KOs) on September 12 at Las Vegas' MGM Grand.

There is no way, of course, that Mayweather can hope to come within Hubble telescope distance of the staggering numbers he posted for his largely disappointing May 2 conquest of Manny Pacquiao. Even now, those grotesquely swollen figures -- $600 million in total revenue, 4.4 million pay-per-view subscriptions, somewhere around $220 million to the winning fighter – must seem like misprints to regular Americans struggling to meet their monthly mortgage payments. But the six-fight sweetheart deal Mayweather signed with Showtime/CBS in February 2013, the last installment of which is against designated fall guy Berto, guarantees that he be paid no less than $32 million even if it's for little more than a glorified sparring session.

As a legitimate boxing match, Mayweather-Berto is of almost zero interest to the average fight fan; Berto is a 40-to-1 longshot, and even those Grand Canyonesque odds would seem to be conservative. Berto, though he is himself a former world welterweight champion, probably has about as much chance of claiming Mayweather's WBC, WBA, lineal and *The Ring* welter titles as he does of winning the Powerball Lottery.

The 38-year-old Mayweather, in a sense, has already won the Powerball Lottery – several times over. According to *Forbes* magazine, he again is guaranteed to be the highest-paid athlete in the world, having already made $285 million this year before he throws his first punch at Berto. His current net worth is an estimated $500 million, which seemingly ensures that he won't – can't – suffer the same financial ruin that befell such riches-to-rags boxing greats as Joe Louis, Sugar Ray Robinson, Mike Tyson and Evander Holyfield. Pacquiao lags far behind in second place, at $160 million earned in 2015, with the third athlete on the list, soccer's Ronaldo, a semi-pauper at $79 million. Even basketball superstar LeBron James, in sixth place, seems like he should be clipping discount coupons and shopping in thrift stores at a mere $64.8 million.

What's more amazing is that none of Mayweather's income comes from product endorsements; the last such gigs he had were way back in 2009, when he did minor TV spots for AT&T and Reebok, with neither company electing to renew its association with him in 2010.

"You can't deny people want to watch him, and people have been waiting a long time to see this fight (against Pacquiao)," Bob Dorfman, editor of *Sports Marketers Scouting Report*, said earlier this year, before the biggest money-generating fight of all time. "But it doesn't mean you'll buy a product he is endorsing or believe him as a spokesman."

Not being a compensated pitchman for Madison Avenue, though, does not seem to bother Mayweather in the least. He almost revels in his anti-establishment, bad-boy persona. What you see is what you get, he insists, and if that includes the occasional homophobic and sexist rant, and at least three domestic-violence convictions, so be it.

"I am always the villain," Mayweather said before his June 25, 2005, brutalization of Arturo Gatti in Atlantic City. "That's all right. I know how boxing works. You have to have a good guy and a bad guy. I don't mind being the bad guy."

Is "Money" actually a villain? Or does he merely play one because it helps embellish his brand? Either way, it doesn't seem to matter much from a bottom-line standpoint. The way he looks at it, has always looked at it, if someone plucks down enough cash for a ticket or a PPV subscription to watch his bouts, it is of no concern to him if that person desperately wants to see him win or lose. Income streams play no favorites.

For a Showtime special he did last year with former *Lifestyles of the Rich and Famous* host Robin Leach, Mayweather explained why he'll never be broke, despite profligate spending habits that make even Tyson's conspicuous consumption in the 1980s and '90s, which saw him blow through a reported $300 million, seem semi-miserly.

"I've got plans for real-estate ventures in New York and film production in Los Angeles," Mayweather, who has vowed that the Berto fight will be his last, told Leach. "I've invested wisely over the years, and I'm not going to wind up broke. I set a goal of $12 million a year coming in at a million a month in interest alone. We've reached that – and I still sign my own checks."

The only problem with that is Mayweather, who bets hundreds of thousands of dollars on sport events (he only goes public on those occasions when he collects on wagers), routinely spends more than a million dollars a month. If he had to subsist solely on that interest revenue, he'd have to cut back, drastically, on the extravagances that have made him more intriguing to fight fans and non-fans than his luminescence inside the ropes. Put it this way: it is Mayweather's flaunting of his fabulous wealth that has replaced his undeniable ring skills as the cornerstone of his appeal. At this stage of his career, he doesn't even pretend otherwise.

Keith Thurman, the WBA's "regular" welterweight champion, admits to being disappointed when he lost out to Berto for the slot opposite Mayweather in which the man with total control, or as close as it ever gets in the fight game, adamantly says is his farewell to boxing as an active participant. Then again, Thurman believes that actual bouts no longer are the primary engine that drives Mayweather's notoriety.

"Let's watch `Money' spend his money on a Rolls-Royce and a Bentley," Thurman told reporters at the Barclays Center in Brooklyn, New York, a few hours before Danny Garcia's August 1 rout of Paulie Malignaggi. "Let's watch `Money' go to a strip club. Let's watch `Money' go around with a bag of money and buy some shoes. Whatever he wants to do, America is going to watch; it's called the `Money' Show.

"So right now at the end of his career he's making more money than anyone thought was possible in the world of boxing. And to me that is his goal. That's why he nicknamed himself `Money.' He's focused on the money and he wants to make history – not in the way I want to make history – but he wants to make history on (financial) numbers and numbers alone. So once again, enjoy the `Money' Show. I wouldn't pay for his next fight, but that's on you."

It does appear sometimes that Mayweather has received more attention for his latest lavish purchases than he did for attempting to depict Berto, who has two losses to fighters (Victor Ortiz and Robert Guerrero) that Mayweather dominated, as the guy who might finally smudge the record of the self-proclaimed TBE ("The Best Ever"). Despite the fact that Mayweather already has bought 88 luxury cars for himself and members of his unwieldy entourage, he couldn't resist the urge to fork over $4.8 million in late August for a Koenigsegg CCXR Trevita, a land rocket that can go from zero to 60 mph in 2.8 seconds and has a top speed of 250 mph. It's the perfect vehicle for those occasions when Floyd is running a bit late for an appointment.

Thurman, who, most would agree, would pose a sterner test to Mayweather than Berto figures to, might have reason to be perturbed, but any suggestion that the most-well-compensated fighter in boxing history has been doing it against a steady stream of bums is misleading at best and simply wrong at worst. Twenty-five of Floyd's 48 pro bouts have been for world championships, and his list of victims includes such notables as Pacquiao, Oscar De La Hoya, Shane Mosley, Miguel Cotto, Canelo Alvarez, Diego Corrales, Juan Manuel Marquez, Jose Luis Castillo, Genaro Hernandez, Zab Judah and Ricky Hatton. Even though he seemingly was pressed in majority decisions over Marcos Maidana (the first of their two fights) and Alvarez, and a split decision over De La Hoya, the closest brushes he has had with possible defeat came against Maidana (1), Castillo and Emanuel Augustus.

No wonder Mayweather struts around like the cock of the walk. He figures he's merited his announced position at the top of the all-time heap, and being No. 1 should have its perks.

"No one can get me to say Sugar Ray Robinson or anybody else was or is better than me," he said before the Mosley fight on May 1, 2010. "No one was better. No one is better. Maybe no one else ever will be better."

The extent of Mayweather's greatness as a fighter is a topic that is debated now and will continue to be well into the future. He is, indisputably, a defensive genius. He is also a technician who doesn't always deliver much bang for all those bucks; his most recent win inside the distance came against Ortiz on September 17, 2011, and he might not have ended that one early (the fourth round) had not Ortiz made the mistake of dropping his hands and turning his head to look at the referee. The first rule of boxing is to protect yourself at all times and Mayweather, with as free a shot as he has ever had, took advantage of Ortiz's lapse in judgment with an overhand right that landed flush. But Mayweather's last six fights have gone to the scorecards, a streak he vows will end against Berto.

"There's going to be some knockdowns," Mayweather said when the matchup was made. "A lot. And there's going to be blood. A lot."

Mayweather being Mayweather, though, don't expect him to toss caution to the wind as if it were so much confetti. If he didn't do it against Pacquiao, when so much was expected in terms of excitement and so little delivered, it would be foolish to think "Money" has suddenly become a leopard disposed to change its spots.

"My health is more important to me than anything," Floyd said of the fears raised by the diminished mental capacity of his uncle and former trainer, Roger Mayweather. "It hurts me extremely bad he don't even know who I am anymore."

If this is indeed Mayweather's last rodeo, the decision not to go for win No. 50 might be his and his alone. It also could be that Showtime or his former TV home, HBO, would balk at coming up with another contract the size of a Third World nation's gross national product, and especially if a precondition to any such arrangement would cede to Floyd total control over, well, everything. It's highly unlikely that Mayweather would be willing to mark himself down like bruised fruit at the supermarket. He is accustomed to receiving premium compensation every time he laces up the gloves, and it seems reasonable to assume he won't accept a penny less than what he's been getting on the about-to-lapse Showtime deal.

But if he really is on the verge of retirement, he soon will walk away with a legacy of opulence that any captain of industry would envy. Consider some of the adventures in spending that Mayweather has engaged in during his relentless march toward membership in the billionaires' club, a distinction he might already have attained if he were only a bit more frugal.

*He keeps on staff a personal chef who is paid $4,000 a day to rustle up his favorite meals, and at any time of the day or night. Also on staff is a personal barber, which also might seem a tad excessive in that Mayweather shaves his head.

*He signs contracts with a solid-gold pen.

*He maintains three residences in Las Vegas; one in Sunny Isles, Florida, outside of Miami; one in Los Angeles and one in New York. He keeps a matching set of cars – a fleet that includes 14 Rolls-Royces – at his primary Las Vegas residence (those are white) and the one in Florida (those are black). "I don't want to get confused where I am," he said in explaining the arrangement to Leach.

*He maintains a staff of around 20, including four burly bodyguards, who know better than to question any directive from the boss.

*He has "at least" $5 million in jewelry, including a $1.6 million necklace.

*He wears top-of-the-line underwear (boxer shorts) and sneakers (Christian Louboutins) which are priced anywhere from $795 to $3,595 a pair, depending on the model) only once before discarding them.

*The bars at his various residences are stocked with his beverage of choice (Louis XIII Remy Martin Cognac), which goes for $3,500 a bottle.

If it appears that PPV sales for Mayweather-Berto are lagging, despite the angle of Floyd bidding to match Marciano, there is one surefire way to spur interest in a fight that hasn't exactly caught on like wildfire with consumers who still feel stung for buying into May-Pac.

All it would take is for Mayweather to announce that his trip from his dressing room to the ring will be made as he sits behind the wheel of that Koenigsegg CCXR Trevita and ticket sales would be sure to boom. And why not? Those who have followed Mayweather have gotten used to the notion of his receiving a minimum wage of $32 million. But a chance to see a $4.8 million car … now that really would be something, wouldn't it?

A-Ward Winning
The Ring, March 2012 issue

The ending was the beginning, and if that sounds like something from Jesus' Sermon on the Mount, what else would you expect from a tournament winner whose eyebrow-raising nickname, "S.O.G.," stands for "Son of God."

"This is not the end. It's really the beginning for us," said Andre Ward, who wears his Christianity on his sleeve in much the same manner as Denver Broncos quarterback Tim Tebow, after his unanimous decision over England's Carl "The Cobra" Froch in the finale of the problem-plagued, yet highly satisfying Super Six World Boxing Classic. "We're going to get better. Believe it or not, you guys (media) haven't seen the best Andre Ward. I'm still growing. I'm still a young fighter. I've still got a long way to go.

"I'm looking forward to the next chapter in my life, the next chapter in my journey."

The question for the moment is whether that chapter will be written against IBF super middleweight champion Lucian Bute (30-0, 24 KOs), which would appear to be a natural pairing, or against an opponent of Ward's choosing, possibly a rematch with Denmark's Mikkel Kessler. Or he could have a go at a light heavyweight with name value, such as Bernard Hopkins, who was among the 5,626 in attendance for Ward-Froch in Atlantic City's Boardwalk Hall.

Ward (25-0, 13 KOs) apparently is inclined to look elsewhere until Bute, who declined to participate in the Super Six, "proves himself" against the kind of top-tier opposition that Ward had to wade through since his tournament first-rounder, an upset unanimous decision over the favored Kessler on November 21, 2009, in Ward's hometown of Oakland, California. That victory enabled Ward to wrest the WBA 168-pound title from Kessler, and by beating Froch he added the Briton's WBC belt as well as *The Ring* championship.

Now in possession of three bejeweled belts and the big, shiny Super Six trophy, Ward is the hunted instead of the hunter, and he is determined to employ his newfound clout to his advantage. It is Ward's assertion that Bute, the Montreal-based Romanian southpaw, hasn't done nearly as much heavy lifting as he and Froch (28-2, 20 KOs) did en route to the Super Six wrap party on December 17. For Bute now to have first dibs on the event's survivor – and for equal or near-equal money – just doesn't seem fair to Ward.

"He's been sitting back, waiting, while we've been fighting for the past 2½ years against top competition," Ward said at the post-fight press conference when asked yet again about Bute. "I don't have to go to Lucian Bute.

"We're (promoter Dan Goossen, manager James Prince and trainer Virgil Hunter) going to sit back and see what makes sense. I think I've earned the right to pick the right fight."

To Ward's way of thinking, Bute – who has successfully defended his IBF title six times since the Super Six kicked off – should prove his worthiness against an "A-level" guy, possibly Froch. Sitting at the same postfight dais with Ward, Froch, his face lumpier than day-old oatmeal, said he would gladly agree to mix it up with Bute, whom he also views with some disdain, and for the same reasons espoused by Ward.

"You can't sit back and take your time when everybody else is working hard," Ward reiterated. "It don't work like that."

Well, sometimes it does. Remember, Michael Spinks turned down a $5 million payday to fight Mike Tyson in a heavyweight tournament whose purpose was to crown the undisputed champion in the mid-1980s. By holding out, Spinks wound up with a $13.2 million payday for fighting Tyson in 1988. Had they scrapped earlier, Spinks might have wound up on the wrong end of the same result – he was blown away in 91 seconds – but his much-larger purse more than compensated for any pain and suffering incurred.

The Bute factor was but one of several problems that then-Showtime president Ken Hershman faced when he tried to bring six

121

fighters from five countries together in the boxing equivalent of a harmonious session of the United Nations Security Council.

Three of the original Super Six entrants – Kessler, Jermain Taylor and Andre Dirrell – dropped out at some point, with Allan Green and old reliable Glen Johnson filling two of those vacancies. That made for a situation in which Johnson had to fight and win only once to reach the semifinals, where he dropped a 12-round majority decision to Froch in Boardwalk Hall on June 24.

Despite all the drawbacks, however, the Super Six was as satisfying to fight fans as it was ambitious in scope. The bouts that took place were routinely competitive and interesting, as might be expected when two quality fighters actually deign to test themselves against one another. And there were surprises, with the two European veterans who were expected to rise, like cream, to the top – Kessler and German-based Armenian Arthur Abraham – failing to reach the final.

Ward, who won the only American gold medal in boxing at the 2004 Athens Olympics, was considered a bit of a longshot when the Super Six began, but he emerged as its breakout star, beginning with his relatively easy nod over Kessler (by margins of four, six and six points) and continuing with paint jobs against Green (a shutout on all three cards) and Abraham (12, eight and seven rounds won). He also took an out-of-tournament, keep-busy fight with Sakio Bika in which he again won every round on all three judges' scorecards.

The result was similar against Froch, a very capable fighter who appeared to be moving in molasses against the quicker Ward. One judge – the British one, John Keane – had "S.O.G." running away with it at 118-110, although Canada's Craig Metcalfe and the United States' John Stewart saw it much closer with identical scores of 115-113.

Prince, the rap mogul who is a key member of Team Ward, derided Metcalfe and Stewart as "kin to Stevie Wonder."

Certainly punch statistics furnished by CompuBox indicated a level of dominance for Ward, who landed 243 of 573 (a very good 42%) to just 156 of 683 (23%) for Froch. And Ward was consistent, connecting at the same 42% clip on jabs (107 of 252) and power shots (136 of 321).

"I was in against a very slick, very awkward, very good fighter," Froch conceded. "I take nothing away from Andre Ward. He's very good at not getting hit, very good at keeping himself out of harm's way. He's like a slippery eel at times."

Of the pair of 115-113 scores, Froch said, "The further the fight went on, I was getting into it. I was winning the late rounds. I know it's not 15 rounds ... but certainly I'm a 15-round fighter. To make up for that, what I need to do is start faster and stronger. He was breathing heavy in rounds 10 and 11. He would have been breathing heavy in six, seven and eight instead.

"I think I'm the closest to come to him on the scorecards. Two of the cards were very, very close. Whether he agrees with that, I don't know. All I'm saying is that I'm the man who came closest to defeating Andre Ward."

Ward is now very much in the conversation for recognition as one of boxing's pound-for-pound best, and maybe his handling of Froch makes him the frontrunner for 2011 Fighter of the Year honors from *The Ring* and the Boxing Writers Association of America. As the man said, the journey continues.

Hershman was scheduled to take over as the new president of HBO Sports on January 9, which means he has a much bigger budget to play with, so maybe more Super Six-type tournaments are in the offing, albeit with a bit of tweaking. Perhaps Hershman's successor at Showtime, Stephen Espinoza, will pick another division for another "grand experiment."

Whether Ward or Bute deserves to be king of the super middleweight mountain, the Super Six at least proved that boxing, for all its self-inflicted wounds, sometimes can and does get it right.

Epilogue: The United States' only gold medalist in boxing at the 2004 Athens Olympics, Ward was only 33 when he retired in 2017, with a 32-0 record that included 16 wins inside the distance, after the second of his two victories over Russian mauler Sergey Kovalev. He was 2017's Fighter of the Year as selected by *The Ring* magazine and the Boxing Writers Association of America, and is now a commentator for ESPN boxing telecasts after a similar stint with HBO.

Remembering Joe `Old Bones' Brown
TheSweetScience.com, August 21, 2017

He had a common name and an elegant ring manner. His career is justly celebrated, but also largely forgotten. Anyone seeking to summarize in a few concise sentences the life and times of long-reigning lightweight champion Joe "Old Bones" Brown, who was 71 when he passed away on December 4, 1984, is apt to be frustrated. The New Orleans native who held the division record with 11 successful defenses until Roberto Duran (who had 12) came along requires thoughtful and thorough examination, a pugilistic doctoral dissertation as it were, to be fully appreciated. In this instance, a Cliff's Notes condensation of what he did and how he did it simply won't suffice.

Brown, who bore a physical and stylistic resemblance to the much-more renowned Sugar Ray Robinson, won the lightweight championship on a gritty, 15-round split decision over Wallace "Bud" Smith in New Orleans' Municipal Auditorium on August 24, 1956. Fighting from the second round on with a broken right hand – post-fight X-rays confirmed the fracture – Brown's long-delayed bid for the title might have ended in still more disappointment had he not decided to ignore the pain and fire the overhand rights he had kept sheathed since incurring the injury. Brown scored a pair of knockdowns in the 14th round on big connections with his damaged paw, which proved to be the difference, at least in terms of public perception.

Although referee Robert Brown and judge Charles Dabney had Brown cruising by respective margins of 12-3 and 9-3-3 in rounds, the other judge, Freddie Adams, had Smith up by 7-6-2. The unofficial Associated Press scorecard had Brown barely ahead at 8-7, while United Press International favored Smith by the same margin.

"I broke the right hand in the second round when I popped him on the chin," Brown said. "I gambled in the 14th round by throwing the first right since the second round and it really hurt. I had to gamble; it was the only way to win."

Although Smith's trainer, Adolph Ritacco, complained that his fighter had been the victim of a "hometown decision," Brown so dominated the rematch, on February 2, 1957, in Miami Beach that

124

Ritacco beseeched the ring physician to halt the bout after 10 rounds with Smith battered and bleeding on his stool. The request was granted, giving Brown his third victory over Smith in as many tries, including a 10-round unanimous decision in a non-title bout on May 2, 1956, in Houston.

Once perched upon the lightweight throne, Brown – who turned pro at 17 on September 3, 1943, thus making for a 13½-year, 99-bout journey to his title shot – was determined to reign a long time. And he did just that, logging those 11 winning defenses (six by KO or stoppage) against some of the finest lightweights during a bountiful time for the 135-pound division. He was much more effective than he had been on the way up, too, having demonstrated increased punching power after taking on a new trainer, Bill Gore, in 1955. Although Brown still maneuvered as nimbly as such other New Orleans-reared dandies as Willie Pastrano, Pete Herman and Ralph Dupas, he now knew when and how to sit down on his punches for maximum leverage.

"I think Joe Brown, once he added that knockout punch, was phenomenal," said Les Bonano, 73, a longtime New Orleans promoter and manager. "He was a master technician with a great sense of spacing. Call me biased or whatever, but, as a lightweight, I really don't think Floyd Mayweather would have beaten the best Joe Brown."

Still, there are those who contend that history has not been as kind to Brown as his achievements merit. "He never got the attention or the glory that some other guys who maybe weren't as good got," Bonano said. "He should have been so much bigger than he was."

That could be because of the years Brown, who served honorably in the Navy for 21 months during World War II and participated in seven Pacific invasions, squandered by fighting for miniscule purses on the Deep South "Chitlin Circuit" during the Jim Crow era. Even the night he dethroned Smith, before a sellout crowd of 8,000, the referee and both judges were black and the seating was segregated, with whites on one side of the ring and blacks on the other. It could have been because of the unadorned plainness of his name, which Sugar Ray Robinson's trainer, George Gainford, suggested he spruce up with something catchy. Sensing that Gainford might have been onto something, Brown promptly dubbed himself "Old Bones," a moniker which did serve to elevate his profile somewhat, as the "Old Mongoose" had done for Archie Moore.

Mostly, though, Brown was bogged down by the burden of having fought so often against so many tough customers in the formative stages of his boxing life, incurring occasional defeats that suggested he was a good, honest tradesman but not someone who was destined to become a living (or even deceased) legend. The night he took on Smith for the title, his 70-18-11 record, with 29 victories inside the distance, hardly hinted at someone who had the makings of an all-timer. At 30, it seemed improbable that he would suddenly find a way to not only move up to his sport's highest level, but to do so by leaps and bounds.

Writer Mike Plunkett, in describing Brown's delayed-reaction breakthrough, put it thusly:

Sometimes greatness is obvious. It explodes out of the gate, often with a particular look and feel to it while other times the ascent of a great fighter in the making is more gradual, punctuated by moments that over time reveal something special.

But other times greatness shows up in disguise, arriving before it is recognized and missed when it is gone. Where prizefighting is concerned, the less obvious sort of greatness can sometimes kick-in for a fighter after years of setback and disappointment, the end result the finished product of lessons learned at the school of hard knocks, and for a time such a fighter bears little to no resemblance to the struggling pugilist he once was. Such was the career of former world lightweight champion Joe "Old Bones" Brown, an example of unlikely and unexpected ring greatness.

Father Time, of course, is the opponent no fighter who doesn't retire while still on top can stave off indefinitely. The sands in the hourglass of "Old Bones'" exhilarating prime were about to run out the night he took on a young, hungry challenger from Puerto Rico, Carlos Ortiz, on April 21, 1962, in Las Vegas. Ortiz – who would go on to fashion a splendid 10-2 record with seven KOs, spread over his two lightweight reigns – easily dispatched Brown's surprisingly creaky old bones en route to a one-sided unanimous decision.

Brown would not fight for a world title again, but neither would he return to the pre-boxing profession, carpentry, he had learned as a boy from his father. He hung around for eight-plus years as an international vagabond who took bouts in Mexico, Mozambique,

South Africa, Finland, Italy, Puerto Rico, Colombia, England, Jamaica, Panama, Venezuela, Brazil and Argentina while again taking short-end money by trading on what remained of his reputation. During his long goodbye, Brown, who was three months shy of his 44th birthday for his final fight, a 10-round, unanimous-decision setback to 23-year-old Dave Oropeza in Phoenix on August 24, 1970 – exactly 14 years since his dethronement of Smith – went a scuffling 20-24-2. And it wasn't just the aging process that marked his deterioration as a fighter. His heart apparently had gone out of his work as well.

Popular British heavyweight Henry Cooper, who had seen Brown at his best, and also bore witness to his professional death throes, noted in *Henry Cooper: An Autobiography*, that there came to be "little pride left in (Brown's) performance" as he tried to compensate "for all the hungry years when he had been forced to fight for peanuts."

When the bad times for Brown ended, as had the good times, all that was left was for a verdict to be rendered for posterity. For the most part, that decision has been far more positive than negative. Among the many highlights of Joe Brown's incredible journey are:

*Induction into the International Boxing Hall of Fame in 1996

*Induction into the Louisiana Sports Hall of Fame in 1976

*Induction into the Greater New Orleans Sports Hall of Fame in 1977

*Being named *The Ring's* Fighter of the Year for 1961

*Participation in *The Ring's* 1961 Fight of the Year (a rousing 15-round unanimous decision over England's very capable Dave Charnley on April 18 of that year in London)

*Getting the No. 36 slot on NOLA.com's list of the 51 greatest Louisiana athletes of all time in 2014, which is especially notable as he is the only boxer to make the cut

*Breaking the legendary Benny Leonard's lightweight record of nine successful title defenses, with 11, since broken by Roberto Duran with 12

If there is anything to still debate about "Old Bones," it's an indisputably accurate reading of his final record. BoxRec.com lists it at 116-47-14 (52); the IBHOF at 104-44-13 (47) and Wikipedia at 105-46-13 (47).

132,000-Plus ... An Attendance Record Unlikely to be Broken
TheSweetScience.com, February 17, 2020

You always hear that records are meant to be broken, but, barring a stunning change in national policy by a communist country unwelcoming to outsiders, the 132,000-plus that turned out to see Julio Cesar Chavez pummel Greg Haugen on February 20, 1993, at Mexico City's *Estadio Azteca* likely will forever stand first for live attendance for a boxing event.

Chavez's intentionally cruel thrashing of the lippy Haugen enabled the Mexican national hero variously known as "JC Superstar" and *El Gran Campeon* to successfully defend his WBC super lightweight title for the 10th time. That fight was the capper to an incredibly deep card dubbed the "Grand Slam of Boxing" by promoter Don King, which also featured title retentions by such top-shelf attractions as Azumah Nelson, Terry Norris and Michael Nunn. But make no mistake, those outstanding fighters – Nelson and Norris, like Chavez, have been inducted into the International Boxing Hall of Fame – merely served as fillers until the main event. The massive crowd might have been nearly as huge and boisterous had the only scheduled bout been the white-hatted Chavez vs. Haugen, the presumptive American villain.

The announced attendance of 132,247 for a showdown fast approaching its 27th anniversary shattered the previous high for a boxing event, the 120,470 that filled Philadelphia's Sesquicentennial Stadium on September 23, 1926, to see Gene Tunney lift Jack Dempsey's heavyweight title on a 10-round unanimous decision. (A crowd estimated at 135,000 turned up in a public park in Milwaukee to see Tony Zale fight Billy Pryor on August 16, 1941, but that doesn't count as there was bleacher seating for only a few thousand and the event was free to everyone.)

The recent incidence of stadium bouts with impressively large gatherings – 90,000 jammed London's Wembley Stadium on April 29, 2017, to watch Great Britain's Anthony Joshua retain his WBA and IBF heavyweight titles on an 11th-round TKO of long-reigning previous champion Wladimir Klitschko – hints at more large throngs willing to leave the comfort of their living rooms to see live boxing, but no promoter can fit a gallon into a quart bottle. Live attendance at least partially hinges on how much space there is in a place, and

128

there is only one stadium that presently has a seating capacity larger than that of *Estadio Azteca* in 1993. That would be Rungrado 1st of May Stadium in Pyongyang, North Korea, which has a capacity of 150,000. But that huge facility is used primarily as a means of the country's populace dutifully assembling for the purpose of feeding the ego of dictator Kim Jong Un.

It's a sharp drop from Rungrado 1st of May Stadium to the 110,000-seat capacity of Sardar Patel Gujarat Stadium in India, known mostly as a cricket venue, and the 107,601-seat Michigan Stadium, the "Big House" of college football in the United States. Sesquicentennial Stadium (later known as John F. Kennedy Stadium) was demolished in 1992, and even *Estadio Azteca*, which was erected to host the soccer matches at the 1968 Mexico City Olympics, has been downsized, having undergone renovations in 1999, 2013 and 2016. It now lists a capacity of "only" 87,523.

All of which likely stamps Chavez-Haugen as a pugilistic equivalent to Woodstock as a you-had-to-be-there human magnet in the estimation of renowned ring announcer Jimmy Lennon Jr., whose memories of the literally biggest event he has ever worked are as vivid now as they were then.

"I can't remember if they had large projection screens like they do now, but I'm assuming they didn't have them then," recalled Lennon, who joined referee Joe Cortez in sharing their recollections for this story. "Here you had this vast sea of people. I saw these little fires high up in the stands. People brought their own food and were cooking way up in the more distant seats. I remember thinking this was more of a mass celebration than a sporting event. Whether or not a lot of people could really see much down in the ring, it certainly seems that they were enjoying themselves. It was kind of like the huge crowd at Woodstock; just being there was a part of it."

Cortez, now 76 and retired from refereeing, said he also was amazed by the gargantuan crowd. "Walking into the stadium that day was like walking into a different world," he said. "You had to be there to believe it, an event with that many fans, almost all of them rooting for Chavez.

"When Chavez was making his walk to the ring, the cheers were incredibly loud. I almost had to cover my ears, and the boos for Haugen when he was making his walk to the ring were just about as loud. It was an intense feeling, I think, for everybody. I knew it was for me. I never had been in a situation like that. I remember thinking, 'What the hell can the people in the seats farthest away from the ring see, unless they have binoculars?' The fighters must have seemed like two little ants, with me as the third ant, in a tiny box. I knew then it was going to be an experience I would remember the rest of my life, and I still feel that way."

Even though Chavez was and is the most popular Mexican fighter ever, the scene might not have been so incredibly jam-packed or emotional were it not for the opponent. The ill will Chavez harbored toward Haugen, a onetime "Tough Man" contestant who had risen above those humble circumstances to win world titles at both lightweight and super lightweight, was palpable, and had been simmering for three years. Each new affront by Haugen only served to harden JCC's determination to someday make him pay.

The feud began behind closed doors, when Haugen showed up at a Chavez sparring session. As Chavez left the ring, Haugen approached him and sneeringly said that his sparring partners were "nothing but young little girls with dresses on."

"I hated him from that moment on," Chavez would later say, with Haugen seemingly enjoying any occasion by which he could verbally torment a fighter who the trash-talking antagonist knew would represent his biggest payday.

The stakes were raised on December 13, 1992, moments after Chavez had scored a sixth-round TKO of Marty Jakubowski at The Mirage in Las Vegas. Haugen entered the ring and again confronted Chavez, telling him that his 84-0 record with 72 wins inside the distance had been crafted against "Tijuana taxi drivers that my mom could whip." But this insult was heard on television, a flung gauntlet that Chavez was only too glad to pick up. He would make Haugen, who came in 32-4-1 with 16 KO victories, regret such impudence.

"I will not have mercy on you," Chavez told Haugen. "I will rip your head off."

King immediately realized that this fight called for the biggest possible setting, and what could be bigger than *Estadio Azteca*? His Hairness played up the revenge angle to the hilt, which was to be expected, except that it wasn't standard pre-fight hype this time. Chavez, who was known to inflict as much pain as possible on any opponent who did not pay him his due as a great fighter, was on a mission to hurt and humiliate Haugen more so than anyone he had faced. There is little doubt that Chavez's making the bout personal imbued his many supporters with the determination to be there so they could someday regale their children and grandchildren with the tale of how they witnessed their glorious knight slay the mouthy dragon.

"I arrived very early at the stadium, maybe 1 p.m. or 1:30," Lennon recalled. "I was in my tuxedo and practicing my announcements, but even then, maybe nine hours before the main event went on, there had to be 15,000 people in the stands. They were cheering as I practiced my introduction of Chavez. It's always kind of awkward to practice your introductions in an empty arena, but it sure wasn't empty then. Of course, all 132,000 hadn't shown up either."

Cortez, as was the case with almost everyone there except the few hardy souls who had come to support Haugen, figured Chavez to win. But what if the brash underdog from Washington state pulled off the upset that could spoil the festive mood of all those JCC idolators?

"The security was unbelievable," Cortez said. "There were so many police officers and military people with their plastic shields, and a lot of them had German Shepherds on leashes. If a riot broke out, which nobody wanted, the security people were ready, but how ready could they have been with a crowd that big?"

Fortunately for all concerned, maybe even Haugen, the hordes of Chavez fans who had come anticipating another sterling performance by their hero got it, which enabled all of them to go home happy. Chavez dropped Haugen with an overhand right just 25 seconds into the first round, the first time the challenger had been decked as a pro, and he might have finished him off shortly thereafter had he pressed the issue. But Chavez eased his foot off the gas pedal, the better to do what he had vowed, which was to prolong the pain he was so intent on dishing out. That plan must have seemed obvious to everyone, even to the folks in the nosebleed sections who had paid only 5,000 pesos for their bargain tickets, then the equivalent of about $1.65 U.S.

"He has no way to keep Julio Cesar Chavez off, except mercy on the part of Chavez, and he has none," TV commentator Ferdie Pacheco said of the systematic disassembly of the unfortunate

Haugen, a fighter who had no chance of winning but was too proud and determined to quit.

"I remember the way Chavez punished Haugen to the body instead of getting him out of there quickly," Lennon said. "But that was the way Chavez was. You had the sense he was controlling every moment of the fight and could have ended it whenever he wanted to."

Finally, after an elapsed time of 2 minutes, 2 seconds in the fifth, Chavez decided Haugen had had enough. Or maybe it was the compassionate Cortez who chose to intervene, wrapping his arms around the valiant but thoroughly beaten-up American.

Asked what he thought about all those "Tijuana taxi drivers" who he had characterized as Chavez victims, Haugen said, "They must have been very tough taxi drivers."

No fight is made memorable solely by the number of butts occupying the seats. Upon reflection, Chavez vs. Haugen was utter domination of a good fighter by a clearly superior one. There have been many of those in the annals of the sport. But still …

"That is definitely one fight I won't forget," Lennon said. "When people ask me about the most memorable fights I've done, that one is right up there. If it isn't No. 1, it's pretty close, if only for the size of the crowd."

When Carbajal-Gonzalez I Made Ounce-For-Ounce Magic
TheSweetScience.com, March 12, 2018

Pound-for-pound? How about ounce-for-ounce? On March 13, 1993, two exceptionally talented and courageous light flyweights, Michael "Little Hands of Stone" Carbajal and Humberto "Chiquita" Gonzalez – with a combined weight of 214½ pounds, or a quarter-pound less than WBC heavyweight champion Deontay Wilder came in for his most recent title defense against Luis Ortiz – demonstrated that a really big fight need not require the participation of even moderately large men.

In adding Gonzalez's WBC 108-pound title to the IBF strap he already possessed, Carbajal roared back from knockdowns in the second (not exactly flash, but close) and fifth (he was legitimately buzzed) rounds to drop the even tinier (5'1" to the winner's 5'6") Mexican standout with a textbook-perfect left hook in the seventh round in the Showtime-televised bout at the Las Vegas Hilton. Chiquita, who was leading by four points on all three official scorecards at the time, collapsed onto his right shoulder before rolling over onto his back, where he was counted out by referee Mills Lane. The elapsed time was 2 minutes, 59 seconds.

"I knew that if I knocked him down he wouldn't get back up," a jubilant Carbajal told Showtime commentator Al Bernstein minutes after he struck the decisive blow. "The way he went down, I knew he wasn't going to get up."

Carbajal's confidence, if indeed he was as sure of the eventual outcome as he professed, was not universally shared. Although Gonzalez suffered a nasty cut above his left eye in the third round, a gash that would continue to worsen with each succeeding round, the switch-hitting whirlwind – ostensibly an orthodox fighter, he changed to and from a southpaw stance early and often – succeeded at taking the fight right to Carbajal, where he frequently got the better of the furious inside exchanges. Had Gonzalez not been stopped at some point because of the severity of the cut, he might have put himself beyond the reach of a Carbajal victory on points had he just continued to do what he had been doing from the opening bell.

"One of the main differences here is simple: Carbajal is not hurting Gonzalez with his big power punches," Bernstein noted as the seventh round began. "Gonzalez is hurting him." But Chiquita, who had been advised by his trainer, Justo Sanchez, before the fateful seventh that Carbajal was "very tired" and primed to be taken out, soon was reintroduced to an immutable truth of boxing: some fighters, like wild animals, are most dangerous when their back is against the wall. Michael Carbajal, like Matthew Saad Muhammad, Arturo Gatti and any number of others who consistently found a way to escape the danger zone as often as they found themselves in it, proved that night that he was a card-carrying member of the club.

It wasn't very long after hostilities commenced that the seemingly reasonable fight plan laid out by Carbajal's older brother and trainer, Danny – lots of movement and extensive use of the jab – was scrapped, the result of Gonzalez's incessant pressure, effective and borderline illegal body attack (he twice was warned by Lane for low blows) and, truth be told, Michael's own determination to stand and trade.

"They don't want Carbajal on the inside all the time with Gonzalez … I don't care how many times they tell Carbajal to jab in this fight, I don't know that he's going to do it," Bernstein opined. "I think he wants to slug it out with Gonzalez, and I think he's going to do it no matter what."

Not that punch statistics are the most accurate gauge of any fight's ebb and flow, but CompuBox statistics substantiated what everyone in the arena and in the Showtime viewing audience already knew. This opening act of a soon-to-be-legendary trilogy was an instant classic, one for the record books and memory banks, with Gonzalez landing 206 of 456 for an exceptionally high 45% accuracy rate while Carbajal connected on 167 of 326, an even higher 51%. Had Apollo Creed and Rocky Balboa gone at it with comparable physical dimensions, this would have been the result.

Not surprisingly, *The Ring* named Carbajal-Gonzalez as its 1993 Fight of the Year. The epic clash might have won the magazine's triple crown, had it also garnered nods as Knockout of the Year and the sensational fifth as Round of the Year. Those designations, respectively, instead went to Gerald McClellan's fifth-round stoppage of Julian Jackson and the second round of the Terry Norris-Troy Waters fight. But the repercussions of Carbajal-Gonzalez I would be felt for years to come, on several levels.

Perhaps most notably, Carbajal (who posted a 49-4 career record with 33 knockouts) and Gonzalez (42-3, 31 KOs), who won the succeeding segments of their rivalry on split and majority decisions, each were inducted into the International Boxing Hall of Fame on June 5, 2006. Theirs was a three-act passion play that was a replication in miniature of Johansson-Patterson, Ali-Frazier, Bowe-Holyfield and Gatti-Ward, and it offered conclusive proof that jockey-sized fighters could cut it at the box office in the United States, a vast, mostly unexplored frontier that previously had not been welcoming to them. Carbajal-Gonzalez II became the first fight in which men their size earned seven-figure purses, and the fact it happened on American soil (on February 19, 1994, in Inglewood, California) made the achievement all the more significant.

But the milestones they established, separately and in tandem, owed in no small part to another little guy, former WBA bantamweight champ Richie Sandoval, being insistent that his boss, Top Rank founder and CEO Bob Arum, take a flier on Carbajal, the

Phoenix, Arizona, resident who was a silver medalist for the U.S. at the 1988 Seoul Olympics.

Despite his status as an Olympic medalist (Carbajal should have come home with a gold, failing to do so because of a scandalously unfair decision that went to Bulgaria's Ivalio Hristov in the final), no major U.S. promoter viewed Carbajal as a potential valuable addition. The old adage that good things come in small packages might refer to rings, but not the kind that are roped off and occupied by two fighters and a referee.

"When Richie Sandoval brought Michael to my office, I thought he was out of his mind," Arum said in May 2006 prior to Carbajal's induction into the IBHOF. "I had seen Michael in the Olympics, but he was, like, 106 pounds. What the hell were we going to do with someone that little? But there was something about Michael that intrigued Richie, and he pleaded for me to take him on.

"The more I listened to Richie make his case, the more I came around. Finally, I said, `I don't know if we can make this work, but what the heck, I'm going to give it a try.'"

It was a leap not only of faith, but of hope and charity. American fight fans have always been infatuated with heavyweights, and their enthusiasm for any division south of lightweight has tended to drop off precipitously. Carbajal could fight, all right, but, physically, he was what he was. There was no way he could eat, stretch or contort himself into something bigger, if not necessarily better.

"The first fight we put him in was a four-rounder, in Atlantic City, against this kid, Will Grigsby, who went on to win a world championship and probably was the second-best 108-pounder in the United States," Arum recalled. "Some matchmaking, huh? But we didn't know what to do with a 108-pound fighter. We had never handled anyone that small before.

"But gradually we worked our way into it. I remember one night in Phoenix when (heavyweight) Tommy Morrison was on the card with Carbajal. This casino executive, who shall forever remain nameless, came to the fight to check out Morrison. He was sitting right near me and he said, when they introduced the Carbajal fight, `You ought to be ashamed of yourself, promoting midgets.' I'll never forget that."

Arum was right; it was difficult finding quality opponents for American fighters Carbajal's size. But, as Arum noted 13 years ago,

"Where there's a will, there's a way There are a lot of great Thai fighters, Filipino fighters, Japanese fighters and Mexican fighters at 108 pounds. We found them. And, of course, Chiquita came later."

Perhaps, because of the Michael Carbajal experiment that paid major dividends, Top Rank has continued to plumb the lower weight classes, from which it imported such precious gems of more recent vintage as Manny Pacquiao and Vasiliy Lomachenko. Many credible pound-for-pound lists nowadays include super flyweight titlists Srisaket Sor Rungvisai (WBC) and Naoya Inoue (WBO), with Thailand's Sor Rungvisai establishing himself with U.S. audiences on the basis of his two victories over Roman "Chocolatito" Gonzalez and another over Juan Francisco Estrada.

Given the trend that he helped create, you'd think that Carbajal, now 50, would be basking in the glow of his status as a Hall of Fame pioneer. But not every mostly happy story has a feel-good ending, and the "Little Hands of Stone" story serves as a cautionary tale of what can happen when a fighter places too much trust in the wrong person.

Most of the $7 million Carbajal earned during his professional career is gone, siphoned by the very man he so often credited with facilitating his success. Older brother Danny Carbajal was released from an Arizona prison in August 2011 after serving 3½ years for stealing hundreds of thousands of dollars in retirement and property accounts from his estranged (and then murdered) wife, Sally. Although there was insufficient evidence to convict him of the 2005 murders of Sally and her then-boyfriend Gerry Best, Danny's greed led him not only to rip off Michael for millions, but to order the eviction of their mother from a house whose deed was in Danny's name.

"He fooled me more than anybody," Michael said of the love and trust he once unwaveringly gave to a brother who proved undeserving of such devotion.

But nothing and no one can take away Michael Carbajal's legacy, or the doors he helped open for little fighters with big talent, or the night when he went to hell and back with Chiquita Gonzalez and had the satisfaction of having his hand raised.

Luck of the Non-Draw
The Ring Gatti-Ward Special Issue, August 2020

Branch Rickey, who as the general manager of the Brooklyn Dodgers had the foresight and courage to integrate Major League Baseball by calling up Jackie Robinson from the minors in 1947, once remarked that "luck is the residue of design." And it is true that, sometimes, Mr. Rickey's description of fortuitous fortune absolutely does owe to meticulous planning. But just as often as something attributable to "luck" turns out well, it also can have less-than-beneficial results.

I thought about the seemingly random nature of the ongoing craps game that life represents while writing the story of the first Arturo Gatti-Micky Ward fight that appears in this issue of *The Ring*, the opening act of a memorable three-fight series that quickly became the stuff of legend among boxing fans. That trilogy, the only one in which Gatti participated during his 16-year, 49-bout professional career, may have been what raised the profile of the very popular action hero enough to gain him posthumous induction into the International Boxing Hall of Fame in 2013 while forever tying him to gritty journeyman Ward, now widely regarded as "Thunder's" primary wingman. There are only two other opponents that Gatti fought twice – Tracy Harris Patterson, whom he defeated both times, and Ivan Robinson, who edged him in back-to-back thrill-fests that matched the incredible excitement level generated throughout the epic triple feature with Ward.

But, having something of a natural contrarian streak, I couldn't help but play a mental game of "what-if," especially after Gatti's longtime manager, Pat Lynch, told me about what might have occurred had that first war with the victorious Ward (by razor-thin majority decision) ended in a draw, which it very easily could have. Had Ward not won the first bout, Lynch likely would have passed on a rematch, which would have rendered Gatti-Ward another one-and-done, as was the case with Gatti's epic slugfest with Wilson Rodriguez. If the outcome had been a draw, "we would not have had that trilogy," Lynch said. "There's no way I would go to another fight with Micky. I would say, 'Forget it, we don't need that. We take the draw and move on.'"

137

Wow. That statement says so much, and it casts new light on the prevailing circumstances of a time when both Gatti and Ward were viewed in some quarters as being on the downhill side of their respective careers. Always a crowd-pleaser if not at an elite level, Ward was 36 years of age when he was first paired with Gatti and had a lot of hard miles on his boxing odometer. Gatti, although just 30, had gone to hell and back so often that he, too, was likely facing the prospect of precipitous decline, which is often the case with blood-and-guts fighters whose shelf life as a major attraction is stylistically abbreviated. It had happened with Matthew Saad Muhammad and later with Ruslan Provodnikov, which is why astute trainer Buddy McGirt had been brought in to help sharpen Gatti's underutilized boxing skills in an effort to extend what remained of his diminishing prime.

And while what was known of Gatti and Ward was that their tendency to take risks almost guaranteed a certain amount of give-and-take, creating good television for HBO viewers, the Gatti camp had to believe that the toll on their guy would not sap too much from him in a physical sense. Except that it did, with the decision for Ward virtually dictating that a rematch be made quickly. That, too, tuned out to be a slugfest, mandating a rubber match that raised the trilogy then and forever to sacred status.

But consider what *might* have happened to alter the course of ring history. Ivan Robinson's edging of Gatti necessitated a do-over, but had Gatti won the rematch, there almost certainly would have been a third fight which, given what had already transpired between the two, likely would have been similarly dramatic. Would Gatti-Robinson now hold the place of honor reserved for Gatti-Ward? And even if there had never been a woulda, coulda, shoulda rubber match pairing of Gatti and Robinson, it stands to reason that a Gatti victory in his first bout with Ward, or even a draw, would have precluded the second and third installments in the series from taking place. By his own admission, Lynch said that might have been the most prudent career option he would have chosen for Gatti, whom he had come to regard as a virtual family member.

In the end, things probably worked out for the best for both Gatti and Ward, if not necessarily for Robinson, who for years unsuccessfully lobbied for a high-paying third go at Arturo. Apart from what took place inside the ropes, the Gatti-Ward trilogy had storylines that have become an entrenched part of the narrative. Their mutual respect led to a friendship that endured up to the time of Gatti's tragic death in 2009. Not only did they occasionally play relatively unartistic golf together, but, after McGirt had withdrawn as Gatti's trainer, Ward consented to serve as his former rival's chief second for his July 14, 2007, bout against Alfonso Gomez in Atlantic City. It was as if a scene from *Rocky III*, with Apollo Creed training Rocky Balboa for his rematch with Clubber Lang, was being played out in real life.

But real life doesn't always have the upbeat flourishes of scripted "reel life." A used-up Gatti in his final fight was stopped in seven rounds, his second consecutive loss and third in four bouts. If life were fair, he would have retired from boxing and into a new phase of his journey as happy and fulfilling as it has been for Ward, who, despite dealing with a diagnosis of chronic traumatic encephalopathy, has never reached for anything he deemed to be reasonably beyond his grasp. "Irish" Micky isn't an inductee into the IBHOF, unlike Gatti, and doesn't expect to ever be, but he has the satisfaction of knowing that he gave all of himself every time he offered up his body and spirit to a blood sport that greedily siphoned bits and pieces of both.

"As a fighter, I was about giving my all every time," he told me. "I always walked out of the ring knowing I did just that. I know in my heart what I did, and that's all that matters."

Gatti was the same. That tells me that the entirety of the trilogy, and the "luck" of immortality it brought to both fighters, actually might be the residue of design.

Section E
Screenings

Rocky's Legacy Complete
Philadelphia Daily News, June 11, 2011

CANASTOTA, N.Y.

Aspiring authors are always urged to "write what you know." It thus probably made sense for a struggling actor and screenwriter named Sylvester Stallone to crank out a story about a down-on-his luck boxer who caught lightning in a bottle and proved to the world he wasn't just another bum from the neighborhood.

Not that Stallone – who will be inducted here tomorrow afternoon into the International Boxing Hall of Fame (Observer category) – ever actually boxed, but just like Rocky Balboa, the pug he created from the hardscrabble Kensington section of Philadelphia, he was from the wrong side of the SEPTA tracks, so to speak, and on the express line to nowhere. The chances of Stallone or his fictional alter ego ever hitting it big were probably so long that any Las Vegas oddsmaker worth his salt would have made either an off-the-board proposition.

But the low-budget *Rocky*, which was released in 1976, won three Academy Awards, including Best Picture, and established a film franchise that, as they say in the industry, has very long legs. Maybe the closest thing to *Rocky*, which spawned numerous sequels, is the James Bond series. But six actors have played the suave British secret agent. Try to imagine any of the later treatments of the so-called "Italian Stallion" with someone other than Sly in the lead role. Can't be done, right?

Stallone also hit a home run, but maybe not a grand slam, with the four-flick *Rambo* series, but, taken on balance, his celluloid career probably includes more misses than hits. He has made some astoundingly bad choices in the selection of roles that might have

140

established him as something other than a two-trick pony, but whenever the box-office take and critical acclaim began to dry up, there were always those old reliables to fall back on.

"I'll just go on making *Rambo* and *Rocky*," Stallone, now 64, said a few years ago, during one of his periodic lulls. "Both are money-making machines that can't be switched off."

But as profitable as the John Rambo character was for Stallone, his heart – and the world's – is more readily given to the guy who fell in love with the pretty but shy Adrian, who made ends meet by serving as a kindhearted enforcer for a loan shark, who was always loyal to his crusty trainer, Mickey, and unaccountably so to his schlub of a brother-in-law, Paulie. Change any of the elements of the original story – which Stallone wrote in only three days after being inspired by Chuck Wepner's failed challenge of heavyweight champion Muhammad Ali – and maybe some or all of the *Rocky* magic disappears.

Even Sly himself is sometimes at a loss to explain why Rocky Balboa became as integral and enduring a part of the public consciousness as any movie character ever has. Upon being told in December 2005 that the Boxing Writers Association of America had selected him to receive an award for "lifetime cinematic achievement in boxing," Stallone said he could not have anticipated his fictional creation's ability to keep going the distance.

"People accept Rocky Balboa as authentic," said Stallone, who was putting the finishing touches on 2006's *Rocky Balboa* when told of that honor. "I can't tell you how many people have come up to me and asked about my boxing career. It's like they really want to believe that Rocky exists.

"You know, I'm amazed by all of this. At one time, I thought people would get over (their fascination with the character) and move on. Didn't happen. After 30 years, Rocky has taken hold to a degree I never could have imagined."

It's still taking hold. A statue of Balboa, a prop from 1982's *Rocky III*, might have been viewed with disdain by certain board members of the Philadelphia Museum of Art, whose steps Rocky so famously climbed, to the strains of *Gonna Fly Now*.

But so many locals and visitors clamored for it to be put on display there that it was permanently relocated from the about-to-be-demolished Spectrum to a place near the base of those steps in 2006.

It is now, and probably always will be, one of Philly's top tourist attractions.

Stallone also is collaborating with Tony Award winner Thomas Meehan, who wrote the librettos for *Annie* and *Hairspray,* on *Rocky: The Musical.* Plans call for the play to be first performed in Germany in the fall of 2012 before debuting on Broadway in the spring of 2013.

What could possibly top all that? Well, maybe a biographical movie about an even longer longshot than Rocky, namely Stallone himself.

Born Michael Sylvester Gardenzio Stallone in the gritty Hell's Kitchen section of New York to an Italian hairdresser father and an astrology-obsessed mother, the future Rocky was expelled from 14 schools before age 13 for antisocial and violent behavior. At 15, his classmates voted him the one "most likely to end up in the electric chair." Much of Sly's defiant ways were acted out in Philadelphia, where the family moved in the early 1960s, or its surrounding areas; he never completed the 10th grade at Lincoln High before enrolling in Devereux Manor High in Berwyn, Chester County, a school for emotionally troubled youths.

Stallone was homeless and sleeping most nights in New York's Port Authority bus terminal when he accepted $200 for his first starring role, a soft-porn movie called *The Party at Kitty and Stud's,* which was released in 1970. He appeared naked in nearly all the scenes.

Having determined that writing his own scripts might boost his flagging acting career, Stallone wrote the screenplay and co-starred in 1974's *The Lords of Flatbush,* whose cast included a pre-Fonzie Henry Winkler, in which he portrayed a leather-jacketed '50s tough guy. But, a year or so later, it's said he had only $106 in his bank account when United Artists executives – who reportedly envisioned Ryan O'Neal in the lead role – green-lighted *Rocky,* with no expectations that it would be anything close to the international smash that it became.

So impressed by Stallone's star-making turn (Sly was nominated for Best Actor and Best Screenplay Oscars) noted *Chicago Sun-Times* film critic Roger Ebert predicted he could become "the next Marlon Brando."

What has followed has been ... well, no one compares Stallone to Brando anymore. One warts-and-all bio of Stallone reports that he passed on the lead role in 1978's *Coming Home* that went to Jon Voight, who won the Academy Award for Best Actor. He also declined the role accepted by Christopher Reeve in 1978's *Superman*, as well as the ones that went to Harrison Ford in 1994's *Witness*, to Eddie Murphy in 1984's *Beverly Hills Cop*, to Bruce Willis in 1988's *Die Hard* and to Dudley Moore in 1992's *Arthur.* But he signed on to such ill-fated projects as 1984's *Rhinestone* and 1992's *Stop! Or My Mom Will Shoot.*

That kind of decision-making played no small part in Sly being nominated a record 30 times for the Golden Raspberry Awards, usually in the "Worst Actor" category, which he's won 10 times. The Golden Raspberry Foundation named him "Worst Actor of the Century" in 2000.

But Stallone could live comfortably off the megamillions he's already banked from the *Rocky* and *Rambo* series, with large checks continuing to come in from residuals, the gift that keeps on giving. One of his more recent action flicks, 2010's *The Expendables*, grossed $266 million worldwide.

And as of tomorrow, he joins the company of Sugar Ray Robinson, Joe Louis, Muhammad Ali, Joe Frazier and any number of boxing legends whose fights were not choreographed.

Yo, Adrian, he did it.

Joey Giardello: The Reel Victim
Philadelphia Daily News, January 11, 2000

The silver-haired senior citizen, unnoticed and unrecognized, settled into his seat for yesterday's 12:30 p.m. screening of *The Hurricane* at UA Riverview Plaza 17 on Columbus Boulevard.

But Joey Giardello, 69, was not just any member of the matinee audience. A former middleweight champion of the world, Giardello was inducted into the International Boxing Hall of Fame in 1993 and just last year was named the fourth-greatest Philadelphia fighter of all time by the *Daily News.*

Giardello (real name: Carmine Tilelli), disturbed by reports his December 14, 1964, title bout against Rubin "Hurricane" Carter in Convention Hall had been severely misrepresented in the film –

143

which is drawing Oscar buzz for lead actor Denzel Washington – had vowed not to add to *The Hurricane's* box-office gross. But he agreed to accompany me and critique Hollywood's version of his bout with Carter, which is briefly depicted but crucial to the storyline.

What he saw was more hurtful than anything he might have imagined. Giardello said his reputation as a tough guy who never ducked anyone, painstakingly crafted during 19 years in the ring, has been permanently damaged by the filmmakers.

"I don't really want to, but for them to come out with something like that … I almost feel like I have to sue somebody," a shaken Giardello said after viewing three minutes of what can only be described as revisionist history. "I think maybe I will look into it."

A publicist for Universal Studios, distributor of *The Hurricane*, declined comment on Giardello's assertions regarding the film.

The two youngest of Giardello's four sons, Paul Tilelli, 37, and Steven Tilelli, 34, said they are attempting to counteract *The Hurricane's* campaign of misinformation against their father by establishing a website, which went online yesterday. As of Saturday, it will include video footage of Giardello's unanimous decision over Carter and his title-winning bout against Dick Tiger.

"Obviously, people who only see the movie are going to think (Carter) got robbed," Paul said. "The movie people were going for the most entertaining angle, which is why they did what they did. We just want to set the record straight."

Giardello and his family will have their work cut out for them. *The Hurricane* tells the tale of the wrongly incarcerated Carter, the former No. 1 contender who spent 19 years in prison for the 1966 murder of a white bartender and two white patrons in Paterson, New Jersey. Carter, who is black, always insisted he was innocent, and a federal court eventually agreed the evidence against him had been coerced, repressed or altered for racial reasons.

As depicted in the film, Carter's loss to Giardello not only was the biggest robbery since the Brink's job, it was tainted by the same sort of overt racism that kept landing Carter in prison on increasingly trumped-up charges.

"I am not a racist, OK?" Giardello said. "There were four guys I could have given that title shot to. One was Joey Archer, who was white. Another was Carter. The other two guys, I can't remember

144

their names off the top of my head. But the fact is, I picked Carter. I gave him the opportunity to be a world champion. The promoter wanted me to fight Archer. I said, 'No, Carter is ranked No. 1, he earned his shot. Give it to him.'

"So what thanks do I get? For people to spread a pack of lies about me 35 years later? This is serious business. I kind of feel my reputation is at stake here."

Giardello was incredulous, then angry, as he watched the film version of himself, played by Ben Bray, take a fearful beating from the unmarked, clearly superior Carter.

"Oh, please," Giardello said as the movie Carter pounded "him" along the ropes. "I don't believe this. This is a joke. He never hit me that much in 15 rounds."

Giardello shook his head as a ringside broadcaster, after proclaiming that "Joey Giardello is about to lose his crown to Rubin 'Hurricane' Carter," explodes in dismay after the decision is given to the champion.

"They must have been watching a different fight, because in the one we just saw, Hurricane Carter took the title," the broadcaster says amid boos from a pro-Carter crowd.

"I can't believe what I'm seeing," Giardello's wife of 50 years, Rosalie Tilelli, 67, who attended the actual fight, said to her husband. "They made it seem like he beat the hell out of you.

"I never thought it would be like this. I thought they would make it seem, you know, a little bit controversial. But this is ridiculous. It's so unfair."

Said Giardello: "They got the crowd booing me. How could they do that? Nobody booed. Those were my people there, from South Philly. They were happy I won. And I did win. I won, he lost. End of story.

"End of the fight, Carter congratulated me in the ring. He wasn't complaining because he didn't have anything to complain about. I was better than him. I know it, he knows it, everybody who was at the fight that night knows it. It's just too bad all the people who see this movie won't know it."

Giardello, who was puffy around the left eye after the real fight with Carter, said he couldn't recall ever being as bloodied and battered as he was made out to be in *The Hurricane.*

"I didn't get nicked up by too many guys," Giardello said. "Maybe two or three. Who were they, hon? You would know."

"Spider Webb did a pretty good number on you," Rosalie replied.

"Spider Webb, yeah," Giardello said. "He did about the best. But Hurricane Carter? He never hurt me once.

"Look, that Denzel Washington is a good actor. He played the part good. I just wish they would tell the truth. If somebody beat me, I'd say they beat me. Why can't (Carter) do the same? I don't like it when people who didn't beat me say they did.

"If you can't get that fight right, how can you believe anything in the movie?"

Epilogue: Joey Giardello, who was 78 when he passed away on September 4, 2008, from complications of congestive heart failure and diabetes, in September 2000 received what was termed a "substantial" sum to settle his lawsuit against the makers of *The Hurricane*. As part of that settlement, a voice-over by director Norman Jewison in the DVD version of the home video says that " ... going back over it, there's no doubt that Giardello won it." Jewison also says that "the truth is a moving target" when making a film about real people, an indirect refutation of the comments by the movie's blow-by-blow TV announcer that the decision for Giardello was blatantly unjust, and were not based on fact.

Section F
Farewells

Emile Griffith's Veil of Drama Often Overshadowed His Deeds
The Ring, November 2013 issue

It is often said that a particular person was "ahead of their time," a designation usually reserved for innovators, trailblazers and bold thinkers who help set the tone for following generations. Such nonconformists are often ignored or even vilified for much of their lives and only appreciated much later for the stances they took.

By those standards, boxer Emile Griffith was ahead of his time. Fighters before him had the misfortune of delivering the blows that killed an opponent. There most likely were fighters before and during Griffith's *machismo*-drenched era that were homosexual or bisexual. To think otherwise is to ignore human nature and the laws of probability. But Griffith, who was 75 when he died on July 23 at an extended-care facility in Hempstead, New York, was defined more for these two aspects of his life – the death of Benny "Kid" Paret under contentious circumstances and his sexual orientation – than for the five world titles (three at welterweight, two at middleweight) he won during an exemplary professional career that stretched from 1958 to '77 and culminated with his induction into the International Boxing Hall of Fame. And, fair or not, he was scorned for quite a few years by those unable or unwilling to accept who he was and what he had done.

Griffith's fatal bludgeoning of Paret on March 24, 1962, at the old Madison Square Garden in New York, in the rubber match of their three-bout series, is probably the most infamous of boxing's deaths. It is the subject of producer-director Dan Klores' acclaimed 2005 documentary, *Ring of Fire: The Emile Griffith Story*, which has frequently been rebroadcast and was televised again by the Madison Square Garden Network 10 days after Griffith succumbed to dementia and failing kidneys. An opera based on Griffith's life, *Champion*, premiered on June 15 in St. Louis.

Paret's death and the lingering toll it exacted not only on his family but on the normally gentle-natured Griffith would have been tragic regardless of the circumstances. But what set that fateful night apart, then and now, is the homophobia that might have fueled Griffith's 29-punch onslaught as the defenseless Paret lay tangled up on the ring ropes, unable to fall, referee Ruby Goldstein looking on and seemingly frozen into inaction.

Was it rage on Griffith's part for Paret's public denouncement of him as a *maricon*, gutter Spanish for homosexual, fed his furious, 12th-round bombardment? Or was it the admonition of Griffith's trainer, Gil Clancy, delivered to his fighter after the sixth round? Clancy had told Griffith, "Emile, look, when you go inside I want you to keep punching until Paret holds you or the referee breaks you! But you keep punching until he does that!"

Maybe it was his strict adherence to Clancy's instructions that prompted Griffith, a master boxer who was not known as a particularly powerful puncher, to deliver one of the most savage knockouts in boxing history. Maybe it was, to some degree, a desire to exact revenge upon an archrival who had relentlessly taunted him. Griffith, who scarcely attempted to conceal his flamboyant lifestyle, said, "I got tired of people calling me a faggot."

The fallout from Paret's death 10 days later was both immediate and long-term. New York Governor Nelson Rockefeller appointed a seven-member commission to look into boxing violence and to make recommendations as to how to make the sport safer. Some called for its immediate abolishment. In any case, televised boxing – the fight was beamed nationwide on ABC – for the most part disappeared from American airwaves for the next 10 years. Goldstein, a Hall of Famer who had been widely recognized as the best referee in the business, came away from that fight with a reputation so scarred that he never again was the third man in the ring.

Noted author Norman Mailer, a big fight fan who was ringside that night, described what he had seen:

Paret lay on the ground, quivering gently, a small froth on his mouth. The house doctor jumped into the ring. He knelt. He pried Paret's eyelid open. He looked at the eyeball staring out. He let the lid snap shut. He reached into his satchel, took out a needle, jabbed

148

Paret with a stimulant. Paret's back rose in a high arch. He writhed in real agony. They were calling him back from death. One wanted to cry out, 'Leave the man alone. Let him die.' But they saved Paret long enough to take him to the hospital, where he lingered for days. He was in a coma. He never came out of it. If he lived, he would have been a vegetable. His brain was smashed.

Paret's wife and children were left to deal with the loss of a husband and father who, by all accounts, was a good and decent man aside from his apparent prejudice toward homosexuals. But Griffith also came away forever damaged, for reasons external and internal. The specter of 1962 hovered over him like a radioactive cloud for the rest of his life.

"People spit at me in the street," he said in *Ring of Fire* of his transformation from popular champion to instant villain. "We stayed in a hotel. Every time there was a knock on the door, I would run into the next room. I was so scared."

That fear – of what might happen to him in a hotel room or on the street – tugged at Griffith's sleeve for the rest of his days. It also compromised his ability to perform inside the ropes with as much intensity as he might have needed to fully maximize his considerable abilities. Some say fighters who hesitate to seize the moment when they have the other guy in trouble are lost souls. It is like a golfer coming down with a bad case of the yips, sweating and afraid to attempt any putt with shaky hands. The big difference, of course, is that golf balls don't jump up and hit you back if you delay in striking them first.

"I was never the same fighter after that," Griffith said of the melancholia that enveloped him following Paret's death. "After that fight, I did enough to win. I would use my jab all the time. I never wanted to hurt the other guy. I would have quit, but I didn't know how to do anything else but fight."

Griffith fought well for someone as constrained as he was. That he was able to fight for another 15 years is remarkable. But he was correct: He never again was quite the same fighter. Of his 24 post-Paret III championship bouts, 17 went the 15-round distance. Only five ended in Griffith victories by knockout, and three of those came in the 12th round or later. He retired with an 85-24-2 record, with 23 wins by KO and one no-contest. He still holds the record with 339 world championship rounds, 51 more than Sugar Ray Robinson.

Every boxer understands the occupational risks he must accept, but it is not easy to be the guy who is able to walk away when an opponent goes down and never gets up. Former WBA lightweight champion Ray "Boom Boom" Mancini, reflecting on the death of South Korean challenger Duk-Koo Kim, who died four days after their November 13, 1982, bout at Las Vegas' Caesars Palace, said that he, too, was haunted by his memories of that fight.

"You can tell yourself this is the business you chose," Mancini said years later. "You seek answers, but you don't always get them. Mostly, I asked myself, 'Why him and not me?' I'd only recently won the title. I had the opportunity to financially secure my future, and I, fortunately, was able to do that. But after that fight, I lost my zest for boxing. And without that zest, that passion, I knew it was the beginning of the end for me. I was already looking to get out."

Griffith, of course, had far more to deal with than did Mancini. Although he was for a time married to a woman, Mercedes "Sadie" Donastorg (Joe Frazier served as his best man), and never came all the way out of that proverbial closet, he was brutally beaten almost to the point of death by a group of pipe-wielding teenage thugs after he left a gay bar in New York in 1992. Did they recognize him as the fighter who had so battered Benny Paret 30 years earlier? Perhaps. But the greater likelihood is that they bore such malice toward "faggots," real or perceived, that they felt their actions were somehow justified.

In a *60 Minutes* segment titled "The Homosexuals" that aired in 1967, Mike Wallace described the charged atmosphere in which Griffith and others like him were obliged to exist:

"The dilemma of the homosexual: Told by the medical profession he is sick; by the law that he's a criminal; shunned by employers, rejected by heterosexual society. Incapable of a fulfilling relationship with a woman, or for that matter, a man. At the center of his life, he remains anonymous. A displaced person. An outsider."

Which brings us back to the concept of Griffith as a man before his time. In this, the 14th year of the 21st century, gays no longer are told they're "sick" by doctors. They're no longer considered criminals but consenting adults with many if not all of the same rights as straight people, although a few states still have anachronistic anti-sodomy laws on the books. They can live their lives openly and legally marry in an increasing number of states.

Collectively, they command burgeoning political power. Indeed, times have changed.

Orlando Cruz, who on October 4, 2012, became the first active boxer to publicly announce his homosexuality, will fight Orlando Salido for the vacant WBO featherweight championship on October 12 in Las Vegas. Neither Cruz's announcement nor that of NBA player Jason Collins in *Sports Illustrated* made much of a ripple. Both have been acclaimed as heroes in some quarters for having the courage to no longer hide that part of their identities.

Griffith, in the April 18, 2005, issue of *SI*, continued to insist that he was not gay, or at least not completely.

"I go to gay bars to see my friends," he is quoted as saying. "What's the difference? I don't know what I am. I don't like that word: homosexual, gay or faggot. I love men and women the same, but if you ask me which is better ... I like women."

Maybe Griffith was right. In our determination of who is or who is not worthy of our respect and admiration, what really is the difference? Those who knew him well say Griffith was a good friend and fun to be around, in addition to being a highly gifted boxer deserving of every honor he received. So remember him, if you must, for his fatal encounter with Paret, or for his refusal to adhere to the societal mores of his era. But if you do that, you also must remember that he was one of the best ever to ply his brutal trade.

Floyd Patterson: a Gentlemanly Champion
Philadelphia Daily News, May 12, 2006

It's hard to believe now, but Floyd Patterson was on his way to becoming Mike Tyson before Mike Tyson was even born.

The parallels between the young Patterson and the young Tyson are almost eerie. Patterson, the two-time former heavyweight champion who was 71 when he died yesterday at his home in New Paltz, New York, after a lengthy bout with Alzheimer's disease and prostate cancer, was trained by Cus D'Amato, as was Tyson. His trademark style, later taught by D'Amato to Tyson, was the peek-a-boo, in which he held his gloves in front of his face and, bobbing and weaving forward, was always in position to launch leaping left hooks.

Perhaps more significantly, Patterson – one of 11 children born into desperate poverty in Waco, North Carolina, before the family made its way north to Brooklyn – was, like Tyson, a troubled youth. He was only 10 when he was sent to a juvenile detention facility, where he learned to box. That also was the path Tyson followed into boxing.

But, unlike fellow Brooklynite Tyson, the perpetually lit fuse who replaced him as the youngest man ever to win the heavyweight championship, Patterson had a gentle nature that survived his hardscrabble days on the street. And while that penchant for kindness might not always have served Patterson well in the ring, it established him as one of the most beloved gentlemen in a blood sport that always had tended to more reward the violent and profane.

"While not one of the great heavyweight champions, I put him at the very top of the nicest men I've ever met," boxing historian and author Bert Randolph Sugar said of Patterson.

Once, when informed that he held the rather dubious record of having been knocked down 17 times in heavyweight title bouts, Patterson smiled and said, "That's true, but I also hold the record for getting up the most times."

Patterson – who weighed as much as 200 pounds only once in his 64 professional bouts – was a lithe, graceful athlete whose dignity, if not his talent, eventually won over almost everyone who once mocked or doubted him.

He was a virtual unknown on New York's fiercely competitive amateur boxing scene when he burst into prominence by winning that city's Golden Gloves championship in 1951 and '52. Patterson was just 17 when he made the U.S. Olympic team that traveled to Helsinki, Finland, in 1952. Fighting in the 165-pound weight class, he won four consecutive bouts, the last of which, a first-round knockout of Romania's Vasile Tita, earned him the gold medal.

Upon his return to America, Patterson turned pro under D'Amato, who had begun working with him three years earlier at the legendary Gramercy Gym. Patterson rocketed up the ratings, compiling a 30-1 record, with 20 knockouts, to earn a spot opposite Archie Moore for the heavyweight championship vacated by Rocky Marciano.

The fans' favorite was the 42-year-old Moore, then the oldest man ever to fight for boxing's most prestigious title, but it was Patterson,

21, who walked away with the prize when he stopped the "Mongoose" in five rounds on November 30, 1956, in Chicago.

It has been noted that, once in possession of the championship, Patterson was overly protected by D'Amato, whose preference was to pair him with the least dangerous challengers he could sell to the public. Patterson's first four defenses came against Tommy "Hurricane" Jackson, Pete Rademacher (the 1956 Olympic heavyweight champion who was making his pro debut), Roy "Cut and Shoot" Harris and Brian London, hardly a murderer's row.

Nonetheless, Patterson's June 26, 1959, title bout in New York against Sweden's Ingemar Johansson was the most widely anticipated heavyweight bout in years. Johansson, whose nickname for his crushing overhand right was the "Hammer of Thor," knocked Patterson down seven times in the third round before referee Ruby Goldstein finally stepped in and stopped it.

Noting that actor John Wayne had a front-row seat for the bout, Patterson, in what to become a recurring theme, apologized for not having performed better.

"This famous American hero had come to watch me fight, and I was losing the title to another country," Patterson said. "It was the most embarrassing moment of my life."

The rematch with Johansson on June 20, 1960, was billed as a grudge match, but, when the Swede was left stretched out and unconscious on the canvas, his right leg shaking from the effects of a perfectly timed left hook, a compassionate Patterson knelt over his vanquished foe.

That gesture made Patterson, once a villain in Sweden, hugely popular there. After he won the rubber match with Johansson in six rounds on March 13, 1961, he fought four times in Stockholm.

But, following another easy defense against Tom McNeeley (whose son, Peter, later would fight Tyson), Patterson no longer could put off a bout with fearsome No. 1 contender Sonny Liston. Much bigger and more powerful, Liston knocked out Patterson in the first round, as he did in the rematch.

Seemingly anticipating defeat in each instance, Patterson brought disguises – a false beard and glasses – to the Liston fights. It was almost as if he had to constantly apologize for being not quite good enough.

153

"Fear was absolutely necessary," he once said of his skittish style. "Without it, I would have been scared to death."

Patterson – the first man to lose and regain the heavyweight title – got his last shot at a belt in 1968, when he lost a decision to Jimmy Ellis for the vacant WBA crown. His most memorable post-Liston bout, however, came against Muhammad Ali, whom Patterson had continued to refer to by his birth name, Cassius Clay.

Before their November 22, 1965, meeting, Ali called the former champ an "Uncle Tom" and, instead of going for the quick stoppage, mocked, humiliated and punished him before knocking him out in the 12th round.

Patterson (55-8-1, 40 KOs) later served as chairman of the New York State Athletic Commission, but, by 1998, the effects of Alzheimer's no longer could be overlooked. He resigned shortly after it was reported that a three-hour video deposition he gave in a lawsuit revealed that he couldn't recall important events in his boxing career.

To the end, however, Patterson remained upbeat. Sugar recalled a lunch at Patterson's New Paltz home that also was attended by former world champs Jose Torres and Gene Fullmer.

"We were in Floyd's living room,' Sugar recalled. "He had a grandfather clock that struck once. Bong. And then there was silence.

"After about a minute, Floyd looked up and said, `If anyone else will admit they heard that, I'll admit it, too."

Politics Aside, Passionate Boxing Fan John McCain was an American Hero
TheSweetScience.com, April 28, 2018

Definition of a "hero," from the Merriam-Webster dictionary: "A person admired for achievements and noble qualities; one who shows great courage."

Senator John McCain, the difficult-to-categorize, at least in a political sense, Republican from Arizona, was four days shy of his 82nd birthday when on August 25 he finally succumbed to the ravishing effects of gliobastoma, a rare form of brain cancer he was first diagnosed as having on July 14, 2017. Those with aggressive GBM, as it is known in its shortened form, have a median survival period of 14 months, meaning the combative former Navy pilot did not outlive normal projections for those similarly stricken.

For those familiar with the incredible true story of a genuine American hero, Senator McCain's adherence to any kind of norm must seem odd. His admirers – and they are many, including those who often opposed his positions as a two-time presidential candidate, two-term congressman and six-term senator – can be excused for somehow believing that a man who had survived as much as John Sidney McCain III had could somehow do it again if only through the force of his will and, maybe, his genetic makeup. Among his surviving family members is his 106-year-old mother, Roberta.

"It's been quite a ride," McCain, acknowledging the inevitability of his latest confrontation with the specter of death, wrote in a memoir published in May. "I've known great passions, seen amazing wonders, fought in a war, and helped make peace. I've lived very well and I've been deprived of all comforts. I've been as lonely as a person can be and I've enjoyed the company of heroes. I've suffered the deepest despair and experienced the highest exultation.

"I made a small place for myself in the story of America and the history of my times."

A small place in the multifaceted story of John McCain, one that almost surely will not be mentioned this week by former Presidents George W. Bush and Barack Obama, among those expected to speak at McCain's Thursday funeral service at Washington National Cathedral (a private funeral is planned for Saturday at the U.S. Naval Academy in Annapolis, Maryland) is the former USNA boxer's unabashed love of the sport, and his relentless championing of its participants.

McCain co-authored, along with Senator Richard Bryan (D-Nev.), the Professional Boxing Safety Act, which became law on July 1, 1997, and he also sponsored the Muhammad Ali Boxing Reform Act, which became law on May 26, 2000. He would have preferred to go even further, but his vision of providing pension and unionized protections for professional boxers ran into the sort of legislative roadblocks that have become all too common in a political landscape marked by increasing partisanship. The biggest impediment to a boxers' union and pension plan is the international aspect of boxing, with two of the four major world sanctioning bodies headquartered

155

abroad: the WBA in Venezuela and the WBC in Mexico. It can be argued that the WBO, based in Puerto Rico, also is under "foreign" purview, although the Caribbean island is a territory of the United States.

"As long as there is not a pension plan or a union – and I say that as a conservative Republican –I don't believe you in any way can compare what the fighters receive to that of other professional sports," McCain said in 2000, during his first presidential run that ended in his party's nomination going to George W. Bush. "Every other major professional sport in this country has unions and pension plans."

McCain's failed push for unionization in pro boxing ran contrary to the prevailing mood of the Republican hierarchy, and so was his advocacy for a bill that would have created the formation of a three-person commission within the Commerce Department to regulate the sport in America. On November 16, 2005, the U.S. House of Representatives voted, 233-190, against the proposed bill. Interestingly, Democrats voted for the proposed legislation by 146-50, but the GOP shot it down by a 183-43 margin. It is one of several instances where McCain, considered something of a political maverick, reached across the aisle on matters he considered to be of enough importance to transcend party orthodoxy.

But if American at large paid little heed to McCain's hit-or-miss boxing crusades, the fighters whose circumstances he strove to improve took notice. Among those who lauded him was IBF middleweight champion Bernard Hopkins.

"Senator McCain is a true hero in my eyes," Hopkins said in July 2000. "I know his history. You have to know who you're dealing with, right? This is a man who was in a prison camp and could have been released early, but he didn't want to leave his friends. That tells me something."

The son and grandson of Navy admirals also named John McCain, there is a strong likelihood John III (one of his sons, John IV, is a fourth-generation Naval Academy graduate now serving as a Navy helicopter pilot) would have remained in the military until he reached mandatory retirement age and risen in rank to join his distinguished forebears were it not for the events of October 26, 1967, when a surface-to-air missile struck his Skyhawk dive bomber on a mission over Hanoi. Its right wing destroyed, the crippled aircraft hurtled toward Truc Bach Lake when McCain parachuted to … well, not exactly safety. The force of his ejection from the plane broke his right leg and both arms, knocking him unconscious. Sinking to the depths of what might have been his watery grave, McCain came to, ignoring the pain as best he could, and somehow was able to kick his way to the surface with his good leg and activate his life preserver with his teeth.

Pulled ashore by some North Vietnamese, one of his captors slammed a rifle butt into his right shoulder, shattering it. Another bayoneted him in the abdomen and foot.

The severely injured McCain was then transported to Ho Loa Prison, which was derisively nicknamed the "Hanoi Hilton" by its 500 or so prisoners. At first denied medical attention, McCain, who by that time was also suffering from dysentery, was described by one of his fellow POWs, Air Force Major George "Bud" Day, as looking "like he absolutely was on the verge of death." His tale might have ended there, in that squalid setting, had not prison officials learned of his two-admiral lineage.

The North Vietnamese, hoping to score a propaganda victory, not only provided him delayed if substandard medical attention – he underwent surgery on his broken leg, but several ligaments were damaged in the process – but offered him early release. Adhering to the military code of "first in, first out," McCain said he would only accept if every man captured before him was released as well.

McCain's refusal to take the accelerated release, as well as his steadfast refusal to give interrogators any more information than his name, rank, serial number and date of birth, so infuriated prison officials that they moved him into solitary confinement in March 1968, several months before his father was named commander in chief of all U.S. Pacific forces. Thus began the systematic torture he was to endue beginning in August 1968, during which his once-dark brown hair turned snowy white and his body weight dropped alarmingly, the result of being put on a diet of stale bread and thin pumpkin soup. But, he said, the torture ended around October of 1969 and his solitary confinement concluded in March 1970. After the signing of the Paris Peace Accords on January 27, 1973, putting an end to the Vietnam War, McCain was released on March 14, 1973.

He came home with a body so irretrievably broken that he would walk with a limp for the rest of his days, and unable to raise his arms above his shoulders. There would be personal recriminations as well, with McCain, at the point of suicide and after four days of prolonged torture during the worst stretch of his incarceration, agreeing to write a confession of his "crimes" against the North Vietnamese people.

"I felt just terrible about it," he recalled. "Every man has his breaking point. I had reached mine."

Perhaps it was the forced signing of that confession that prompted Republican nominee Donald J. Trump, of whom Senator MCain was not a fan, to take an egregiously distasteful shot at his tormentor from Arizona during an appearance at the Family Leadership Summit in Ames, Iowa, during the 2016 presidential campaign. Asked about McCain's service to his country while in the Navy, Trump responded, "He's not a war hero. He was a war hero because he was captured. I like people who aren't captured."

Although Trump – who never served in the military and received four deferments from 1964 to '67 – quickly recanted, he was widely criticized by Democrats and Republicans alike for comments so seemingly inappropriate for someone aspiring to become Commander in Chief of all U.S. military forces. While it is not obligatory for a sitting president to have donned a uniform in defense of his country, to have done so would appear to be beneficial; of the 45 individuals who have held the nation's highest elected office, 22 saw combat or served in combat zones while another eight served in other capacities.

Although a frequent critic of Trump, McCain considered the late Ronald Reagan his hero and political role model. Thus was McCain paradoxical in many ways, forever, in the words of Winston Churchill describing Russia, a riddle wrapped in a mystery inside an enigma. To left-leaning boxing promoter Bob Arum, McCain was a "great American" and "terrific boxing fan" whose politics were a bit too conservative for his own taste, while to Trump backers he was a gadfly who too often strayed left of their preferred right-of-center moorings. He was in his own way that rarest of politicians, true to his own somewhat alterable beliefs, a fighter for his constituents who kept him in office and a steadfast proponent for that most under-represented minority, the boxers with whom he so readily identified.

"There are some issues that need to be tackled because it's the right thing to do," he once said of his obsession with eliminating or at least minimizing some of the ills linked to professional boxing. "I'm very proud to be involved in the movement to effect some real change in the boxing industry. I believe that boxers are the most exploited of all professional athletes. They come from the lowest rung, and generally are the least educated. They're the only major sport that's not unionized.

"I can't force boxers to invest their money, but I sure think I can prevent them from being exploited by unscrupulous outsiders."

Perhaps my most enduring memory of Senator McCain is the one time I had a chance to speak to him, in a brief interview that was more like two fight fans having a chat, despite the fact I was holding a tape recorder. It was August 25, 1998, and the senator and Pennsylvania's Republican governor, Tom Ridge, were part of a capacity-plus, sweat-soaked crowd of 1,350 at Philadelphia's Blue Horizon for a sort-of notable event, the final *USA Tuesday Night Fights* telecast, which ended the cable network's 17-year run. In the main event, heavyweight novelty attraction Eric "Butterbean" Esch blasted out journeyman Tim Pollard in the first round of a natch, scheduled four-rounder.

It didn't take long for the two politicians, who arrived wearing suits and ties, to doff their jackets and ties and to loosen their collars. But they nonetheless appeared to be enjoying themselves immensely; for Senator McCain especially, this suffocatingly hot night was a chance to let his hair down and indulge in his not-so-secret passion.

"It's my first time here, but I've seen the place on television a hundred times," he said. "I'd heard about the incredible atmosphere and everything I heard is true. This is one of the great, classic places for boxing."

Rest in peace, Senator McCain. The symbolic 10-count has sounded and you take your earthly leave having scored a couple of victories on points in the ongoing quest to make things better for fighters and those who care about them."

One of the finest and most iconic of American sports writers, longtime *Miami Herald* columnist Edwin Pope, was 88 when cancer claimed him the evening of January 19, with his family by his side, in Okeechobee, Florida. Mr. Pope – briefly a colleague of mine, when I was on the *Herald's* sports staff in 1970 – had been in ill health for several years. But even after I moved on from Miami to jobs at other newspapers, we would on occasion amicably cross paths, in the press box for a football game or, more likely, at ringside for a major boxing event.

A former boxer during his college days at the University of Georgia, Mr. Pope recalled making "hundreds" of trips to Miami Beach's famous 5th Street Gym, where he developed close relationships with Muhammad Ali and Angelo Dundee, both of whom, sadly, are also now gone.

"I loved boxing because I boxed in college and grew up on boxing listening to Joe Louis on the radio. I was fascinated and enchanted by it. (But) never did I ever want to be anything else (than a sports writer) from the time I was 11 years old, except the brief time in college at Georgia when I wanted to be a fighter," Mr. Pope – I knew him too little on a personal level, and respected him too much in a professional sense, to have the temerity to address him by his first name – said some years ago.

Although Mr. Pope did not focus on the sweet science often enough to be primarily classified as a "boxing writer," when he did, his work was so exquisite that he deservedly if somewhat belatedly was the co-recipient, along with former *Sports Illustrated* senior writer William Nack, of the A.J. Liebling Award for Outstanding Boxing Writing at the 82nd Boxing Writers Association of America Awards Dinner in 2004. I consider it one of the highlights of my tenure as president of the BWAA that I successfully championed his candidacy for the Liebling. But make no mistake, Mr. Pope did not receive that prestigious award because of my endorsement; he got it strictly on merit.

I know what some of you are thinking, if you have managed to make it through the first few paragraphs of another of my tributes to the dearly departed. Who really cares about the authorship of stories about our favorite sport? Boxing is first and foremost about fights and fighters, and that is undoubtedly true. But it is also about fights and writers, who serve as the conduits that allow the public to look beyond the obvious and get a sense of things that only the most discerning eyes ever get to see, and then convert that insight into well-crafted prose. The best of the best do so with fairness and equanimity, which sometimes is easier said than done.

"I had the ax, I held the gun. I didn't want to fire it randomly," Mr. Pope said of the responsibility he felt whenever he sat down to write. "I always wanted to be fair, even to people who didn't deserve it."

The true giants of my profession, never that numerous in any case, have become an even more exclusive fraternity with Mr. Pope's passing. My first sports writing role model, longtime New Orleans columnist Peter Finney (who received the Liebling in 2012), was 88 when he died on August 13, 2016. I first met Peter when I was 16, the summer before my senior year in high school, when I had the good fortune to be hired as a minimum-wage copy boy at the *Times-Picayune*, also getting my first bylines in a real newspaper for covering American Legion baseball games. When my hero-worshiping younger self told Peter – who became a friend of long-standing – that I wanted to be just like him, he offered advice that I have always tried to follow, and have passed along to younger writers who over time have come to consider me something of an elder statesman.

"Find your own voice," Peter told me, "and your own style."

Edwin Pope, in Miami, and Peter Finney, in New Orleans, were as identifiable, and probably more so, than the most heralded athletes ever to have starred in those cities, if for no other reason than the fact that their incredible longevity matched their talent. Mr. Pope became sports editor of his hometown *Athens (Ga.) Banner-Herald* at the impossibly young age of 15, mostly but maybe not entirely because, as he noted, "every able-bodied man was in the service" during World War II. Peter Finney began writing for the then-*New Orleans States* in high school, the launch of an illustrious 68-year career.

Clearly, these men and others of their ilk were not late bloomers. They were blessed with their gift at an early age, and, upon recognizing it, had no choice but to happily follow their destiny.

"Peter was generous as a mentor to his colleagues," former *Times-Picayune* editor Jim Amoss said of Finney. "He had an eye for what was interesting and a voice that was distinctive and irresistible. Even if you weren't a New Orleans sports fan, you read Pete for his take on what mattered in our world."

It is a familiar tale of sustained excellence played out by other dedicated men in other towns: Jim Murray of the *Los Angeles Times*, who was 79 when he died in 1998; Shirley Povich of the *Washington Post* (92 when he died in 1998); Blackie Sherrod of the *Dallas Morning News* (96 when he died in 2016); Stan Hochman of my paper, the *Philadelphia Daily News* (86 when he died in 2015). Other writers might have assumed their duties, but, really, all were irreplaceable, in the manner that a Sugar Ray Robinson or an Ali is irreplaceable.

So let me take this opportunity to acknowledge my appreciation for some of the remaining members of an emperors' club who have helped shape my career in ways both great and small: my dear friend Jerry Izenberg, 86, columnist emeritus for the *Newark Star-Ledger*, whose latest book, *Once They Were Giants: The Golden Age of Heavyweight Boxing,* will soon be in bookstores, and *New York Times* columnist Dave Anderson, also 86, who won the Pulitzer Prize for "distinguished commentary on sporting events" in 1981. Both have been inducted into the International Boxing Hall of Fame in the Observer category.

Regardless of the line of work any of us are in, we all compete. We all seek to become the best that we can be. As I approach the figurative championship rounds of my own 47-year career in sports journalism, I know that I have been fortunate to have stood in the shadow of such sports writing legends as Peter Finney, Edwin Pope, Jerry Izenberg and Stan Hochman, as well as to still go head-to-head with the formidable likes of Thomas Hauser, Ron Borges, Springs Toledo, Mark Kriegel and others. One thing all of the aforementioned have in common: they always held firm to the belief that their next story would be better than the one that preceded it, and that the status quo is never quite good enough for those who continually strive for perfection and realize it is always just beyond their grasp.

Sadly, Edwin Pope is likely not the last fighter, writer or other boxing notable whose life I will be obliged to commemorate for The Sweet Science. In 2016, I tried to find the right words to say goodbye to Muhammad Ali, Aaron Pryor, Alex Stewart, Jack Obermayer and Richie Giachetti. Similar farewells were extended in 2015 to Howard Davis Jr., Izzy Burgos, Tony Ayala Jr. and Gene Fullmer; in 2014 to Ed Derian, Matthew Saad Muhammad, Rubin "Hurricane" Carter and Jose Sulaiman; in 2013 to Tommy Morrison, Craig Bodzianowski and Carl "The Truth" Williams; in 2012 to Hector "Macho" Camacho and Emanuel Steward; in 2009 to Arturo Gatti, Jackie Tonawanda and Ingemar Johansson, and in 2008 to Joey Giardello and Toby Gibson.

All of those stories were worth telling, and my fervent hope is that I have done them justice.

Angelo Dundee Was Boxing's Will Rogers
The Ring, May 2012 issue

Will Rogers was only 55 when he died in a crash of a small airplane in Alaska on August 15, 1935. But the man who at various times in his life was a cowboy, humorist, vaudeville performer, social commentator, politician and motion picture actor was one of the best-liked and most-admired persons in America during his time in the public eye because of his unflagging optimism and penchant for wry observations.

Perhaps Rogers' most famous epigram concerned his belief that everyone had some good in him, or at least enough positive aspects for a keen-eyed observer to spot them if he looked closely enough. "When I die, my epitaph, or whatever you call those signs on gravestones, is going to read, "I joked about every prominent man of my time, but I never met a man I didn't like," Rogers once wrote. "I am so proud of that, I can hardly wait to die so it can be carved."

Angelo Dundee, the Hall of Fame boxing trainer who was 90 when he died on February 1 in Oldsmar, Florida, might or might not have met someone he didn't like. Lord knows, there are more than a few people walking around who are so obnoxious it would be difficult for even Will Rogers to take much of a shine to them. But a variation of Rogers' famous take on the human condition applies to the pixieish chief second for Muhammad Ali and Sugar Ray Leonard, so much so that it *should* be etched into Dundee's headstone.

There simply isn't anyone who ever met Angelo Dundee who didn't like him, a lot. He was the perpetually cheery guy whose effervescent personality could lift anyone's spirits. Engage Angelo in even a minute or two of conversation and you'd come away with a smile on your face and a bit more pep in your step, even if you'd never met him before. It was a rare gift that stamped him as special, maybe even more so than the ability to coax winning performances out of his fighters. And make no mistake, Dundee's Hall of Fame credentials are legitimate; Ali and Leonard were only two of the 15 world champions to have benefited from Angelo's expertise and genial manner, a list of ring greats that also included Carmen Basilio, Jose Napoles, Willie Pastrano, Ralph Dupas and, deep into his career, George Foreman.

"Angelo touched so many people," said Ed Brophy, executive director of the International Boxing Hall of Fame in Canastota, New York, which inducted Dundee in 1992, the IBHOF's second year of existence, and welcomed him back on a nearly yearly basis thereafter. "He was truly a goodwill ambassador for the sport of boxing. He was filled with enthusiasm for the sport, and for life in general. Being around him would just energize you. When I hung up the phone after our last conversation, I know I felt 10 feet tall. And he had that effect on just about everyone."

While Brophy is probably correct, that the spirit of Angelo Dundee will continue to live on for years to come, the harsh reality of his absence will be evident from June 7-10 at the IBHOF's 23rd Induction Weekend. Fans that have made the annual pilgrimage to the picturesque central New York hamlet won't have Angelo to spread his special brand of sunshine. They won't get to see him embrace and talk over old times with new inductee Thomas Hearns, whose September 16, 1981, fight with Leonard was one of the most-anticipated matchups of all time.

"I'm no big deal," the humble and self-deprecating Dundee would frequently say of his participation in some of boxing's most memorable moments. It was almost as if he considered himself something of a real-life Forrest Gump, a fortunate but ordinary individual who somehow managed to be in the right place at the right time for all that history-making.

To a certain extent, that is at least partially true. Angelo – who was christened as Angelo Mirena when he came into this world on August 30, 1921, in South Philadelphia – was a master of taking advantage of the opportunities that presented themselves to him with astounding regularity. But there is a saying that winners make their own luck, and maybe the chain of events that led to Dundee's becoming a celebrated international figure in his own right would never have gathered momentum had there been a misstep early in his career.

"As a kid growing up in Philly, I never traveled further than Atlantic City," Dundee said upon his notification in January 1992 that he'd been selected for induction into the IBHOF. "Never had a car. Nobody in the neighborhood had a car back then."

America's entry into World War II greatly expanded Dundee's worldview. He enlisted in the Army Air Corps, took up boxing in basic training and served in England, France, Belgium and Germany. Upon his release from the service in 1946, he returned home before heading up to New York in '48, where his older brother, Chris, was a boxing manager and promoter.

Chris Dundee moved to Miami Beach in 1950 and Angelo, by now a full-time trainer – he'd learned his craft from the wizened likes of Ray Arcel, Charlie Goldman and Chickie Ferrara, among others, while in New York – followed in 1952. As was to prove the case so often in subsequent years, Angelo found himself in the right place at the right time. A girl he had dated in New York, Helen Bolton, traveled to Florida with the intention of breaking off the relationship.

"Two days later we were married," Angelo said, happily reminiscing about a union that would endure until December 2010, when Helen, the mother of the couple's five children, passed away.

Dundee's career, as it turned out, was every bit as fortuitous as his personal life. In February 1952, he brought one of his fighters, Bill Nen, to New Orleans for a bout with a promising 16-year-old pro named Ralph Dupas.

"I met Dupas' trainer, Whitey Esneault, when I was over there," Dundee recalled. "He said, 'Ange, I got these two kids, they're underage, they can only fight six-rounders here. If I send them to you, would you work with them?' I said sure, no problem."

Both of the fighters Esneault turned over to Dundee, Dupas and Pastrano, wound up winning world championships.

Another twist of fate brought Dundee and future world champion Basilio together. Basilio was set to fight Baby Williams when his trainer took ill and Dundee was asked to fill in.

"Carmen got all busted up, but I took care of it and his managers (Joe Neto and John DeJohn) were very happy with my work," Dundee said. "Anyway, they kept asking me back. I'd come in two weeks before a fight to calm Carmen down, take him to church, tell him jokes."

Dundee was in the corner on September 23, 1957, when Basilio, a two-time welterweight champion, won the middleweight title on a 15-round decision over Sugar Ray Robinson in Madison Square Garden. "What a great night that was," Dundee said. "I remember thinking, `Man, it can't possibly get any better than this.'"

Except, of course, that it did. Dundee became the best-known cornerman in boxing through his association with Ali, the brash gold-medal winner from the 1960 Rome Olympics who went on to win the heavyweight title three times and everlasting fame as "The Greatest."

And when Ali was nearing the end of the line, Dundee hit it big again with another Olympic hero, Leonard. "What a ride I had with those guys," Dundee said.

But Ange was not just a passenger; he helped chart the course of legend. In the foreword to Dundee's autobiography, *My View From the Corner: A Life in Boxing*, co-authored with Bert Randolph Sugar, Ali praised Angelo for letting him "be exactly who I wanted to be, and he was loyal. That is the reason I love Angelo."

Ali's endorsement of Dundee was enough for Leonard, the breakout boxing star of the 1976 Montreal Olympics, to also entrust his professional development to the little guy who knew what buttons to push, and when.

"I was told to get Angelo Dundee, and that was through the advice of Muhammad Ali," Leonard said in an interview with National Public Radio. "And from Day One, I knew I had made the right choice."

Leonard recalled his epic welterweight unification fight with Hearns, who was ahead on the scorecards through 12 rounds of the scheduled 15-rounder.

"I was totally spent," Leonard said. "I mean, it was over 100 degrees in that ring, and you're so exhausted. Your legs, your lungs, everything's burning and on fire. At that point, most guys would quit. And Angelo said, 'You're blowing it, son. You're blowing it,' which made me just get up there and try one more time. And with that little boost of confidence, I won the title."

Most obituary-type tributes to deceased dignitaries would at this time include a message for them to rest in peace. But that wasn't Angelo Dundee's style; he's no doubt inside the pearly gates right now, chatting up Saint Peter or even the Big Guy Himself, telling riveting stories of fights won and bringing smiles to celestial faces.

Sad Final Chapter for a Great Action Hero
TheSweetScience.com, May 26, 2014

Some call boxing the "sweet science," which conjures images of intricate strategies and balletic movements more reminiscent of a Nuryev or a Baryshnikov than of tough guys punching for pay. And make no mistake, there are fighters whose grace and fluidity of movement hinted at or even screamed that they were actual scientists of pugilism: Willie Pep, Miguel Canto and any number of other stylistic dandies weren't exactly nerds, but they executed a more physical version of *The Big Bang Theory*. Imagine, if you can, Dr. Sheldon Cooper with nimble feet, quick reflexes and a snappy jab.

There are those, however, whose claim to fame owed more to indomitable will than to extraordinary skill, to power more than prettiness. The blunt-force trauma guys come forward relentlessly, taking punishment to dish out punishment, their most memorable bouts recalled as bloody wars of attrition that bespeak the beauty that can be found even in the fiercest, most primeval of boxing battles.

Former WBC light heavyweight champion Matthew Saad Muhammad was such an acclaimed warrior, wearing down opponents in two-way action classics that left a deep impression on anyone who saw him dig inside himself to find, time and again, some last ounce of courage which marked the difference between victory and defeat.

167

Now Saad Muhammad, 59, is gone, having succumbed to the debilitating effects of amyotrophic lateral sclerosis, more commonly known as Lou Gehrig's disease. Saad passed away early Sunday morning in the Intensive Care Unit of Chestnut Hill Hospital, in his hometown of Philadelphia.

Funeral arrangements are pending.

"He had been battling the illness for the last couple of years, but then he took a turn for the worse," said a longtime friend and associate, Mustafa Ameen. "Those of us who knew him will miss him. He was a good man. Sure, he had his ups and downs – a lot of ups, and a lot of downs. But at least now he isn't suffering any more. Hopefully, he's in a better place, and I'd like to think that he is."

Saad Muhammad was a first-ballot inductee into the International Boxing Hall of Fame in 1998, which tells the story of who and what he was more than his final won-lost record, which is a deceiving 49-16-3, with 35 knockouts. But, like many fighters who hang around too long, he was just 5-7-1 in his last 13 bouts, with four of his eight losses inside the distance coming during that span. He was by then a shell of his former greatness, and he knew it. But what's a used-up fighter to do when he has made too many wrong choices, financial and otherwise, and has no way to earn a living but to keep putting himself in harm's way?

"Toward the end I started losing my power," Saad recalled in 1998, a few days before he was inducted into the IBHOF. "You can't fight the way I did unless you got something to back it up. I couldn't back it up any more. But you know what? I have no regrets. I was like Frank Sinatra. I did it my way."

Well, maybe he did, at least professionally. As far as the rest of it … well, that's another matter. Saad – abandoned as a child, homeless as a toddler and later as an adult, his $4 million fortune eroded to nothing by a profligate lifestyle and leeching entourage – surely would have done some things differently if life had afforded him a couple of discretionary mulligans.

"I was in a state of shock," he said of the gut-wrenching decision he made in the summer of 2010 to walk into the RHD Ridge Center, Philadelphia's largest homeless shelter. "I thought to myself, `Am I really going to go into this shelter?' But I had to go somewhere. My money had run out. I was going hotel to hotel, bills piling up. I went into the shelter because I hoped it could help me make a change."

It is hardly a unique situation, boxing history liberally dotted with sad stories of the rapid descent of good and even great fighters who treated their ring earnings as if they were a permanently sustainable asset, like a backyard fruit tree that periodically renews its natural bounty.

By today's exorbitant standards, Saad's estimated $4 million fortune was more of a nice-sized molehill than a mountain. Floyd Mayweather Jr. has made 10 times that amount for a single bout. But it was significant swag for the 1970s and '80s, and Saad admitted to living large – too large. He had a Rolls-Royce, a mink coat and a swarm of hangers-on he estimates at up to 60 people.

"I was putting my people up in hotels, buying them cars," he said. "I would be nice to other people, help other people out, give to other people. Never once did I think, 'Who's going to take care of me when I'm broke?' Stupid me."

Perhaps Saad – his birth name was Maxwell Antonio Loach, although he didn't rediscover that until he was an adult, and he won his 175-pound title when he was still known as Matthew Franklin, before his conversion to Islam – would have made more prudent choices had he not endured a childhood as harrowing as anything to be found in the pages of *Oliver Twist*. Even though boxing gave him a sense of purpose, he wandered through a lost-and-found life, seemingly a perpetual victim of circumstance.

Saad was introduced to hardship at an early age. Living with an aunt after his mother died, his childhood could have come out of a Charles Dickens novel. He was five years old, he said, the day his aunt told him to go out for a walk with an older brother, who was nearly eight.

"They just didn't have enough money to take care of me, so they got rid of me," Saad said. "I was so scared. Then a policeman found me at night and asked me my name. I said, 'M-m-m-m-m.' I was so scared, I was stuttering."

The frightened child was taken to Catholic Social Services, where the nuns named him Matthew Franklin, after the saint and the thoroughfare (the Benjamin Franklin Parkway) where he had been abandoned.

"When people ask me to describe the greatest triumph of my career," he said in 1998, "I tell them it was just surviving what I went through as a kid."

Having been found, Franklin soon found ways to become lost again. He got into trouble early and often, some of the arguments ending in fistfights, a means of expression at which he proved to be quite adept. He was sent to reform school, where one of his teachers, whom he knew as "Mr. Carlos," suggested he channel his pent-up rage into something more useful, like boxing.

After compiling a 25-4 record as an amateur, Matt Franklin – his man-strength enhanced through work as a longshoreman before he turned pro in early 1974 – began his career in search of a signature style that fit both his temperament and gift for hitting hard. Following a 10-round unanimous-decision loss to Eddie Gregory (now Eddie Mustafa Muhammad) on March 11, 1977, Franklin decided that his most productive course of action was to ditch any notions of stick-and-move. He would stand and slug, and may he who came equipped with more concussive power and a higher threshold of pain have his hand raised at the end.

There have been more gifted fighters, to be sure, but by either of his professional names, Matthew Franklin or Matthew Saad Muhammad, the man would have to rank at or near the top of any crowd-pleasing favorites. He was at once an updated Jake LaMotta and a precursor to Arturo Gatti. Anyone who purchased a ticket for one of Saad's fights was sure to get lots of bang for his buck. He won his 175-pound title on an eighth-round stoppage of Marvin Johnson on April 22, 1979, in Market Square Arena in Indianapolis, a virtual replay of his even-more-rousing 12th-round TKO of Johnson on July 26, 1977, in Philly. But if the Johnson bouts represented Saad at his blood-and-guts best, there were other fights that rose nearly to that level, such as his 14th-round TKO of Yaqui Lopez and his fourth-round stoppage of John Conteh in their second matchup.

"I was in a lot of wars," Saad conceded in 1998. "People would see me get hit and not know how I could take the kind of shots I took. Sometimes I don't even know how I did it myself. It's like God told me to get off that canvas and keep going.

"The (first) fight with Marvin Johnson had to be the fight of the century. It was like rock 'em, sock 'em robots all the way. Same thing with my fight with Yaqui Lopez and the second fight with John Conteh. It was fights like that that made me who I am."

Lou Duva, the legendary manager and trainer who also was inducted into the IBHOF in 1998, said Saad's constantly attacking, never-say-die approach would have made him a difficult opponent for anyone, including the best light heavyweight in the world at that time, Roy Jones Jr.

"Saad Muhammad was an outstanding fighter," Duva said. "He's the one guy who I think, if he were around today, could beat Jones. His style would just wear you down. It wore down a lot of good fighters, and I think it would wear Jones down."

Told what Duva had said, Saad agreed with his assessment. "I think he's right," Saad said. "When I was at my best, I think I would have had a chance to beat any light heavyweight because of the way I fought. I got in trouble sometimes, but I always came right back at you."

Not surprisingly, Saad sought to fill in the blank spaces in his life story with as much determination as he always exhibited inside the ropes. Who was he, really? Why had he been cast aside at such an early age? So he offered a $10,000 reward to anyone who could offer information as to the identities of those who had deemed him expendable.

Also not surprisingly, stepping forward to put in a claim to the reward money were the aunt who had abandoned him and the older brother who had left him alone on the street, crying and frightened.

It might be argued that Saad's plunge from wealthy champion to destitution (at one point he was unemployed and owed $250,000 to the IRS in back taxes), while self-inflicted, was a desperate bid to buy a form of love to replace the family he didn't have in his formative years, and didn't want him even when he was around. It is a reasonable theory, although he exacerbated the situation by botching his later attempts at being a reasonably good husband and father. He was married and divorced twice, and his relationship with his children was also rocky at times.

Speaking of rocky, Saad was one of several actual fighters up for the role of Clubber Lang in *Rocky III,* but he lost out to a scowling bouncer from Chicago named Lawrence Tero – you now know him as Mr. T – because his vanity would not allow him to shave his head (Saad's version) or because he objected to the script calling for him to lose the climactic fight to star Sylvester Stallone's Rocky Balboa character (Ameen's version). So Saad was obliged to sit back and watch as Mr. T became an instantly recognizable figure on the big and little screens.

Nor did a proposed film of Saad's seemingly Hollywood-friendly tale ever gain traction beyond the discussion stage. Polly Wilkinson, who was for a time Saad's business manager, kept pitching his story to the studios, but it never found a buyer. Thus was Saad reduced to working as an itinerant roofer, a sometimes trainer of fighters, and ultimately as a homeless person.

"Anyone can fall down," he said of his difficult decision to admit he had hit bottom. "The important thing is whether you can get back up. You have to make commitments and do the right thing."

If that sounds like a line from a *Rocky* movie, well, so be it. It wouldn't be the first time life has imitated art. Or is that the other way around?

Rest in peace, Saad. You fought like a man possessed every time you stepped inside the ring, and the guess here is that you left this earth the same way.

RIP, Toby Gibson
TheSweetScience.com, November 26, 2008

Richard Green, 46, suicide by handgun on July 1, 1983
Mitch Halpern, 33, suicide by handgun on August 20, 2000
Toby Gibson, 61, suicide by carbon-monoxide poisoning on November 25, 2008
Three Nevada referees. Three deaths by their own hand.

In the aftermath of still another referee's irreversible decision to give up on life, questions abound. Why and how did these men, so respected within the boxing community, come to feel such overwhelming personal despair? Is there any correlation, any pattern, that links them beyond their profession? Or is this just another instance of cruel coincidence?

"I 100% believe that there was nothing boxing-related that contributed to the deaths of Mitch Halpern and Toby Gibson," someone who knew both men, but asked not to be identified, told me. "Their only common denominator was that they were referees. But whatever was bothering them, and something obviously was, had nothing to do with boxing. I'm absolutely convinced of that."

Gibson, who worked two undercard bouts of Saturday night's lineup at the MGM Grand headlined by the junior welterweight clash between Ricky Hatton and Paulie Malignaggi, did not give any outward indication he was troubled when he worked the final fights of his 23-year refereeing career.

"He seemed normal, and everything was fine when I saw him on Saturday," said Keith Kizer, executive director of the Nevada State Athletic Commission.

But something must not have been fine with Gibson because, two days later, he went into his closed garage, started the engine of his car and remained in the driver's seat until there was no more oxygen left to breathe. His body was found by his wife, Barbara.

Was Gibson experiencing marital or family problems? Had the economic downturn dealt his stock portfolio or 401k account a knockout blow? Was he keeping secret any depression he might have been feeling?

My source said Gibson recently had lost his regular job, but he was uncertain if that could have spurred him to take his own life.

"He'd been learning mixed martial arts," the source said, indicating Gibson was preparing to branch out into refereeing work in another combat sport. "I know he had lost his job with the State of Nevada penal system. He was taking some inmates up into the mountains where they were doing forestry work. But whether that was a factor in this, I couldn't say."

Gibson, a native of Youngstown, Ohio, had served as the third man in the ring for boxing events in Nevada since 1985. He was generally considered to be a competent referee, if not necessarily an elite one.

Higher on the pecking order for major assignments were Green and Halpern, both of whom were regarded as among the best in the business.

Halpern got his start as a referee in March 1991 and he went on to work 87 world championship fights and hundreds of non-title bouts around the world. Among the signature events he worked were Evander Holyfield's 11th-round stoppage of Mike Tyson on November 9, 1996, the welterweight championship unification fight between Oscar De La Hoya and Felix Trinidad on August 18, 1999, and the second fight between Lennox Lewis and Holyfield on November 13, 1999.

Controversial endings are endemic in boxing, and any referee who works long enough or often enough can find himself in the harsh glare of public scrutiny. Although Halpern was rated as the second-best referee in all of boxing by *The Ring* magazine just months before he pointed a gun at his head and squeezed the trigger, he had been widely criticized for his work in the March 3, 2000 fight between WBA super welterweight champion David Reid and veteran power-puncher Felix Trinidad.

Although a gold medalist at the 1996 Atlanta Olympics, Reid was, despite his championship belt, something of a neophyte professional with only 14 bouts when he entered the ring against Trinidad. By the time Reid made it to the final bell, he had been knocked down four times, thrice in the 11th round, and was clearly in distress. Reid was never the same fighter after that, and, fairly or not, Halpern was criticized for allowing him to absorb more punishment than was necessary in a matchup the Philadelphian did not appear to have any chance of winning from the middle rounds on.

Could Halpern have been driven to the brink by a sense of guilt that he had not done all he could to protect the valiant but stricken Reid? Not likely; Reid kept attempting to fight back whenever he found himself in trouble, and referees, for the most part, are made of hard bark that is resistant to boos and putdowns.

"Was there ever anybody more vilified than Richard Steele?" my source said of another Nevada referee who found himself embroiled in more than a few disputed conclusions to high-profile fights. Steele, however, took the occasional slings and arrows and was adamant that he always had done his duty as he saw the light to do that duty.

More likely, it was personal issues that bedeviled Halpern, who was involved in a child-custody case at the time of his self-inflicted death. Those who knew Halpern, who did not leave a suicide note, believe that "woman problems" were at the core of his despondency.

But the referee who most likely was consumed by grief stemming from his work in the ring was Green, who drew the assignment for the November 13, 1982, bout at Caesars Palace between WBA lightweight champion Ray "Boom Boom" Mancini and South Korean challenger Duk Koo Kim.

Green, a Louisiana native who had been a Golden Gloves boxers in the 1980s, had earned generally high marks for his work in a number of big-time fights, including the October 2, 1980, pairing of Larry Holmes and Muhammad Ali. Serving as the third man in the ring for Mancini-Kim, though, haunted him as much as it did Mancini, whose 14th-round stoppage of Kim in a bloody, two-way battle has weighed upon him like an anvil.

Kim slipped into a coma and died four days after the fight. His mother flew from South Korea to Las Vegas to be with her son before the fight and was the one who tearfully consented to having the life-support equipment turned off. Three months later, she took her own life by drinking a bottle of pesticide.

Green, who blamed himself for allowing the fight to go on and thus for Kim's death, also committed suicide after his depression deepened.

"What really tortured me that night was it could have been me," Mancini said in an ESPN special that was shown on the 25th anniversary of his fight with Kim. "I was looking at my hands going, `I can't believe I did that.'

"My faith in God is the only thing that carried me through that. I said my prayers, `God, please help me to find the answers. I need answers. Help me to find the peace in this.'"

Green apparently never found his answers or his peace.

Maybe there is no common thread that ties Green to Halpern, or Halpern to Gibson. But some things need to be taken into consideration when assessing the pressures that referees occasionally find themselves under.

Take, for instance, the prison sentence recently meted out to disgraced NBA referee Tim Donaghy for conspiring to provide assistance to gamblers, a scandal that threatened to undermine public confidence in pro basketball.

There are sports books in Nevada, and it is not uncommon for large wagers – sometimes in seven figures – to be placed on boxing matches. If approached by anyone attempting to influence a fight's outcome, a referee or a judge would be obligated to report such a contact to the Nevada State Athletic Commission and to the FBI.

But what if a losing bettor blamed the referee and threatened to do harm to him or to his family? And what if a boxing ref, as was the case with Donaghy, developed a gambling problem that made him susceptible to bribes and coercion?

A referee can work hundreds of bouts without incident and all it takes I one tragedy to forever taint him. If Green or Ruby Goldstein were here, you could ask them. Goldstein, who died in 1984, was inducted posthumously into the International Boxing Hall of Fame in 1994. But despite his 21 years of exemplary service, he probably is best known for momentarily freezing in the March 24, 1962, fight in which Emile Griffith battered Benny "Kid" Paret into a coma and, a few days later, death.

Another referee of note, Joe "Firm but Fair" Cortez, doesn't have an inkling as to why Gibson took his own life. "Toby and I posed as part of a group photo Saturday at a seminar we did with some doctors," Cortez said from Hawaii, where he and his family went to celebrate Thanksgiving. "It didn't seem that anything was wrong with him then."

But there is stress related to the job that has the potential to become dangerous when it runs headlong into the travails of everyday living. Cortez understands that referees are human beings, too, and subject to anxieties the rest of us face. His daughter was left paralyzed after an automobile accident, and his wife contracted breast cancer. How difficult can it be to have all that on your mind when you're giving instructions to the fighters before the opening bell sounds?

"With criticism comes hurt," Cortez acknowledged. "Sometimes it seems as if you're damned if you do, damned if you don't. Even when you follow the rules to a 'T,' the fans don't want to hear that. Fans are fans; they have a rooting interest in a particular fighter.

"Every referee knows what it's like to have people say he's no good, he's biased, he ought to be run out of boxing. Whenever I hear that a referee made a judgment call that is somewhat controversial, I'm the first one to pick up a phone and call him to offer my support. See, I know what he's going through; I've been through it.

"Like I always say, you got to have a thick skin to be in this business because the pressure is just tremendous. Fortunately, I can deal with pressure. But Toby ... I don't know what was going on with him when he decided to do what he did. You never know what's going through someone's head at any given moment."

Section G
Personals

The Night Smokin' Joe Fought Terry Daniels (But I Missed It)
TheSweetScience.com, January 13, 2015

They say it takes two to tango, and in no sport does that old axiom hold true more than boxing, the ultimate one-on-one confrontation. We remember the great fights, even cherish the thought of those very special occasions when the combatants are highly skilled, determined to give their all, and are more or less evenly matched.

But classic slugfests are just prettier swatches in the patchwork quilt that is the entirety of any boxer's career. For every unforgettable confrontation, there are two or three pairings, and sometimes a lot more, that are as non-competitive as George Armstrong Cuter vs. the Sioux at the Little Bighorn. But history has carved out a place of honor for the gallant but doomed Custer, and maybe cynical fight fans shouldn't be so quick to sweep into the dust bin of memory those no-hopers who were offered up as human sacrifices to vastly superior champions.

January 15 marks the 43rd anniversary of one such fight, and one that by all rights I should have witnessed from ringside. In his first title defense since outpointing Muhammad Ali in the "Fight of the Century" on March 8, 1971, in Madison Square Garden, heavyweight king Joe Frazier took on mystery man Terry Daniels at New Orleans' Rivergate Arena. The following afternoon, in Tulane Stadium a few miles away, Super Bowl VI would take place between the Dallas Cowboys and Miami Dolphins.

Why am I still a bit sad, all these years later, that I missed watching Smokin' Joe floor the willing but outgunned Daniels five times before referee Herman Dutreix stepped in and waved off the massacre 1 minute, 25 seconds into round four? Well, part of it is that I was then, as now, a boxing guy, the son of former welterweight Jack Fernandez, and whose childhood was spent watching flickering, black-and-white telecasts of the *Gillette Cavalcade of Sports* as my dad gave his own running commentary alongside that of the inimitable Don Dunphy.

But another part of it is the fact that, as the Boy Wonder (I was all of 24 then) sports editor of the *Houma Courier*, a Louisiana newspaper in a town about 45 miles southwest of my hometown of New Orleans, I somehow had been credentialed to cover Super Bowl VI by the nice folks at the NFL. I would be among hundreds of approved media members in the chilliest Super Bowl (game time temperature: 39 degrees) played to that point, part of a near-capacity crowd of 81,000 that would watch the Cowboys dominate the Dolphins, 24-3, to an extent that nearly matched what Frazier had done the night before to Daniels.

Alas, my application to cover Frazier-Daniels – which was viewed live by 8,500 or so spectators, a sizable portion of whom likely were football fans taking a break from Bourbon Street – was denied. No reason was given for my exclusion, but it has been suggested that maybe the seating area for the press was much more limited than for SB VI, and, well, the *Houma Courier* and its kid reporter didn't come equipped with the prestige granted representatives from the major metropolitan media centers. Oh, sure, I knew Frazier was an overwhelming favorite, but I had watched Ali-Frazier I via closed-circuit at a New Orleans theater, and it disappointed me mightily that I had been denied the opportunity to see the left-hooking wrecking machine up close and personal. There was, of course, no way of knowing that someday I would become the boxing writer for the *Philadelphia Daily News*, in Smokin' Joe's adopted hometown, and on close enough terms with the great man and his family that I was invited to functions that otherwise were off-limits to other media types.

Terry Daniels? He was merely The Opponent, a pale-hued, reasonably warm body imported from Texas to take his expected walloping from Frazier for a career-high purse of $35,000 (the champ was paid $350,000) and then to slink away, probably never to be heard from again.

It did sort of work out that way, but Daniels had a tale to tell, as does every ham-and-egger who is offered a dream shot at the title knowing that his vision of glory probably will dissipate into blood, pain and the realization of his own limitations. But, hey, 18 years after Frazier-Daniels, a 42-1 longshot named James "Buster" Douglas went to Tokyo, took down the seemingly invincible Mike Tyson and again reminded everyone that lottery tickets sometimes are cashed.

At 6'1", 191½ pounds and with a deceptively impressive record of 29-4-1 that included 25 victories inside the distance, Daniels might not have been a complete fraud. But, in retrospect, he can now be described as a precursor to Peter McNeeley, who served as Mike Tyson's first designated victim after Tyson served three-plus years in prison on a rape conviction.

In an interview a few days before he was to swap punches with Frazier, Daniels spoke boldly of his intention to shock the world. Asked if he possessed the wherewithal to douse Smokin' Joe's fistic inferno, Daniels said, "I don't think I do. I know I do. I feel confident. I feel I've done everything I can do to get ready for this fight. I know I'm ready. I'm in the best shape I've ever been. I feel strong. I feel good."

Perhaps Daniels bought into his own bravado, or maybe he was just whistling past the graveyard. But he was going to be fighting for the title and, well, anything can happen in the fight, right? In any case he was going to come away with the kind of purse he never could have gotten for fighting other semi-anonymities on the far fringes of actual contention. Sometimes all it takes for a guy like Daniels to float into wider public consciousness is to be in the right place at the right time, and New Orleans on January 15, 1972, was definitely the right place, and not just because of the Super Bowl that would be played the following day.

Much was made of the fact that Frazier-Daniels was to be the first heavyweight championship fight to be held in the Big Easy since reigning champ John L. Sullivan was stopped in 21 rounds by "Gentleman" Jim Corbett at the Olympic Club on September 7, 1892, the first title fight under the Marquess of Queensberry rules. Forget Buster Douglas, whom nobody had heard of at that point (and why should they have? Buster was still in grade school); could Daniels, hyped by his publicity-savvy manager, Doug Lord, as a "Great White Hope," replicate what Corbett had done to the legendary John L. almost 80 years earlier?

"I told the fight promoters I've got a white kid from Dallas, he's friends with the Cowboys, and everyone knows the Cowboys are going to the Super Bowl in New Orleans," Lord said. "They loved it. They bought it. For us, it was a fantasy world."

Daniels had his own connection to football, having gone to SMU to play that sport as well as baseball, until a knee injury crushed those ambitions and steered him into boxing. Although Daniels might not have been anybody's idea of the real deal, he wangled his dream shot at Frazier with a third-round stoppage of Ted Gullick, who was rated No. 9 in the world and was coming off a 10-round, majority-decision loss to a once-very legitimate contender, Cleveland "Big Cat" Williams.

Maybe Daniels wasn't in as futile a situation as universally accepted. Although Frazier had temporarily displaced Ali as the king of boxing, he was enjoying himself, perhaps a bit too much, in the afterglow of his electrifying victory in the Garden. Three months after his leaping left hook in the 15th round sent Ali crashing to the canvas, and served as an exclamation point to his unanimous-decision victory, Smokin' Joe was in the south of France, enthralling miniscule European audiences with his musical group, the Knockouts. The tour mercifully ended when the Knockouts -- who were hardly the second coming of the Temptations or the Four Tops – drew 50 paying customers for one concert, obliging their chastened lead singer to get back to his real job.

In December 1971, Frazier was hunkered down in the dark and frigid (11 degrees below zero) predawn hours at his training camp at the Concord Hotel, in Kiamesha, New York, getting ready to go out and do roadwork with a sparring partner, Ken Norton, who would go on to make some noise in his own right. But try as he might, Frazier couldn't quite summon the energy he had marshaled in his preparations for the first Ali fight, when so much more was at stake. Terry Daniels clearly did not inspire the 5'11" champion to push himself into peak condition, and it showed on fight night when he stepped into the ring at a then-career-high 215½ pounds.

Even though Frazier kept bouncing Daniels off the floor as if he were a basketball, this version of Smokin' Joe was set at a comparatively low flame. Former light heavyweight champion Jose Torres was even moved to observe, "I, for one, think that Joe didn't look at all like that indestructible machine. My conclusion is that Frazier has lost interest in the sport of flat noses. He is ready to retire at any time. And now is that time."

Torres wasn't spot-on in his assessment – the best of Joe Frazier emerged one more time, in the unforgettable "Thrilla in Manila" against Ali on October 1, 1975, which ended with trainer Eddie Futch refusing to allow the half-blinded Frazier to come out for the 15th-round – but the unstoppable force of nature that blew through Bob Foster, Jimmy Ellis and Buster Mathis like a Category 5 hurricane was a receding shadow of his former might. His final successful defense came on May 25, 1972, in Omaha, Nebraska, against Ron Stander, a Midwestern version of Terry Daniels. The "Council Bluffs Butcher" lasted four rounds, but wasn't allowed to come out for the fifth by a ring physician who disapproved of the multiple cuts on his swollen face, which would require 17 stitches to close.

It should be noted, however, that both Daniiels and Stander – whose wife at the time was so dismissive of her husband's chances that she said, "You don't take a Volkswagen into the Indy 500 unless you know a hell of a shortcut" – stung the champ with jolting punches, which perhaps presaged Smokin' Joe's next, far less successful defense, in which he was dropped six times by George Foreman in losing on a second-round TKO on January 22, 1973, in Kingston, Jamaica. There is a good chance Foreman would have won anyway, but Big George was seated at ringside for Frazier-Daniels and maybe he saw something he believed would be useful whenever he and Frazier got around to rumbling.

I had hoped to contact Daniels for this story, but my inquiries drew blanks. But he once admitted he was so impressed by Frazier, and the aura of impending violence the Philadelphian wore like a comfortable robe, that "I felt like shaking his hand when he stepped in (the ring)." It is a familiar feeling among standard-issue fighters who have the privilege of being battered by the very best; Stander kept a small, autographed and laminated photo of Frazier in his wallet, and Seamus McDonagh, who went on to run a shoeshine stand in San Francisco, handed interested customers photos of himself landing a hard right to the jaw of future heavyweight champion Evander Holyfield.

What we do know of Terry Daniels is this: Unlike the Miami Dolphins, who were thrashed so soundly by the Cowboys in Supe VI but came back to go 17-0 and win the Super Bowl the following season, there would be no second chance at redemption for a fighter whose first real shot at the big time would also be his last. Daniels, who would now be 68, finished his career with a 35-30-1 record that includes 28 KO wins, but 13 such losses. After the pummeling he took from Frazier, he lost his next five fights, and 18 of his final 20.

There would be good moments for Daniels, too. He married twice and helped raise three sons, but he later was diagnosed with traumatic brain injury, which some have called "pugilist Parkinson's." It is the sort of sad closing chapter that often is written about fighters who linger too long at the fair, and there can be no denying that destiny sometimes deals the same unhappy cards to the great and the mediocre.

So celebrate the best of Joe Frazier and the Ali who threw down with, among others, Sonny Liston, Foreman, Norton and so many other top-tier opponents. But remember, too, Daniels and Stander, as well as such passers-by as Dave Zygiewicz and Manuel Ramos (other Frazier title foes when he was the New York State Athletic Commission "world" champion and Ali's non-taxing conquests of Juergen Blin, Rudi Lubbers, Jean-Pierre Coopman and Richard Dunn.

They all had a brief moment in time when they were allowed to bask in the reflected glory of actual ring royalty. It's not quite heaven, but it's closer than most fighters ever get.

Marvis Frazier, Bikers and Hot Dogs in the Ring
TheSweetScience.com, July 28, 2017

If you cover boxing long enough, you're apt to see a lot of strange stuff, and I have. A riot following a foul-filled disqualification where tensions between the opposing fan bases ran high (the first of two Riddick Bowe-Andrew Golota bouts, on July 11, 1996, in Madison Square Garden). A motorized white parachutist nearly landing in the ring and then being pummeled by walkie-talkie-wielding bodyguards for Nation of Island minister Louis Farrakhan during a heavyweight title bout (the middle episode of the three-fight Bowe-Evander Holyfield trilogy, on November 6, 1993, at Las Vegas' Caesars Palace). And, perhaps most notably, a part of a heavyweight champion's ear being gnawed off by his toothy opponent (the infamous "pay-per-chew" bout where an enraged and unhinged Mike

Tyson went after Holyfield's ear as if it were a filet mignon in their June 28 1997, rematch at the MGM Grand in Vegas).

But there are other, less-high-profile matches where the sights and sounds would seem to come straight out of the fertile imagination of Rod Serling, creator of *The Twilight Zone*. Some of them I was able to chronicle for readers of my media outlet of the moment. But one, I wasn't. Until now.

Inspired by the side journeys taken by my TSS colleague, Ted Sares, down some of boxing's darker streets, the most recent being his mesmerizing profile of fighter-turned-Mafioso hit man Joe Barboza, I figure it's time to finally tell the story of the last professional fight of the son of a renowned heavyweight champion, a group of peeved and tattooed bikers, a beer-and-mustard-splashed television cameraman and a harried referee trying to kick hot dogs out of the ring even as the principals continued to pound away at one another amid the edible debris.

It all happened the night of October 27, 1988, in the sparsely attended Tucson Convention Center in Tucson, Arizona. I would have loved to have written about it, too, for the amusement and edification of readers for my newspaper, the *Philadelphia Daily News,* except for a directive from the sports desk back in Philly to under no circumstances write more than my allotted 14 column inches because of space limitations. Faced with a quandary of choosing which way to go – telling the tale of the bikers, beer-soaked cameraman, hot dogs frantically kicked away by referee Ron Meyers and, oh, yes, round card girl who had ducked underneath the press table and nearly had her chin in my lap – I decided to devote those 14 column inches to a straight report of what proved to be the final ring appearance by Marvis Frazier, son of the great "Smokin'" Joe Frazier (his trainer and chief cornerman), in which Marvis won a close and somewhat uneventful 10-round unanimous decision over Philip Brown, a decently skilled journeyman with an impressive record.

To this day, I continue to wonder if I made the right call. But like Ted Sares, able to rummage through the attic of a lifetime of memories and come up with dusty gems like the one on Barboza, a good and true yarn told late is better than one never told at all.

Marvis Frazier, who turns 57 on September 10, has unfortunately been given short shrift as a boxer because he bore the heavy burden of forever being compared to his legendary father. But Marvis was the best and most accomplished male descendant of the fighting Fraziers' family tree, a list that includes heavyweight Rodney Frazier, son of Joe's sister Rebecca; super middleweight Mark Frazier, son of Joe's brother Tom, and junior welterweight Hector Frazier, another of Joe's sons who campaigned as "Joe Frazier Jr." And although he was not a blood relative, some might recall that Tyrone Mitchell Frazier, a protégé of Smokin' Joe who claimed to be the great man's nephew (with his tacit approval), once traveled to Bismarck, North Dakota, to challenge WBA light heavyweight titlist Virgil Hill. Although he lost a wide unanimous decision, the *faux* Frazier kin managed to go the distance. Also trying her hand at her dad's demanding profession was Joe's daughter, Jacqui "Sister Smoke" Frazier-Lyde, who went 13-1 with nine KOs and whose only loss was a majority decision against fellow celebrity daughter Laila Ali. Frazier-Lyde is now a municipal court judge in Philadelphia.

As an amateur trained by future Hall of Famer George Benton and Val Colbert, Marvis compiled an impressive 56-2 record, winning the 1999 National Golden Gloves title as a heavyweight. A bit taller than Joe at 6'0½", he was the spitting image of his father with one notable exception – he was more of a technician, a strong jabber with a solid defense, his more conservative style reflecting the values espoused by Benton, whose pupils included such accomplished champions as Evander Holyfield, Pernell Whitaker and Meldrick Taylor.

Upon turning pro, however, Marvis – whose devotion to Joe was absolute, with that deep and abiding affection clearly returned in kind – turned his career over to his pop, whose method of training was to instruct all of his fighters to fight just as he had, always boring in and firing left hooks. The only problem was that Marvis might have had the right genes for such a sudden transformation, but he was otherwise a poor fit to undergo a radical makeover.

Although Marvis earned a world rating, went 19-2 with eight victories inside the distance, several of his successes coming against such accomplished heavyweights as James Broad, Joe Bugner, Bernard Benton, James "Quick" Tillis and future WBA heavyweight champ James "Bonecrusher" Smith, he is best known for his two defeats – one-round blowouts against WBC heavyweight king Larry

Holmes (Marvis was just 10-0 when he got a title shot he was clearly unprepared for) on November 25, 1983, and a fast-rising force of nature in the big-man division, Mike Tyson, on July 26, 1986, in Glen Falls, New York. Tyson nearly decapitated the younger Frazier with a ripping right uppercut in the opening seconds of that bout, and connected with a couple of unnecessary follow-up shots as Marvis was sliding to the canvas. Elapsed time: 31 seconds, the fastest win recorded by Tyson in a career liberally dotted with quickies.

Prior to Marvis' ill-fated go at Tyson, observer Lou Duva told *New York Times* boxing writer Phil Berger how and why he expected Frazier the Younger to fail.

"He's a stubborn, opinionated guy. But a good guy," Duva said of papa Joe. "But the question is, does he book his fighters' matches from here (Duva tapped his heart) or here (tapping his head)? Who's coming to fight: Joe Frazier or his fighter? He'd like them to fight as good as Joe Frazier could, but there's only one Joe Frazier."

It appeared that the creeping realization he could never quite fill his Pop's shoes that made Marvis' fight against the 6'3", 218¼-pound Brown (Marvis actually outweighed the taller man by three-quarters of a pound) of special interest to followers of both Fraziers. Rumors already were beginning to circulate that Marvis' heart had gone out of his impossible quest to join Joe at the top of the heavyweight mountain, and that the Brown fight might be his final appearance in the ring.

I was already booked for a somewhat extended trip out West – Thomas Hearns was to square off against James "The Heat" Kinchen for the vacant WBO super middleweight crown on November 4, at the Las Vegas Hilton, with Sugar Ray Leonard taking on Donny Lalonde for Lalonde's WBC light heavyweight title as well as the vacant WBC super middleweight belt three days later at Caesars Palace –so why not, I suggested to my executive sports editor, Mike Rathet, let me head to Tucson a few days earlier for Frazier-Brown, which could have significant implications for the Philadelphia fight scene? Rather said OK, so off I went.

Frazier-Brown was not the main event – former WBC featherweight champion Juan Laporte's defense of his NABF super featherweight belt against Lupe Miranda was – but Marvis' fight was the opening half of a regionally televised doubleheader. It was the delayed arrival of a determined and hardy cameraman that set the stage for the (mostly) off-TV drama that helped nudge Frazier-Brown, at least to on-site spectators who knew what was going on, into a production of the theater of the absurd.

Seated directly behind one of the neutral corners were several biker types, perhaps mistakenly identified as such because of their full beards, bandanas, wide array of tattoos and apparel that suggested all were members of the same motorcycle club. They were obviously fight fans, and no one could dispute that they were enjoying the action during the non-televised undercard bouts. But their collective mood grew surly as the cameraman mounted the ring apron for Frazier-Brown, partially blocking their view. And by the time two of their buddies returned from the concession stand with cardboard trays laden with cups of beer and hot dogs, the situation seemingly was headed toward critical mass.

Concession items don't come cheaply, but that didn't stop the biker guys from dousing the cameraman with beer and pelting him with frankfurters. The poor guy had mustard in his hair and he smelled like a brewery. All this happened just a few yards from where I was sitting as one of just two members on press row (the other was a young reporter from the *Arizona Daily Star*) and the round-card girls, who weren't digging developments.

Apparently unaware of what was going on outside the ropes, Marvis and Brown were fighting their way toward the problem area. Across the way, a phalanx of rent-a-cops (arena security guards, not regular police) was forming to confront the bikers. One of the round-card girls, anticipating Armageddon, had crawled under the press table without properly introducing herself to me despite our sudden proximity. The referee, Meyers, had the unenviable task of trying to follow the give-and-take between Marvis and Brown, while kicking the hot dogs away, as if he were practicing field goals. When I watched the YouTube replay of the fight on Thursday night, Meyers' fancy footwork is clearly visible, although the TV commentators chose not to mention why hot dogs had made their way onto the canvas or why the cameraman appeared to have shampooed with yellow mustard.

Fortunately, because of the far-from-capacity crowd, an arena official offered to move the biker guys to comparable seats where their view would be unobstructed. They agreed to move, avoiding a confrontation that the rent-a-cops and at least one round-card girl were fervently hoping would never advance beyond the theoretical.

The postfight interviews – Marvis prevailed on the scorecards by margins of 96-94 (despite being docked a point in the sixth round by Meyers for low blows), 96-95 and 95-94 – stuck to the straight and narrow. "He ain't bruised, he ain't bumped, so let's go," said Joe, who seemingly was anxious for Marvis to fight again as soon as possible. "This game is for hit men only. What Marvis needs is to get right back to the gym. If he's going to fight, he needs to fight."

For his part, Marvis expressed the same eagerness to keep on keeping on. "I need the work," he said. "If it was up to me, I'd fight every three or four weeks ... enough to get my sharpness back."

Seven months after edging Brown, Marvis had yet to fight again, although he never did get around to formally announcing a retirement. It wasn't until many years later, long past the point where he might have considered a comeback, that he acknowledged the obvious. "Pop said when it starts feeling like a job, do something else," he said. "It started feeling like a job. You got to know when to get out of the game. It didn't feel like I was there. The spirit left me."

At various times, Marvis also repeated the mantra that had originated with Joe about why the fight game isn't for everybody, and shouldn't be unless there is a full commitment to the demanding task at hand. "You can get your brain shook, your money took and your name in the undertaker's book," both Fraziers noted.

Joe, beset with physical problems, was 67 when he passed away on November 7, 2011. His memorial service was attended by 3,500 or so admirers, including Muhammad Ali, Don King, Jesse Jackson and other notables. Marvis became an ordained preacher, ministering to prison inmates and also working as a security guard. Forever the dutiful son, he never questioned the wisdom, or lack thereof, of Joe's tinkering with the style that had made him so successful in the amateur ranks. Few fighters have lived their lives with as much class and dignity as he has.

I couldn't track down Meyers for his memories of what had to be the most unusual fight in his abbreviated, 20-bout refereeing career. He worked only one fight after Frazier-Brown. And speaking of Brown, who entered the ring that night in Tucson with a 31-2-2 (18) record, the loss to Marvis was the first in a streak of 10 consecutive defeats to close out his career, although no one can accuse him of

187

looking for soft touches; some of the guys who beat him down the stretch included Riddick Bowe, Jorge Luis Gonzalez, Mike "Hercules" Weaver, Johnny Du Plooy, Pierre Coetzer, James Broad and Joe Hipp. The attractive round-card girl who crawled under the press table very well might be a grandma by now, telling the kiddies her own version of what happened the night of October 22, 1988, and the bikers' beards likely have gone gray as they now park their posteriors in rocking chairs instead of on the seats of Harley-Davidsons.

Boxing, like life, rolls on like a river to the sea. Just when you think you've seen it all, something comes along that breaks new ground. Sometimes, that ground even is covered with hot dogs.

The Bite Fight ... And the King of the Cowboys
TheSweetScience.com, May 30, 2013

The review copy of *The Bite Fight: Tyson, Holyfield and the Night That Changed Boxing Forever* arrived in the mail a couple of weeks ago. The promotional flyer that accompanied the 222-page book called it "an unparalleled account of the infamous bite felt 'round the world."

Written by George Willis, the excellent *New York Post* sports columnist, this behind-the-scenes account of one of the most bizarre nights in boxing history delivers on that heady promise. Everything you know, or think you know, about that fateful night of June 28, 1997, is in there as well as some stuff you might not have heard.

But even George, gifted wordsmith and hard-digging reporter that he is, doesn't know every tiny detail of what went on after Tyson's teeth sank into Holyfield's ears as if they were a menu item at one of the MGM Grand's fine dining establishments. I have my own particular recollections of the aftermath of the "Bite Fight," and they can't be found in any book, magazine or website.

Until now.

TSS readers, you are about to learn of the (mostly) secret connection between Holyfield-Tyson II (Holyfield won the first matchup, and Tyson's WBA heavyweight championship, on an 11th-round TKO on November 9, 1996) and the "King of the Cowboys," Roy Rogers.

Well, at least there is a connection as far as my wife Anne, our younger daughter Amy, our foreign-exchange student, Izumi Tirado, and I are concerned. When Tyson got the munchies and the spit hit the fan, he altered what I somewhat foolishly had presumed would be a working vacation, with three days scheduled to be spent with my female entourage in and around the Los Angeles area following the big bout. I had arranged for lodging at a nice hotel in Marina del Rey, California, where the plan was for our group to do Disneyland, Universal Studios and, you know, the whole tourist bit in the brief time allotted. I'd been to L.A. before, of course, but this was to be the first such experience for the missus, Amy and Izumi.

But then Tyson chewed off a one-inch chunk of Holyfield's right ear in the third round, prompting no-nonsense referee Mills Lane to disqualify him prior to the start of round four, and ... hey, you know what they say about the best-laid plans of mice and men.

June 29 was not spent by our group in southern California; I was required to remain in Las Vegas, as was the army of media types who changed their travel plans to accommodate the post-bite set of circumstances. Anne, Amy and Izumi hung around the MGM Grand while I tried to find out what the very perturbed members of the Nevada State Athletic Commission planned to do in terms of disciplinary action for Tyson. On July 9, the NSAC socked him with a "lifetime suspension" subject to annual review (his boxing license was reinstated on October 18, 1998) and a record $3 million fine, the maximum allowable under Nevada law.

So we got a late start for SoCal, on June 30, traveling by rental car across the desert. I can't recall whether I possessed a cell phone in that technologically unadvanced age -- if I did, the reception in the desert must have been pretty bad – so I stopped en route to call my editors at the *Philadelphia Daily News* to find out if there was anything new and interesting about the ongoing story on which I might need to be brought up to speed. It was like asking if the sun is hot and it gets dark at night. Of course there were fresh developments; I was told to check into the nearest hotel so I could make a few calls, gather any pertinent information and crank out another story or two or three.

On the way to that hotel, in Barstow, California, we passed a sign advising us that just ahead was the Roy Rogers Museum, where it was said that Roy himself and wife Dale Evans (birth name: Lucille

189

Wood Smith), the "Queen of the West," were on-site nearly every day, regaling visitors with tales of their many screen adventures amidst a treasure trove of memorabilia, including Roy's stuffed palomino, Trigger.

"Oh, we have to stop there!" exclaimed Anne, who, like me, was an unabashed fan of Roy --- born Leonard Slye on November 5, 1911, in that noted Wild West outpost of Cincinnati, Ohio – through our constant Saturday-morning exposure to his movies and TV shows when we were children.

"Sorry," I had to tell her. "I have to get to work on this Tyson stuff as quickly as I can. We can catch Roy the next time we're out this way."

You can probably guess the rest. Our three days in Los Angeles had been reduced to part of a single day, which meant the only place I got to take Anne and the girls was nearby Universal Studios. Amy seemed to particularly enjoy that experience, probably because she spotted comedian/actor Pauly Shore on the grounds, which must have seemed like a big deal to your average 15-year-old. Pauly Shore? All I could think was, he's no Bob Hope. Or Roy Rogers, for that matter.

We flew back to Philadelphia from LAX, which meant no return trip across the desert to Vegas and no stopping off at the Roy Rogers Museum. Then, on July 6, 1998, it was reported that Roy Rogers was dead at the age of 86. He was physically beyond our reach, at least in this dimension.

To this very day, I don't think Anne has forgiven Mike Tyson for the missed opportunity for which he was unwittingly responsible.

The Roy Rogers Museum in Victorville, California, closed a few years later and in 2003 its contents were moved to Branson, Missouri, where another museum was operated by Roy and Dale's son, Roy "Dusty" Rogers Jr. But Roy Sr. had left instructions to Dusty to shut everything down once the museum started to operate at a loss, which it did, and it closed its doors permanently on December 12, 2009. A public auction of Roy's most treasured keepsakes was held in New York City on July 15, 2010, with sales totaling $2.98 million. Among the items which sold at much higher prices than the auctioneers had expected were Roy's 1964 Bonneville, which went for $254,500; an even more cherished ride, stuffed Trigger, was purchased by a Nebraska cable TV network for $266,500. Trigger's fancy saddle and bridle fetched a staggering $386,500, one of Roy's shirts sold for $16,250 and one of the beloved hero's favorite cowboy hats – white, of course – for $17,500.

Which got me to thinking: What would the most distinctive memento from the front end of our Bite Fight adventure, the chewed-off piece of Holyfield's ear, be priced at if it still existed and were somehow made available to a collector looking for that extra-special piece of boxing history?

I went through my own voluminous files – sorry, George, you weren't the only reporter to assiduously chronicle the event – and rediscovered that the missing part of Holyfield's ear was, in fact, really missing. To the best of anyone's knowledge, it still is.

Mitch Libonati, a member of the MGM Grand's Convention Services staff, took possession of the severed piece of flesh, at least temporarily. "A buddy of mine said Evander had been bitten," Libonati said. "I didn't see it, but I did see that Tyson had spit something out. There was a melee in the ring after the fight and when it cleared up, I found it. I picked it up, put it in a latex glove and ran back to the locker room.

"I told some of Evander's people, `I have a piece of Evander's ear. I'm sure he wants it.'" According to Libonati, heavyweight Michael Grant, a member of the Holyfield camp, took the piece of ear and placed it in an ice bucket that included several other latex gloves.

"But the piece didn't get (to Valley Hospital)," Tim Hallmark, Holyfield's conditioning specialist, said on June 29. "Somewhere in the locker room to the ambulance to the hospital, it never turned up. The plastic surgeon (Julio Garcia) and I were rooting around in three or four gloves in the ice pack, but we never found it.

"I'm not a doctor, but I imagine if somebody found it at this point, it wouldn't be in very good shape."

I'll leave it to George to provide additional details, which he does in Chapter 12 of his book, cleverly entitled *Ear Piece*.

Garcia, who was born in Cuba and came to this country with his father, an orthopedic surgeon, 37 years prior to the Bite Fight, was watching the pay-per-view telecast at a pool party in southwest Las Vegas when Holyfield and the upper portion of his right ear became separated.

"Some poor guy is going to get called in to sew him up," Garcia, in Willis' book, recalled thinking. Five minutes later, Garcia's beeper began to buzz. He was being immediately summoned to the emergency room at Valley Hospital.

"Traditionally, human bites are the most prone to infection," Garcia said of the task he was being asked to perform. "They're worse than a dog bite. We have more bacteria in our mouth than a dog has."

But Garcia had an even more daunting task. The latex glove containing the piece of Holyfield's ear had been placed in a red biohazard bag, but when Garcia examined the bag's contents, he found only a piece of skin, not the cartilage. And matters got worse from there; after Garcia left to change into operating garb and to scrub, he returned to find the red biohazard bag missing. He suspects it might have accidentally been thrown away, but who knows for sure? Perhaps a souvenir-seeking hospital employee or bystander grabbed it.

"It's not a locked facility," said Garcia, who nonetheless performed a 45-minute procedure to repair, as best he could, Holyfield's raggedy ear. "Any person could have come into that area and taken it."

One story that has made the rounds is that someone from Holyfield's camp wound up with the cartilage and sold it in New York where it was purchased for $25,000 by a stockbroker. Another has it that the cartilage lies in a trophy case displayed in the memorabilia section of a restaurant in Cincinnati (Roy Rogers' hometown!) although the granddaughter of the founder of the restaurant says the grisly thing on display there is actually from a chicken and was placed in the glass case as a joke.

Perhaps you have heard of the "Six Degrees of Separation" theory involving Kevin Bacon, in which virtually every actor you can think of can be linked to fellow actor Bacon or one of Bacon's movies within six easy-to-connect dots. For our family, that premise more or less holds true with Mike Tyson.

But first let it be noted that where we missed out on seeing the "King of the Cowboys," we did not miss out on seeing the "King of Rock 'n' Roll," Elvis Presley, in an eerily similar situation. Anne and I, natives of New Orleans, were living down South in the 1970s when an entertainment reporter friend advised me he could procure tickets for us, if we wanted them, to the May 5, 1975, Elvis concert at the Mississippi Coliseum in Jackson. Elvis diehards were pitching tents days in advance of those ducats going on sale, and Anne was, at best, lukewarm about attending. We liked Presley's music for the most part, but it wasn't as if we thought he walked on water.

"But the guy is not in real good shape," I said of the fat Elvis, whose health was obviously deteriorating. "We better see him now, because we might never get another chance."

It didn't happen quite as quickly as it did with Roy Rogers, but Elvis passed away on August 16 (Anne's birthday), 1977, at the too-young age of 42. Which brings us to …

The night of June 8, 2002, in Elvis' longtime home of Memphis, Tennessee. WBC/IBF heavyweight champion Lennox Lewis – who had had a piece of his left leg chomped by Tyson during a scuffle at a New York press conference to officially announce the much-anticipated matchup – savagely kayoed the erstwhile "baddest man on the planet" in eight rounds. A pundit might say that Lewis had sunk his own teeth into Tyson and chewed off a chunk, without so much as opening his mouth in the ring. Lewis' fists had served as his incisors.

I thought of all this when I made the obligatory pilgrimage to Graceland, Elvis' mansion-turned-museum, a few days before Lewis-Tyson, and every time I grabbed a, um, quick bite at a Roy Rogers restaurant, a chain of fast-food joints in the Northeast and Mid-Atlantic states that, as of August 2012, have been reduced in number to 49 from its onetime high of 650. There probably are more people around today who think of roast beef sandwiches, cheeseburgers and fried chicken rather than blazing six-guns and a galloping Trigger when they think of Roy Rogers, if they think of him at all.

Hard times, it would seem, can descend even on the most heroic of figures, as well as the most villainous. Tyson and Holyfield are bereft of all or most of their nine-figure fortunes, the aura of their fame dimming along with the boxing skills that made them icons. Tyson, now a reasonably placid, mostly stay-at-home husband and father, tours the country as the star of a one-man stage show in which he essentially beats himself up for the snarling pit-bull image he so zealously created when his bite was even more dangerous than his bark. Most of whatever income he brings in these days goes to the Internal Revenue Service and a long line of creditors.

On November 14, I will be one of 14 inductees into the New Jersey Boxing Hall of Fame's Class of 2013, along with – you guessed it – Mike Tyson. I figure the ghosts of Elvis and Roy will be floating somewhere around the room, so connected are they in their own way to Mike and me.

ESPN The Magazine's `Cuba' Issue
TheSweetScience.com, February 24, 2014

The February 17 issue of *ESPN The Magazine*, like so many that preceded it, was largely devoted to a particular theme. In this instance, the cover photo, of the Los Angeles Dodgers' 23-year-old phenom, right fielder Yasiel Puig, hinted at much of what was inside: a series of articles about Cuba, which the publication proclaimed was the launching point for the "opening (of) the next great pipeline of sports."

The pipeline has been free-flowing from Cuba to the United States and other countries for many years, predating the Fidel Castro-led revolution that toppled the admittedly corrupt regime of President Fulgencio Batista in 1959, although any use of the word "free" doesn't come close to describing living conditions in the island nation located just 90 miles south of Key West, Florida. The Soviet Union might have formally dissolved on December 26, 1991, which led to the tearing down of the concrete-and-barbed-wire Berlin Wall and the figurative but no less real "Iron Curtain," but the "Sugar Cane Curtain" that continues to separate Communist Cuba from the U.S. remains in place.

That reality is much to the chagrin of the large Cuban-American population in south Florida and more than a few government dissenters in Cuba's population of 11.3 million, who dream of making it to our shores, or at least of the restoration of the freedoms which are denied them in their homeland.

"Some Americans who have never experienced anything else don't understand how important freedom is," said Maria Alejandra Santamaria, a retired educator in Miami who came to America from her native Havana in 1968. "Freedom should never be taken for granted. You have to fight for what you want. You have to earn your

194

happiness, and that only comes through hard work and dedication. It's not easy; nothing worthwhile ever is. But when you have been through so much to even get to the United States, you realize what a precious gift that is.

"There are so many young Cubans who live there now who are as desperate to leave as we were because they know there is something else, something better, than they have grown up under."

Cubans know there is something better in no small part because of breakout athletes like Miami Marlins pitcher Jose Fernandez and Puig, Cuban defectors who finished first and second, respectively, in the voting for the 2013 National League Rookie of the Year Award, and, in their early 20s, are already millionaires. They know something of the repeated attempts by those players, often at the risk of their own lives or of imprisonment, to reach the U.S. They are familiar with the story of WBA and WBO super bantamweight champion Guillermo Rigondeaux, the two-time Olympic gold medalist (2000 and 2004) who tried on seven different occasions to escape Cuba before he finally reached the U.S. and freedom. In doing so, Rigondeaux – who was incarcerated after one failed attempt and was stripped of his national-hero status and his most prized possession, a car – made the gut-wrenching decision to leave behind his wife, five-year-old son, 15-year-old stepson and seven siblings.

"You are a champion, and it means nothing," Rigondeaux is quoted in the ESPN piece about him and other Cuban boxers who made it out. "We are like dogs. After all your time is over, you end up telling stories on a street corner about how you used to be a star."

What is not so widely known are the success stories of Maria Alejandra Santamaria and her husband Jose (known to his many friends and family members as Pepe), who arrived in New York City with little more than the clothes on their backs and, over time, forged new, prosperous lives for themselves and their three children, all of whom were born in the U.S. Including brothers, offspring and in-laws, there are 18 members of the Santamaria clan who live in and around Miami.

"Many Americans believe that what has happened in other countries, including Cuba, can't happen here," said Roxana Santamaria, the youngest of Pepe and Maria's grown children. "That is the danger."

I know the Santamarias' saga well, because Pepe is my wife's first cousin. My beloved Annie is half-Cuban, her late mother, the former Georgina Ortiz, having met and married my future father-in-law, the late J.E. d'Aquin, in 1948 while he was in Havana as an employee of the U.S. government. Anne and I met on a blind date as high schoolers in New Orleans in 1965 and we married 3½ years later. Although I am not Cuban – my lineage is a hodgepodge of English, Scot-Irish, Filipino, French and Swedish, among other nationalities – our four children are part Cuban, as are our six grandchildren.

Havana is a city that for many years I have felt connected to, although I have never been there and probably never will. Maybe that is because I have become immersed in the Cuban culture through our trips to Miami, which sadly are less frequent than I would prefer. Whenever Anne and I are visiting the Santamarias, Maria – better known by her nickname, "Marita" – makes sure I am always well-fortified with *café con leche*, a particular favorite, and mounds of black beans and plantains. While platters of food are not being passed around the dinner table, tales of what was and hopefully will be again are also exchanged.

"Castro was putting people in concentration camps," Marita told me of the harrowing days for those who opposed the bearded one's totalitarian rule. "I didn't want Pepe to go into a concentration camp. I asked a relative, who used to live here in Miami, to send Pepe money for airfare so he could go to Madrid, Spain. The day before Castro's people came to arrest him, he left for Madrid. He stayed there for a few months before, with the help of the Catholic Conference, he was able to join me in New York.

"It was terrible being separated. Many Cubans went to one country or another and they never were able to get back together with their families. It was hard for Pepe to make the decision to leave, but it was his only chance to stay out of the concentration camp, where I know that some people died."

Anne returned with her parents for a brief visit to Havana when she was an infant, and again in 1955 or '56 (she doesn't recall the exact year), when she was six or seven. What she does recall is the sound of gunfire echoing in the hills when she and her parents went to see her mother's aunt.

"It was machine guns, I think," she said. "We knew that there was fighting between Castro's supporters and Batista's soldiers in the mountains. I remember being terrified. I think we stayed there for just a day or two before we went back to Havana.

"All my life I've wanted to go back there, but after Castro took over we never did, of course. I hope someday, if things are different, I'll be able to visit again."

As a sports writer for these past 43 years, and even before, Cuba and Cuban athletes have drifted in and out of my consciousness with surprising regularity. For reasons I still don't quite understand, one of my favorite pitchers as a kid was Camilo Pascual, the Cuban righthander with the big overhand curveball who performed with distinction for the Washington Senators and Minnesota Twins. I also liked the flair with which outfielder Minnie Minoso played both in the field and at the plate, a style which is replicated by the swashbuckling Puig. Then again, a bit of showmanship has always been an integral part of the Cuban approach to sports. What Minoso brought to the diamond the great welterweight champion Kid Gavilan, with his signature "bolo punch," brought to the boxing ring.

Said Jose Fernandez, the Marlins pitcher, in *ESPN The Magazine*: "I am who I am. I come from a different place. Baseball in Cuba is a lot more emotion, a lot more passion. At the end of the day, it's a game, and you're supposed to have fun, right?"

I'm not sure it was fun I was seeking when I requested the assignment from my editors at the *Philadelphia Daily News* to cover the 11th Pan American Games in Havana, which if nothing else would have given me an opportunity to report back to Anne all that I had seen of the land of her mother's birth. But much to my regret, a columnist with more pull and seniority, Bill Conlin, got that gig.

I did, however, cover the 10th Pan Am Games in Indianapolis, Indiana, in 1987, which produced no shortage of sights and sounds that made clear the wide gap, ideological and otherwise, that existed between Castro's Cuba and the U.S.

One of the stories I wrote was about the conundrum in which members of PAX-I, Indianapolis' Pan Am organizing committee, found themselves while trying to smooth the ruffled feathers of the Cuban delegation after an anti-Castro group paid for a private plan to fly over the Pan Am site towing a banner urging Cuban athletes to defect.

Also on the political front, officials of the American Legion, who had agreed to allow the use of their outdoor mall for the closing ceremony, withdrew that consent when it was learned that a central theme would be the honoring of Cuba, which was to be the site of the 1991 Pan Am Games. The venue for the closing ceremony was shifted to the Hoosier Dome, but even that move wasn't without incident. PAX-I had hired Gloria Estefan and the Miami Sound Machine, a popular salsa-rock group, to provide entertainment sure to please the glut of Spanish-speaking visitors. But the Cuban delegation reacted to the Miami Sound Machine with the same lack of enthusiasm they might have shown Sylvester Stallone had he paraded through the athletes' village dressed as Rambo.

Cuban Olympic Committee president Manuel Gonzalez Guerra noted that Estefan's father once was a bodyguard for Batista's wife. Guerra said the selection of Estefan was a "provocation" of the Cuban delegation and he threated to boycott the closing ceremony. The Cubans did, in fact, attend the party, but when Estefan and the Miami Sound Machine took the stage, Guerra and his athletes stood up, turned their backs and remained still and silent throughout the show. I have sometimes wondered how many of the protesting Cuban athletes later defected, or tried to.

There was intrigue in the competition, too, not the least of which was in boxing. Although the U.S. led the way with 370 total medals and 169 golds, Cuba finished second in both categories, with 175 total medals and 75 golds. Ten of those golds and a bronze went to Cuban boxers, while American fighters were limited to one gold, four silvers and four bronzes.

"Everybody is dwelling on the Cuban thing," one of the U.S. boxers, future WBA super middleweight champion Frankie Liles, said of the bitter rivalry that was developing in the ring between the two countries. "One of the things that's in the back (of the American boxers' minds) is stopping the Cubans – not just beating the Cubans, but stopping them."

Liles and his teammates came up way short, and four years later, at the Pan Am Games in Havana, the Cubans were kicking American butt inside the ropes: 11 golds (no silvers or bronzes) to one gold, four silvers and four bronzes for U.S. fighters. It's little wonder American promoters were so hot to get their hands on some of the more accomplished Cubans.

Then again, not every Cuban superstar, in boxing or baseball, viewed defection as a path to paradise. In 1974, Bob Arum and Don

King each tried to entice celebrated heavyweight Teofilo Stevenson, then 22 and the winner of the first of his three Olympic gold medals, to come to America to fight an aging Muhammad Ali. But Stevenson, who was 60 and pretty much broke when he died last year, refused to be swayed. "What is a million dollars," he reasoned, "compared to the love of eight million Cubans."

The baseball equivalent of Stevenson, according to Conlin, was Omar Linares, whom Conlin observed at the '91 Pan Am Games in Havana. "The best third baseman I have seen not named Mike Schmidt," wrote Big Bill, who also noted that Linares was a "devout Fidelista" who wasn't going to defect for anything so crass as stacks of U.S. dollars.

All I know is that the Havana I have heard about so often, the one of the Santamarias' pre-Castro memories, remains an alluring destination for those of us who have ever read an Ernest Hemingway novel. You don't have to fire up a contraband Cohiba to know something has been lost to Americans who are prohibited from traveling to Cuba, or to realize that even more has been lost to Cubans who haven't been able to make it to this land of the free.

Section H
Other Sports

It was not my intention to become primarily known as a boxing writer, although I did have a deep attachment to fights and fighters because of my dad, a onetime pro welterweight, with whom I would watch the *Gillette Cavalcade of Sports* as a grade-schooler. Those nights we spent together catching the fights on our old Philco TV set helped deepen the bond I no doubt would have had in any case with my late father, who has forever remained my hero and role model. It wasn't until 1987, when I asked for and received the boxing beat for the *Philadelphia Daily News* in that great fight town, that my identity as a sports writer began to inexorably shift toward all matters related to the ring. That now seems to be a really fortuitous development, seeing as how it is generally better to be known and recognized for something than to be overlooked for everything.

But comfortably fitting into a role does not mean that I consider myself a one-trick pony. It has been my privilege, at other newspapers I have worked for as well as the *PDN*, where I spent 28 fruitful years, to have received significant assignments involving sports other than boxing. While *Championship Rounds, Round 2* is first and foremost a boxing book, this section is devoted to work I am proud to have done chronicling other areas of athletic competition. All athletes, superstars or not, have stories to tell, some of which are quite compelling. Here are a few that I hope I was able to tell well.

The Wrong Goodbye? Jordan Wanted More From Last Go-Round
Philadelphia Daily News, April 16, 2003

"Gods do not answer letters"
*Author **John Updike**, writing of Ted Williams' refusal to take a curtain call at Fenway Park in 1960 after hitting a home run in his final at-bat.

WASHINGTON

Nearly 43 years after Teddy Ballgame put the perfect punctuation mark to a career marked by magnificent achievement and haughty defiance, another sporting deity demonstrated that, in this era of instant communication, gods now do not answer emails. Advanced technology still has not brought them close enough for mere mortals to touch.

Instead, the mere mortals are left only to gaze in open-mouthed wonder. Yet even if Michael Jordan can summon one of his signature, game-winning flourishes – nailing a fadeaway jumper or slamming home a double-clutch dunk at the buzzer – in the final act of his flying circus tonight against the 76ers at the First Union Center, it can't qualify as a sendoff appropriate for someone of his stature.

Only one team on the floor has anything to play for, and it isn't his Washington Wizards. For all he had given to his new devotees in our nation's capitol, and to the NBA in this third and presumably final of his league incarnations, the competitor in him had wanted to give so much more than the lottery and its ping-pong balls. At age 40, he could not, by dint of his will alone, transform a roster of mismatched parts into something postseason-worthy.

Perhaps it was because of his inability to hoist the Wizards (37-44) onto his back and carry them to glory, as he had the Chicago Bulls for six NBA championship seasons, that Jordan chose to leave the floor without addressing the crowd Monday night after a 93-79 loss to the New York Knicks in his home finale at the MCI Center. Or perhaps it was a sheepish acknowledgment, amid the waves of adulation that always have washed over him, that even gods can have human frailties.

"Hopefully, I've put enough memories out there," says Jordan, who only briefly lingered for a video tribute of his most gravity-defying moments after his next-to-last performance. "I have another life, and I know I have to get to it at some point in time. I'd like to think the fans can understand that."

Were his Philadelphia swan song somehow to reflect his glorious past, the game would not be in the First Union Center but across the parking lot, in the First Union Spectrum, where many of his most electrifying performances were registered. Although he is averaging

24.5 points in his six career games at the First Union Center, Jordan went off for 753 points in 28 games at the First Union Spectrum; his 35.7-point average is his highest in any NBA arena in which he has played at least two games.

But for every time he frustrated and beat the Sixers, it was impossible for him to be hated even by Philly fans notoriously harsh toward visiting players. He was, well, Michael Jordan, and it was as if every spectator in every city he visited was part of his extended family, reveling in the exploits of a revered patriarch.

Jordan leaves still as one of the best 20 players in the league, but now we are children of a lesser god.

We have, thankfully, been spared the sight of him as tragic figure, a Joe Namath dropping back into the pocket on wrecked knees as a Los Angeles Ram, or a Willie Mays stumbling under fly balls as a New York Met. His Airness remains a formidable presence, but maybe a more sympathetic one now that his aura of omnipotence has frayed around the edges.

Although MJ is finishing up as a Wizard, he no longer is enough of an on-court magician to routinely produce miracles – unless you count the 82 consecutive sellouts of the MCI Center in a town where pro basketball was mostly dead.

Whether the level of his game was atop Mount Olympus or at a lower plateau, Jordan was, and still is, the hottest ticket around.

"Nobody talked about the Washington Wizards," coach Doug Collins says. "All of a sudden, everybody's watching the Wizards on TV. We're the No. 1 road draw in the NBA. Cleveland had two sellouts, and they were for us. That's the way it's been. That's what Michael brings."

On the court and in the standings, however, the going has been more difficult.

This was not how his playing career, which took him on a wild ride through the record books and the sanctums of our minds, was supposed to end and how his team, mired in turmoil and acrimony, was supposed to end up.

Jordan had already issued himself the perfect farewell, on June 14, 1998, shaking free of Utah Jazz defender Bryon Russell with a hard fake to his right before rising up to hit the jumper that gave the Bulls a championship-clinching, 87-86 victory in Game 6 of the NBA Finals. Even as the ball left his hand, the final seconds ticking off,

Jordan stood frozen, his right arm extended, cocksure in the knowledge the ball would swish through.

"My perfect picture was him hitting that shot against Utah," says Knicks guard Allan Houston, who helped spoil Jordan's MCI Center finale with a game-high 23 points. "That's the storybook ending. But he had a hunger for coming back. I would've liked to see that be the last memory because it doesn't get any better than that."

Jordan understands how people might feel that way. But, then, only one person lives inside Michael Jordan's skin, where the itch to excel is never totally scratched.

"I had no expectations for my ending," he says of the moderately satisfying Wizards phase of his hoops journey. "Everybody, I'm pretty sure, would like to see me hit the game-winning shot in the Finals. To some degree, that is the dream ending. But to a competitor, sometimes not being as successful is a great sendoff.

"You know, you've got to move on to do other things and in other ways that will be just as successful. That's how I look at this."

It might be argued that he chose to return, from a second retirement from the Bulls, to become a part of the Wizards organization (he spent 21 months as a part-owner and president of basketball operations before deciding to play) for the very reason that the expectations of him would not be nearly so daunting as they were in Chicago. There, all those championship banners hanging from the rafters of the United Center made him as much a larger-than-life figure as the immense statue of him at the building's entrance.

Jordan loves the Chicago area and still lives there in the offseason, but he was like Elvis in Memphis, having to reserve side rooms of his favorite restaurants so he and his family could dine in peace. In Washington, where politicians dispense the currency of power in a manner no athlete ever could, the space he created around himself was easier to maintain, and not just because he seldom ventured out in public for non-basketball purposes.

"Like Vince Lombardi and Ted Williams before him, Jordan has come (to Washington) much in the way of a traveling art exhibition: highly trumpeted and beautiful to look at, but, ultimately, part of someone else's permanent collection," Rachel Nichols noted in the *Washington Post*.

Not that Jordan was arrogant and aloof as much as private. His corner locker at the MCI Center is not double-wide, nor does it come furnished with a customized recliner and big-screen television, as is the case with Barry Bonds' vanity space at San Francisco's Pac Bell Park. Jordan even is polite and accommodating toward those banes of Bonds' existence, sports writers, because he understands they are the conduits to his public.

In assessing Jordan's legacy, it should be noted that he understood so much more than the bottomless depth of his talent and how to spectacularly market it. He took that gift and forged it with sweat and desire, as if he still remembers the sting of being cut from his high school team as a sophomore.

"Michael is Michael because he always puts his heart on display out there, diving for loose balls and what have you," says injured Wizards forward Charles Oakley, a former Bulls teammate. "He plays every game hard, never short-changes the fans. Guys like him, they make the game better."

It is a lesson Jordan failed to pass on to his younger but somehow less impressionable teammates with the Wizards, some of whom actually complained that he had hindered their progress.

For a while, Jordan tried to fill a role instead of commanding center stage, even coming off the bench the first 16 games of the season. But, in pivotal developments Sixers fans surely can understand, Jerry Stackhouse chafed at not always being the first offensive option and Larry Hughes resisted attempts to be made into a point guard.

Stackhouse and Hughes, both former Sixers, had similar problems meshing their games with that of Philly's superstar equivalent, Allen Iverson.

"Michael and I had a clash in styles," says Stackhouse, who did not relish playing the part of an acquiescent, Scottie Pippenesque squire to Jordan's shining knight. "He needs a set-it-up guy, and I have more of an attacking style. I do think Michael sacrificed, and I sacrificed. It just didn't work the way we planned."

However, as Collins warns, "All these guys who thought he took away from their game, they're going to find out what he brought. Be careful what you wish for. You just might get it."

John Updike, in his *New Yorker* essay on Ted Williams, noted that the Red Sox great "is the classic ballplayer of the game on a hot

August weekday, before a small crowd, when the only thing at stake is the tissue-thin difference between a thing done well and a thing done ill."

Jordan has totally given of himself in games that mean nothing, at a time when his legerdemain is sporadic, because to do otherwise would be a repudiation of all he has ever stood for. It is OK to fail, he has said, but it is never acceptable not to try.

"I've missed more than 9,000 shots in my career," he says. "I've lost almost 300 games. Twenty-six times, I've been trusted to take the game-winning shot and missed. I've failed over and over and over again in my life. And that is why I succeed."

Rising From the Floodwaters
Philadelphia Daily News, January 11, 2007

NEW ORLEANS

In the great 1970 war movie *Patton,* the famed World War II general dismisses the enemy's fixed fortifications as an impediment to his advancing army.

"If mountain ranges and oceans can be overcome," George S. Patton tells a fellow officer, "anything made by man can be overcome."

This below-sea-level city, devastated only 16 months ago by an indiscriminate killer known as Hurricane Katrina, stands in stark testimony to the accuracy of Patton's pronouncement. New Orleans' protective outer shell of earthen levees and concrete seawalls proved woefully inadequate when battered by 125-mph winds and tidal surges of up to 28 feet.

Tourism long has been the epicenter of this fragile economy, with visitors from around the world arriving to sample Mardi Gras, Bourbon Street, Creole cuisine, jazz and the everyday revelry of a place whose French motto is *Laissez les bons temps rouler,* or "Let the good times roll."

Katrina slammed into the Gulf Coast on August 29, 2005, and soon entire neighborhoods were washed or blown away. It transformed the Louisiana Superdome into a refugee camp and international symbol of misery and despair.

Now tourists come not only for the old, familiar lures, but also to inspect the ghost neighborhoods that might never rise from the rubble. A significant chunk of the pre-storm population of 455,000 has scattered. The 200,000 or so residents who remain undoubtedly are less inclined to stage "hurricane parties" and wait out the next big storm whose unpredictable path might veer toward America's most vulnerable metropolitan area. It is about hope and survival, and humanity's refusal to be beaten into submission.

New Orleans is my hometown, so I am as familiar with hurricanes as I am with crawfish etouffee. I was born two days after the great unnamed hurricane that flooded parts of the city on September 19, 1947. The first floor of Lakeshore Hospital was underwater when I came into this world, delivered by a doctor operating in the dim light of lanterns, after electrical and auxiliary power were shorted out by the spreading waters of Lake Pontchartrain. My parents nicknamed me "Stormy," and my mother, now deceased, told me she would have christened me as "Gale" had I been a girl.

In high school, I met a girl named Gale who was born on the same day as I. We laughed that there probably were more similarly named "lantern babies" in the city who arrived on or around the same date, living symbols of what happens when certain atmospheric conditions converge to form natural destruction.

During my freshman year at LSU, another major hurricane, Betsy, again turned portions of New Orleans into fetid wading pools. My girlfriend (now wife) grew up in the Ninth Ward, which is particularly vulnerable to flooding, and her home was largely submerged. Frustrated by his inability to always protect his loved ones from the forces of nature, my future father-in-law moved the family to a new house in a developing section known as New Orleans East. There, he believed, they finally would be safe.

New Orleans East, as it turned out, proved no more resistant to Katrina than the Nazis' network of barbed wire and pillboxes were to Patton's tanks. I have been here several times since Katrina struck, driving with my wife to view the remains of the dwellings of her childhood and adolescence. Doors of wrecked houses in those neighborhoods are spray-painted with X's, some with markings indicating that corpses were found within.

This no longer is the city I know. Let the good times roll? Many residents are angry, so much so that even their NFL team's surprising participation in the postseason can't totally camouflage their frustration. Volunteers for organizations such as Habitat for Humanity painstakingly gut and repair houses one by one, but billions of dollars in federal aid remain held up as politicians argue over how all that relief money should be spent. Insurance companies have canceled policies en masse; there still is no definitive plan on how to rebuild the levees to a Katrina-resistant level; and thousands of front lawns are dotted by FEMA trailers as the homes behind them remain in disarray and unoccupied. Each and every playground once operated by the New Orleans Recreation Department has become a trailer park, the green spaces once occupied by ball-playing children covered by the ugly, white cylinders reflective of a society in transition.

And if all that weren't enough, Saints owner Tom Benson threatened to rip out what remained of New Orleans' heart by relocating the franchise to San Antonio, where he lives. Benson reasoned that the Superdome and New Orleans as a whole were too wrecked for his team to remain economically viable in the long term. Compassion is a wonderful thing, but, hey, business is business.

Outside cynics might argue that relocating the NFL's most historically inept organization should not have been paramount to New Orleanians, who had far more consequential problems to solve than retaining this band of helmeted mercenaries. But that viewpoint does not take into account these residents' love affair with their team, which, even before Katrina, was a symbol of civic pride and another reason to party. Having membership in the NFL club gave residents a reason to believe their town was still major league, despite a shrinking population and flagging economic base.

Then-NFL commission Paul Tagliabue was insistent that his league could not abandon New Orleans and the Saints, who went 3-13 in 2005 as literal orphans of the storm, on loan to San Antonio. The NFL contributed $15 million of the $185 million that went into the swift makeover of the Superdome, and Tagliabue vowed that New Orleans would remain a league member until it demonstrated it no longer could or would support the franchise.

But if Tagliabue was St. Paul, the angel who saved the Saints, he was not the only agent of divine intervention. New coach Sean Payton came in and cleared house of the malcontents and underachievers. He and general manager Mickey Loomis wooed and won free-agent quarterback Drew Brees, who not only set team passing records in the first season of his six-year, $60 million deal, but became active in the community, helping heal wounds in ways that transcended the playing field.

The Houston Texans, who had the first pick in the draft, also chipped in, choosing North Carolina State defensive end Mario Williams instead of the most exciting and marketable player available, USC running back Reggie Bush, who fell to the Saints at No. 2 like manna from heaven.

A perfect storm again was forming, but this one throbbed with positive energy. After the new-look Saints opened with road victories at Cleveland and Green Bay, they returned to the sold-out Superdome for a nationally televised Monday night game against Atlanta that had the feel of Mardi Gras, the Super Bowl and V-E Day all rolled into one. The Falcons were no match for all that mojo and fell, 23-3

The city of New Orleans might not have been all the way back, but that game was a sign that its feisty populace had not given up.

"The atmosphere was indescribable," said starting guard Jahri Evans, the rookie from Division II Bloomsburg University and Philly's Frankford High. "Me coming from Bloomsburg, I had never experienced anything like it. Everybody was so pumped up. It was just a crazy, unforgettable experience."

It could get even crazier and more raucous, should the Saints knock off the Eagles Saturday night and then advance to and win the NFL's ultimate game.

"That Monday night game was ridiculous," said Saints defensive tackle Hollis Thomas, a former Eagle. "But I've never seen this crowd in a playoff atmosphere. I gotta believe our fans are going to be even more jacked up for this one."

For those who see only dark clouds, not silver linings, that Monday night game represented all that remains wrong with New Orleans. Why weren't precious few city and state resources funneled into rebuilding houses instead of a sports palace? Weren't priorities skewed? Is winning a few football games so important when viewed against the backdrop of the ruined Ninth Ward?

What those critics don't realize is that the Saints are a key component of the economic engine that powers New Orleans. There must be something to build upon, a reason for the stragglers to return, a promise of normalcy and better things.

The Eagles, of course, are widely viewed as the Little Team That Could, their five NFC East titles in the last six years notwithstanding. They were given up for dead when quarterback Donovan McNabb went down with a season-ending injury against Tennessee on November 19 and was replaced by 36-year-old retread Jeff Garcia, whose best days were said to have been behind him.

But a resurgent Garcia has helped piece together a six-game winning streak that landed him on the cover of *Sports Illustrated* last week, and title-starved Delaware Valley residents are daring to hope that the Eagles can deliver the first major professional sports championship since the 76ers in 1983.

Throughout most of the rest of the nation, however, the Saints have become America's Team, a phoenix rising not from the ashes, but rather from the receded floodwaters of the worst natural disaster ever to strike this country. They are the balm on a still-festering wound, a cure for what ails an entire region.

Should the Saints win Saturday, expect more than a few fans to fill the French Quarter and make their way to a popular watering hole whose signature drink is known as …

A hurricane.

Off to See the Whizards
Philadelphia Daily News, July 7, 2000

It is baseball's version of *The Picture of Dorian Gray.* When former Phillies ace Robin Roberts looks into the mirror these days, the first thing he sees is what much of the world sees: the face of a 73-year-old grandfather of seven.

But if Roberts so chooses, the reflection that stares back at him is that of an outstanding, 23-year-old athlete forever locked in a wondrous, charmed summer. Perhaps as much as his six consecutive 20-win seasons and 1976 induction into baseball's Hall of Fame, that single summer has conferred upon Roberts and his teammates some measure of sports immortality.

The crow's-feet crinkling his eyes and strands of gray hair signifying that Roberts is not really immune to the aging process

209

cannot obscure the fact that he is, and always will be, part of one of Philadelphia's most exclusive fraternities. He is a Whiz Kid.

"A lot of guys play their entire careers and never are a part of anything like what we were a part of," said Roberts, a 20-game winner in 1950, the last victory being the pennant-clinching 4-1, 10-inning victory over the Dodgers at Brooklyn's Ebbets Field on October 1, the season's final day.

"It was a special time, and a very special team. The Phillies hadn't won a pennant in a long time and we sort of came out of the blue. I don't know what you'd call it. Magic, maybe."

Magic appears out of nowhere and vanishes just as quickly, but legends are forever. Death and illness can never rob the Whiz Kids of their legendary status as one of this city's most beloved teams. But with each passing year that magic in a bottle has evaporated, bit by bit, as the magicians of a half-century ago yield to the same natural laws of diminishing returns that affect us all.

When the Phillies honor the Whiz Kids at 6:30 tomorrow evening in Veterans Stadium, the occasion will be as bittersweet as it is celebratory. As is the case with the Memorial Day parade in Darby Township, which was discontinued this year after 54 years because too many World War II veterans of American Legion Post 845 had died or were too feeble to march, tomorrow's festivities almost certainly will mark the final official gathering of an aging, increasingly decimated team.

The last time the Phillies staged a reunion of the Whiz Kids, in 1975, the turnout was large and the mood exclusively boisterous. Almost everyone made it to the Vet – then all of four years old and regarded as one of the finest multipurpose stadiums in the country – and the mostly fortysomething ex-players got to reprise their glory days in an old-timers' game against a squad of former big leaguers.

"It's always been wonderful when any of us have gotten together," said Roberts, who now fills his days playing a lot of golf in Tampa. "But I'm quite sure this will be the final gathering of this type. It seems like so many of us have passed on in just the last three or four years. I'm sad to say it, but this might be the last time a lot of us will be in the same place at the same time."

Bob Miller, the standout rookie righthander who went 11-6 after an 8-0 start in 1950, agrees.

"We have to face the fact that we're getting older and the fans who actually saw us play are getting older and fewer in number," said Miller, 74, who recently retired as baseball coach at the University of Detroit after 38 seasons. "Memories are dimming. That's just the way it goes, doesn't it? But I do think the Whiz Kids will endure. It's a team whose place in history is going to outlive all of us."

Unless there is an unexpected arrival by an ailing player who had indicated he could not be present, vice president of public relations Larry Shenk is expecting tomorrow's reunion to be attended by 11 players and coaches who made the magic in 1950 – pitchers Roberts, Miller, Curt Simmons, Bubba Church, Paul Stuffel and Steve Ridzik; catchers Andy Seminick and Stan Lopata; infielder Ralph "Putsy" Caballero, outfielder Jack Mayo and coach Maje McDonnell, 78, who has remained with the organization as director of the Phillies' speakers bureau.

There will be much happy reminiscing about that title-clinching victory, one that included centerfielder Richie Ashburn's throw to Lopata that nailed Cal Abrams at the plate in the ninth inning and Dick Sisler's game-winning, three-run homer in the top of the 10th off Don Newcombe. But those sharing the memories will be saddened by the absence of Ashburn, the longtime Phillies broadcaster and 1995 Hall of Fame inductee who died in 1997, and Sisler, who died in 1998. Both were on hand for the 1975 reunion.

"It's like losing a member of your family whenever someone from that team passes on," Miller said. "I remember when Del Ennis died. Then Richie died, which was really a shock. If there ever was anyone I thought would live to 100, he was the guy. I can't tell you how shaken I was by that.

"Those were wonderful guys who I lived with and laughed with. They weren't just teammates. We were so much closer than that. I know it's a cliché to say we were like brothers, but that's exactly what we were."

Seminick, 79, who enjoyed a career year in 1950 when he batted .288 with 24 homers and 68 RBI, said the opportunity to mingle with those who helped him live his dream simply was too important to pass up.

"I canceled a trip to Russia to be there," Seminick said from his home in Melbourne, Florida. "It was going to be, you know, a tourist-type thing. I've always wanted to see Russia. But the Kremlin is going to be there later on, and maybe an opportunity like this won't be.

"My first thought was I better get on up to Philadelphia and see these guys while I can. They might not be there later on. I might not be there later on."

Righthander Bubba Church, 75, had his season and career ruined in mid-September that year when his face was shattered by a line drive off the bat of burly Cincinnati Redlegs slugger Ted Kluszewski. He understands the urgency of getting to Philadelphia this weekend.

"Your outlook changes as you get older," Church said from his home in Birmingham, Alabama. "I think most of us who are still around think in terms of looking for daylight each morning when we get up. That's our goal. If the sun is shining, fine, we can say we made it through to another day.

"My God, it has been 50 years since we were Whiz Kids. So any chance we have to get together is to be cherished."

None of the Whiz Kids can claim to have had an inkling of what would transpire in the best summer of their lives. For decades the Phillies had been almost comically lousy, finishing in the National League's second division 30 times in 34 seasons from 1916 to 1949. Sixteen times they came in dead last. But manager Eddie Sawyer was encouraged by the strong finish of his young, talented '49 squad, which went 32-24 after July 29 to finish a strong third behind the Dodgers and St. Louis Cardinals. It was the Phillies' highest finish since 1917.

"After that last game (in '49) players were milling around, saying their goodbyes," Ashburn said before the 1975 reunion. "Sawyer got everybody together and made a short talk. He said, 'Boys, come back here next year ready to play. We're gonna win it.'"

To be sure, the Phillies had a stockpile of good, young players to go along with a few seasoned veterans, like MVP pitcher Jim Konstanty, the kind every team needs for stability on the field and in the clubhouse. In addition to Ashburn, who caught everything hit anywhere near him and always seemed to be on base, the fresh-faced nucleus included RBI machine Ennis, slick-fielding shortstop Granny Hamner, steady third baseman Willie "Puddin' Head" Jones and, of course, the righty-lefty pitching hammers, Roberts and

Simmons. But the Dodgers were, well, the Dodgers, with all those future Hall of Famers clustered on their roster, giving the Phillies a barrier other than their own sad history to overcome.

"Nobody ever dreamed that our 1950 team would win the pennant, I don't believe," said Church, who finished 8-6 with a 2.73 earned run average that season.

Added Miller: "It was my first year and I never had a sense we were, like, destiny's darlings. We knew we had to go out and play hard every day to have a chance to win."

Seminick, however, said many Phillies knew from the start they had a chance to take down the burgeoning Brooklyn dynasty.

"It started in spring training," Seminick said. "We were very confident about our ballclub even then. We went into Opening Day confident and it carried through."

The Phillies, who were to finish 91-63, held a nine-game lead over the Dodgers with 15 games remaining, an advantage that would have been insurmountable were it not for a series of disasters that seemingly converged at the same point in what had been an extraordinary season.

Miller was never the same after he injured his back tumbling down the steps at the North Philly train station. Church's face got in the way of that wicked liner. And, perhaps most tellingly, Simmons' National Guard unit was called to active duty when the 21-year-old phenom was 17-8 and on pace for a 23-win season.

"In July, August and the first week of September, you wouldn't believe how solid we were and how well we played," Roberts said. "We didn't feel like we were sneaking up on anyone. When we went into a town, it didn't matter which one, we expected to win the series.

"But then Bob got hurt and all of a sudden he couldn't throw anymore. Bubba got hurt. And losing Curt … well, you can't lose someone like Curt Simmons and expect to be as good as you had been."

Said McDonnell: "Curt was overpowering, maybe as good as any pitcher in the league. But there wasn't much you could do in those days when the Army called you up. Pennant race or no pennant race, he had to go."

The Dodgers beat the pain-wracked Miller, 7-3, to cut the Phillies' lead to a single game heading into the October 1 finale. Sawyer, with precious few options, had little choice but to hand the ball to Roberts for his fourth start in nine games.

"I was 23," said Roberts of his ironman duties down the stretch. "It never affected me. I had a good delivery. Nobody was counting pitches back then. Nobody had an agent. It was a different world."

Ashburn, hardly known for his cannon arm, then gunned down Abrams, Sisler homered into the third row of the leftfield bleachers and the Whiz Kids marched off into history. It hardly mattered that the Phillies, their starting pitching threadbare, were swept in the World Series by the lordly New York Yankees. Roberts, Ashburn and Sisler had already given the season the perfect exclamation point.

"You hate to say it, but the World Series was almost anticlimactic," McDonnell said. "We couldn't get much higher than we did winning the pennant like that on the last day."

In a sense, perhaps it's best that things happened exactly as they did. Would the Whiz Kids have been as revered had they won the pennant by 10 games, instead of drawing out the drama to that final, pressure-packed afternoon? Would they occupy their singular spot in Philadelphia's collective heart had they strung together a succession of championship seasons?

Roberts isn't sure, but he has his own ideas.

"For most of us, that was our only shot," Roberts said. "Oh, sure, I wish I could have been like (Yankees catcher) Yogi Berra, with his 22 championship rings or whatever. (Berra played on 14 pennant winners and 10 World Series champions.) That would have been nice. But maybe that 1950 season wouldn't have seemed as special.

"Sometimes a team just puts it all together when they aren't supposed to. I think the Chicago White Sox we're seeing now are like that. They weren't supposed to be this good, and we weren't supposed to be that good in 1950. A lot of people didn't think we compared to the Dodgers and, on paper, I'm sure we didn't."

Injuries, military service (Simmons missed all of the following season while on active duty), dubious trades and failure of several key players to match the career years they posted in 1950 conspired to ground the Whiz Kids. The '51 Phillies tumbled to 73-81, in fifth place. Simmons was released in 1960, but came back to haunt his old club, playing a key role for the pennant-winning Cardinals as they overcame a 6½-game deficit with 12 games remaining, thwarting the '64 Phillies' bid to duplicate the magic of 1950.

Now all that remains are the memories of what was and might have been.

McDonnell, with his front-office contacts, is the primary keeper of the flame, informing the surviving Whiz Kids of any and all developments as they occur.

"When (pitcher) Russ Meyer got very sick – he died about a year ago – I contacted most of the guys and told them," McDonnell said. "They all called Russ, and I knew he appreciated that.

"I do what I can do. For 17 years, we had a basketball team that played games all over the Delaware Valley every winter. Robby, Curt and myself played all 17 years. But the time came when that became kind of impractical. We're not as young as we used to be."

Miller said that reality was driven home every time he appears at a card show.

"You sign your picture for some little kid and you know what he's thinking," Miller said. "He looks at it, then he looks at you, and he's making a face that says, 'Is this the same guy?' And his grandfather is telling him, 'I was there when this man beat the Cubs. I remember it like it was yesterday.' Only it wasn't yesterday. It was 50 years ago."

Tomorrow, that grand and glorious yesterday returns for the Whiz Kids.

`I'm Not Down One Bit'
Philadelphia Daily News, November 1, 2010

Anyone who ever played with or against fullback Kevin Turner knew he was a good person to have on your side on fourth-and-short. He was a powerful inside runner, on the relatively rare occasions when he was asked to carry the football, and a sure-handed target on checkdown and dumpoff passes. But his primary asset was his willingness and even eagerness to, in the parlance of the sport, "put his hat on somebody" as a lead blocker.

"He was a battering ram," one of Turner's former Eagles teammates, linebacker Ike Reese, recalled with obvious appreciation. "That's what fullbacks are. Very often they ram themselves into linebackers.

215

"I remember going up against Kevin in practice. We nicknamed him 'The Anvil' because he brought it every time he took you on as a blocker."

Added defensive end Hugh Douglas, another former Eagles teammate of Turner's: "Kevin always played hard. He was one of the better fullbacks I've seen, at a position that at that time was being phased out of the NFL. He never shied away from contact."

But hammering other players during his eight seasons in the NFL, the last five of which were spent with the Eagles, and being hammered upon, possibly has exacted a cruel toll on Turner. Last week, the Birmingham, Alabama, resident returned from Boston after consulting with a fifth team of neurologists, who confirmed what four others had already told him: the diagnosis of amyotrophic lateral sclerosis, more commonly known as Lou Gehrig's disease, was accurate.

But, this time, Turner has hope, something not commonly found with ALS patients. And Turner is not one to give up without a fight.

He came away from his examination somewhat encouraged that he can beat ALS, to whatever extent it can be beaten. He was evaluated by Robert Cantu, who recently co-authored a research paper about NFL-related head injuries and is the co-director of the Center of the Study of Traumatic Encephalopathy at Boston University, an organization that has studied the autopsied brains of more than 20 former NFL players.

"I'm a little disappointed," said Turner, 41, who admits he was hoping for a diagnosis that the ALS symptoms had miraculously vanished. "Dr. Cantu said what I have is definitely some sort of ALS, but it's atypical in that it isn't in my legs yet, only in my thorax and upper extremities. He said usually, by now, there would be some sign of weakness in my legs if this was your classic ALS.

"It's funny – if any of this can be funny – but I was told by another neurologist just three weeks ago that what I have is classic ALS. I've been to five different neurologists – three in May and June, two more since then. Dr. Cantu is the only one who offered any kind of hope that this isn't quite as bad as it could be. I take it as a positive."

A spokesperson for Cantu said the doctor was ethically prohibited from discussing Turner's medical condition, citing doctor-patient privilege.

216

Dr. Leo McCluskey, head of the ALS department at the University of Pennsylvania, confirmed that there are instances where the disease affects mainly the upper body.

Turner is scheduled to see another doctor today in Washington.

"I'm very happy it's not in my legs, and I certainly hope it stays that way," Turner said. "But there are no guarantees. I've read that there are some ALS patients who have it stop in their upper body. If I'm one of those, that would be great. I'm not down one bit. I'm still very optimistic I'm going to find a good way through this, wherever it leads.

"Whether I regain my strength or the disease stops spreading, who knows? Maybe I'll live 25 more years, but I can't use my arms and hands. That's fine, too. I'll make do. I've done a lot of living in my first 40 years. There's certainly no regrets there."

*****

There is no known cure for ALS, a progressive, fatal neurodegenerative disease caused by the degeneration of motor neurons, the nerve cells in the central nervous system that control voluntary muscle movement. The disorder causes muscle weakness and atrophy throughout the body. Unable to function, the muscles gradually weaken until they cease to function.

Turner was handed what is tantamount to a delayed death sentence – some of the specialists who examined him gave him no more than two to three years to live.

It is possible, of course, that Turner was afflicted with ALS on the basis of random selection – horrible luck. One or two people out of 100,000 in the general population develop ALS every year, most of those stricken being 40 to 60 years of age. Not all of those diagnosed, of course, are football players who use their heads, as Turner describes, as the "tip of the spear."

But the NFL's increased concern about concussions and their long-term effects is worth noting, as is mounting medical evidence that professional and even college players are far more susceptible to eventual neurological problems, including the onset of ALS. A recent study explored a possible link between contact sports, such as football, and an ALS-type illness linked to head trauma.

217

The *Boston Globe* reported that Turner is the 14th former NFL player to be diagnosed with ALS since 1960, a much higher rate than occurs in most adult males.

McCluskey said there is no way to determine if ALS diagnosed in football players is directly attributable to game-related head trauma.

"When I retired (in 1999), they told me I had the spinal column of a 65-year-old man," Turner said. "Any other fullback or linebacker probably has heard the same thing.

"The studies that have come out would seem to indicate that playing football over a period of time can lead to more of certain types of injuries. I think I've always known that. The type of collisions you're involved in ... it's a different type than you get at other positions.

"Fullbacks and linebackers are taking hits in a way that linemen don't, although I would never take anything from anyone on the field. Everybody is going to get hurt at some point. That's just the nature of the game. But fullbacks have to get low and stick their heads in there. You're leading the way at the point of attack. You're the first one in and you've got to go in hard. You're going in with a head of steam, with a running start because you have to dig somebody out of the hole."

*****

Turner was recently honored in his hometown of Prattville, Alabama, at a dinner attended by a number of his former teammates at the University of Alabama, including running back Siran Stacy, who also has known his share of tragedy. Stacy – a former Eagle – lost his wife and four of his five children in a 2007 automobile accident. It would be difficult to say which player is more admiring of the other.

"It breaks your heart," Stacy said of what Turner is facing. "This is our brother, our friend."

For his part, Turner said Stacy has provided a standard to help him live each day as it comes.

"Siran was a different guy in college," Turner said. "I'm not saying he was a bad guy, but he's made a remarkable transformation in his life – even before the car wreck happened. I'm a Christian man, but he is a testament that there is a God. He's doing such good things in his life, and for his daughter that survived, it's an inspiration to me. It's unbelievable that you could lose your wife and four of your kids in the blink of an eye and somehow manage to keep it together."

Such is the fellowship of the locker room, where bonds are formed that frequently extend beyond the limits of playing careers. To be a "good teammate" is the ultimate compliment, one that often transcends the scope of normal friendship. And Kevin Turner was a very good teammate.

"Kevin was the consummate professional," said Juan Castillo, the Eagles' offensive line coach who has kept in regular contact with Turner since his NFL career ended. "We still talk about the good times. Anybody who's ever been around the guy had to like him. KT is the kind of person you'd want your son to grow up to be, the kind of person you'd want your daughter to marry. He's a better person than he was a football player, and he was a very good football player.

"You know, I talked to him about a week and a half ago. He didn't mention his being sick, not once. To this day, he has never brought that up to me. Even after I found out, I thought it best if he was the one to mention it first. But he always talked as if there was nothing wrong with him.

"That's just the kind of guy he is. He never complained about anything when he was with the team. Even with something this big, he wouldn't want anyone feeling sorry for him."

Turner's natural stoicism and reticence aside, he understands that his illness affords him a platform to address certain issues, albeit reluctantly, in the hope that current and future players might be spared the ordeal that has dramatically changed his life.

"We're going to get a foundation started," he said. "We're going to raise awareness of ALS, of spinal-cord injuries, of brain trauma. The people who will be involved will get it done, and done in a way that really makes an impact.

"As football players, we need to know what we can do to protect ourselves. There's a lot of things you can find out about a man on the football field. I don't mean for this to sound like a cliché, but you find out how someone is going to react when things are going your way and when they're not.

"If I knew then what I know now, would I still have played football? Yeah, I would. NFL players get paid good money, but that's not the reason they start playing. That's not the reason they rose to that level. They made it to the top because they loved what they were doing."

But Turner said, if he could go back in time, he'd love the sport by playing it a slightly different way, one that would presumably reduce the head-related injuries that have become the NFL's not-so-hidden curse.

"When you're 25 and playing in the NFL, you kind of feel invincible," he said. "Well, not really invincible, but you're living in the moment. The present is the only thing that counts. The future pretty much is confined to the next game you're going to play.

"I love the game of football. I love everything about it. I knew going in that there was a danger of paralysis, of tearing up your knee, your shoulder, whatever. It's not likely, but possible. But this ALS thing ... It's not something I ever considered. Now I see that the damage doesn't come from one concussion. It's the repetitive nature of taking those kind of hits year after year that cause problems. If I had to do it all over, the one thing I would do different is maybe go in low on linebackers more often, do a little more cutting and less straight-up `iso' blocking.

"With my size (6'1", 230) and (lack of) athletic ability, I probably shouldn't have been playing fullback in the NFL. I guess I was dumb enough to ram myself in there at all times. Look, I don't question why this happened to me. But maybe because it did happen to me, some good can come out of it for other players."

Exacerbating Turner's situation is the fact that he's broke, or nearly so, the money he made in the NFL lost in a speculative real-estate deal gone bad. He also is separated from his wife, who has custody of the couple's three children.

What buoys Turner is the support of people who have rallied around him, some of whom he never got to meet. They are the fans who loved his work ethic, his penchant for getting his jersey dirty.

"I got an email about a month ago," he said. "It was from someone in Philly just sending me good wishes. He said, at the time I was playing, his 10-year-old son was just beginning to watch football and that I was his favorite player. That just blew me away. I wasn't a superstar; I was more of a journeyman.

"You can't truly get a sense of the people you touch a lot of the time when you're someone like me. I shot the man an email back to say I thank him and his son more than they can ever know."

Turner has never attended a game at Lincoln Financial Field, but he hopes to be in the house on November 7, with sons Nolan, 13, and Cole, 7, when the Eagles host the Indianapolis Colts.

"I want them to experience the atmosphere, the passion, of football in Philly," he said. "It really is something special. I feel so fortunate to have been a part of that."

Epilogue: It is a testament to Turner's strength of character that he refused to meekly yield to the disease that continued to ravage his physical being, hanging on until he finally and inevitably succumbed to ALS on March 24, 2016, at the age of 46. His son Nolan entered the 2020 season as a senior safety for No. 1-ranked Clemson, and was a key member of the Tigers' 2018 national championship squad.

Cold War: Hockey Divides Quebec
Philadelphia Daily News, April 25, 1985

Bobby Smith of the Montreal Canadiens is an American, so his opinions aren't particularly influenced by the cultural and economic forces that always have been attendant to hockey in French-speaking Canada. All he knows is that he feels privileged to be an NHL player at this time and in this part of the world.

"When I retire, I think the highlight of my career will be the confrontations with the Nordiques," Smith said Tuesday night, after the Canadiens had dropped a 7-6 overtime decision to Quebec in the third game of the Adams Division final series. The victory gave Quebec a 2-1 lead in the best-of-seven series, which continues tonight at *Le Colisee.*

"It's a good, honest rivalry," Smith added. "I don't have any friends on the Quebec team, and I don't think there's anybody in their locker room who feels all that friendly toward me.

"And that's OK. I agree with what Larry Bird says about Julius Erving. He says people pay good money to see athletes play their hearts out. They don't want to hear about guys from opposing teams having lunch together."

Following that logic, Smith once disassociated himself from his closest friend.

"Tony McKegney and I played junior hockey together," Smith said. "We were as close as two people could be. When I was playing for the Buffalo Sabres, we talked on the telephone at least twice a week.

"When he was traded to Quebec, though, we stopped calling one another. It just didn't seem appropriate. After he was traded away from Quebec (to Minnesota), we started talking again."

******

Welcome to the crowded world of professional hockey in the province of Quebec, where the traditionally powerful Canadiens and upstart Nordiques are embroiled in perhaps the most bitter feud in professional sports.

While there are a number of differences between the two teams – big city vs. smaller city, old vs. new, ownership by rival breweries – the principal point of contention is their close geographical proximity (about 150 miles). Nothing unusual about that, unless you consider the province's status as a closed society unlike any other on the North American continent. Within that society a debate rages: Is there room enough in this hockey-mad region for two NHL franchises?

Although political activists in the province are not calling as strongly for a separation from Canada, Quebec is as culturally removed from the rest of the nation as, say, Fiji is from the United States.

Those differences translate quite literally to hockey. Says Bernard Brisset, director of communications for the Nordiques: "If we have a chance at two players of more or less equal talent, we'll always take the French Canadian. I think it's only logical. A player born in the province knows the environment, he knows the culture. Take a player from someplace like Regina, Saskatchewan, and he'd be lost in Quebec City."

Until six years ago, when the Nordiques gained admission into the NHL, the Canadiens had virtual exclusivity within the province for more than six decades. Although the Nordiques had been in existence since 1972, they were a member of the World Hockey

Association, whose status was roughly equivalent to that of a glorified minor league.

When the WHA went belly up in 1979, few people cared – except the management of the Canadiens, which was outraged at the prospect of nearby Quebec City becoming an NHL rival.

"If they could snap their fingers and make us disappear, they'd do it right now," said Marcel Aubut, the aggressive president of the Nordiques. "They fought to keep us out of the league. They sued everybody they could think of to keep us from getting a network TV contract (which the Nords obtained only this season). We are like a nightmare to them."

******

One team's nightmare, another team's dream. Depending upon whom you ask, the presence of the Nordiques is either the greatest thing to happen to the Canadiens or a tragedy of unfathomable dimensions.

Brisset, a native Montrealer who spent 10 years as a hockey writer for *La Presse* in Montreal before assuming his current duties, believes the competition between the teams is good for both.

"I remember the Canadiens winning four straight Stanley Cups, from 1976 through 1979, and even then there never was the kind of reaction that there was when Montreal eliminated Quebec last year (in the Adams Division finals)," Brisset said. "It was like the celebration in Detroit when it won the baseball World Series, or in San Francisco when it won the Super Bowl.

"So for the public, for the hockey fans in Montreal, the rivalry is great. Hockey would never be the same – well, not for a long time, anyway – if there was no Nordiques for the Canadiens to play. The management of the Canadiens might not think so, but this rivalry is good for hockey."

But Claude Mouton, Brisset's counterpart with the Canadiens, isn't so sure. Like others in the Montreal organization, Mouton seems to view the Nordiques as another penalty imposed upon the Canadiens – who have won 22 Stanley Cups in their 75-year existence – for being overly successful.

"One season (1976-77) we lost only eight games," Mouton said, "and if we had really worked at it, we might not have lost any. That's how dominant we were.

"Well, everyone said that wasn't right, that it wasn't fair. So now we don't have first choice among the players and we have to share our territory."

Montreal's dynasty was built largely on French Canadians. Every kid in Quebec dreamed of becoming a Canadien, and those good enough invariably did because of a territorial draft system that annually granted Montreal first shot at the two top junior players in the province. Since it generally seemed that the best young players were French Canadians, Montreal's success was virtually self-perpetuating.

The territorial draft was abolished in 1967, replaced by the sort of open draft used by the NFL and NBA. That same year the NHL doubled in size, from six teams to 12, and has since expanded to its current membership of 21 teams.

While the Canadiens swallowed hard and grudgingly accepted all those changes, entry of the Nordiques into the league was perhaps the most bitter pill of all.

"They don't want to admit we exist," Brisset said. "They know they have to live with us, but they don't like it. To them, the Nordiques are crap."

******

To understand the impact the Nordiques have had on Quebec City, it is necessary to have some insight into the umbilical cord that long has tied the province's second-largest city to its larger, more cosmopolitan neighbor.

"Quebec City always has had something of an inferiority complex in comparison to Montreal," said Yves Poulin, a sports writer for the Quebec City-based *Le Soleil.* Quebec City is called 'the big village.' Montreal is the big city. Montreal has baseball (the Expos) and football (the CFL's Concordes) and a lot of other things we don't have here.

"In hockey, it is the same. Quebec City has had some great players, like Jean Beliveau, but they always wound up in Montreal.

People here have been raised with the Canadiens. For another team to win fans away from the Canadiens takes time."

Aubut, for one, knew how big a job he had on his hands when it became apparent the Nordiques were about to take on the Canadiens head-to-head. Not only did Quebec City have a small population base (about 500,000) from which to draw, but the Nords had to spend the first five years of their existence without a network TV contract while trying to steal bits and pieces of the Canadiens' massive fan support.

"I have to acknowledge that what we are trying to beat is an incredible dynasty," Aubut said. "It is like trying to beat the New York Yankees or the Boston Celtics. But it can be done, eventually."

The Nordiques took a long step toward parity in 1982, when they stunned Montreal, three games to two, in the Adams Division semifinals.

Oddly enough, some hockey fans in the province that had been inclined to root for Quebec as a second-favorite team became hostile when the Nords showed themselves to be competitive on the ice.

"When we first came into the league in 1979, I'd say we were more popular than we are now," Brisset said. "Why? Because we were new, because we were trying hard. When we beat the Canadiens in the playoffs we became the enemy. The novelty of the Nordiques had worn off, and we finally were seen as a threat – a real threat – to the Canadiens."

Certainly the Canadiens could see that. Carling O'Keefe, the brewery that owns the Nordiques, had only an 18% share of the beer market in the province in 1979 while Molson, which owns the Canadiens, was the runaway leader at 42%. Since then, Carling O'Keefe has closed the gap considerably, the result of an aggressive sports marketing campaign based on the brewery's ownership of the Nords and radio-TV sponsorship of the baseball Expos.

In response, the Canadiens this year hired a marketing and public relations director, Francois Seigneur – a first for the organization.

Seigneur has instituted certain changes, not the least of which was making fans at the Forum feel more welcome.

"In the past, the feeling at the Forum was, `Sit down, shut up and don't do anything,'" Seigneur told the *Toronto Globe and Mail* in a recent interview. "A lot of things weren't allowed in the Forum. They weren't allowed to have banners, they weren't allowed to drink beer in the stands, and weren't allowed to honk horns. We've changed that."

The Canadiens insist the changes were not prompted by competition from the Nords, but one-upsmanship involving the two teams appears to be stronger than ever. During last year's playoff series against Montreal, for instance, Quebec officials treated the media to elaborate pregame meals. The Canadiens, who had felt sandwiches were sufficient to satisfy the writers' hunger, immediately followed suit.

******

But rivalries are not built on four-star dining. While most Canadians see hockey as an art form, one which emphasizes finesse and skill, Montreal and Quebec occasionally have reduced the sport to the level of tag-team wrestling. Two days before Easter last season, the Canadiens and Nords engaged in a bench-clearing brawl that became known as "Bloody Good Friday."

Then, Tuesday night, the violence erupted again as referee Bob Myers handed out nearly 2½ hours' worth of penalties in a game marred by several fistfights.

"You can't back down, they can't back down," said Dale Hunter of the Nordiques, whose goal in overtime ended the game. "There's going to be fights. That's the way it is when Quebec plays Montreal."

"We have to keep the situation under control," said Aubut. "We have to keep those things in the rivalry that are good and eliminate those that are bad."

Nobody ever said that was going to be easy.

Epilogue: Canadiens vs. Nordiques probably never was a fair fight for the hearts and minds of the province's rabid hockey fans, given Montreal's rich history and decades-long head start in establishing its brand. The Nordiques finally acknowledged the reality of their disadvantageous position and relocated to Denver in May 1995, where they were renamed the Colorado Avalanche. Quebec City never did win a Stanley Cup, but Montreal twice more laid claim to Lord Stanley's big trophy since this story appeared, upping its franchise total to an NHL-high 24. Adding insult to injury for disappointed Nords fans, the Avalanche won Stanley Cups in 1996 and 2001 in large part because of the superb play of Quebec City-born goaltender Patrick Roy, who was a key member of the Canadiens for 11 seasons, winning two Stanley Cups, before being traded to Colorado, where he helped win two more.

Agassi Prepared for One Last Run
Philadelphia Daily News, August 28, 2006

NEW YORK

The huge, rectangular sign hanging outside the entrance to the Billie Jean King Tennis Center does not identify by name the likeness of the bald man lunging for a backhand. Then again, it doesn't need to.

"An American Original" read the three words on the sign, and anyone who has not been marooned on the dark side of the moon for these past 21 years knows that the icon depicted is the singularly recognizable Andre Agassi, who begins play in his 21st and final United States Open tonight. Before his appearance at Wimbledon this summer, Agassi announced he would retire from competitive tennis upon his exit from his nation's richest and most prestigious tournament, whenever that happened.

"The more matches I play (at the U.S. Open), the longer I get to be in that environment," the winner of eight Grand Slam events, including all four majors, said several weeks ago. "But regardless of how it ends, it's going to be great.

"I hope when I get back to the familiar sights and sounds of Arthur Ashe Stadium that something takes over, but I don't know what to expect. That's the part of it that's pretty hard to get my arms around."

Tennis being actual sport and not a scripted, made-for-TV drama, there is a very real possibility that the 36-year-old Agassi's much-hyped farewell will prove to be more a cameo than the extended mini-series everyone so desperately wants. Arguably the most popular player ever to wield a racket, Agassi has attempted to play through chronic back pain (he's just 8-7 this year and has not advanced beyond the quarterfinals of any of the seven tournaments he has entered), and fate has handed him an unfavorable draw that might not allow for much indulgence in sentiment.

227

Should Agassi survive his opening-round Andre vs. Andrei pairing – and Romania's Andrei Pavel, 32, is no sure thing to roll over for the older man, who lost to a 346th-ranked Italian in a tournament in Washington last month – he's likely to meet rising star Marcos Baghdatis, the 21-year-old from Cyprus who was the runner-up at this year's Australian Open. If Agassi advances to the fourth round, big-serving Andy Roddick, now coached by the legendary Jimmy Connors, could be the opponent.

"He's got a tough draw," top-seeded Roger Federer said of Agassi, whom he defeated in four sets in last year's U.S. Open final.

But Agassi has bucked imposing odds before. Despite his brilliant shot-making, he was dismissed early in his career as a shaggy-haired, denim-shorts-clad, earring-wearing punk whose dubious dedication never would come close to matching his luminescent talent. The Agassi of the late 1980s might be described as the Anna Kournikova of his era, someone whose pretty-boy appeal was directed more to giggling girls and young male wannabes who sought to replicate his rebellious persona.

Everyone remembers the "Image is everything" global ad campaign for a camera company that featured Agassi as sort of a tennis-playing James Dean, flouting convention and doing what he pleased. And Agassi might have sustained his popularity as the cool, distant outsider until the encroachment of age and male-pattern baldness eventually caused the teenyboppers to turn their attention to someone younger and hipper.

But somewhere along the line the self-absorbed Agassi underwent a remarkable metamorphosis. He acknowledged his receding hairline and began shaving his head. His diet of doughnuts and fast-food burgers gave way to more nutritious fare. Most of all, he realized that his rare gift for playing tennis was too precious to fritter away, that he already had wasted too much time on being fashionable rather than becoming great.

Agassi won his first Grand Slam event at Wimbledon in 1992, a significant feat given his preference for playing from the baseline, and in 1994 he came off a wrist injury to become the first unseeded U.S. Open champ in nearly three decades.

Perhaps even more notably, the former world No. 1 braked a tumble that saw him sink to No. 141 in the computer rankings in 1997 to again become the world's premier player in 1999. Five of his eight Grand Slam titles came after his 29th birthday, and his elongated excellence – Agassi has finished in the top 10 of the year-end computer rankings 16 times, a record he shares with Connors – has seen him swap strokes with three generations of players, from Connors and John McEnroe to Pete Sampras and Jim Courier to, now, Federer and Rafael Nadal.

Not that his look on the tennis court is the only part of Agassi's personal journey. Agassi is married to tennis great Steffi Graf and they have two children. It is his second marriage; actress Brooke Shields was his first wife.

The preening kid who thought only of himself has become a humanitarian whose annual gala, Grand Slam for Children, has raised $52 million for charitable causes. Several million dollars of Agassi's personal fortune have gone into Andre Agassi College Preparatory Academy in a blighted section of his hometown of Las Vegas. The school, now in its sixth year, has 530 students from kindergarten through 12th grade who see Agassi more as a benefactor and path to a better life than as a future Hall of Famer.

Even those players more likely to advance further in this year's U.S. Open realize that Agassi's goodbye will overshadow anything anyone else does during the fortnight. *Sports Illustrated* went so far as to call the Open a "farewell party masquerading as a tennis event."

Roddick said Agassi, whose prime was overshadowed somewhat by Sampras, who won a record 14 Grand Slam tournaments and beat him 20 times in 34 meetings, is most like Connors in the impact they had on the game.

"Jimmy and Andre were both huge crossover stars, probably bigger than tennis itself," Roddick said. "They both stood the test of time, and they both could hold a crowd in the palm of their hands."

Added two-time U.S. Open women's champion Serena Williams: "Andre has meant so much to tennis. He's had that charisma, that great attitude, great personality, great style. I think the game is going to miss him more than probably they miss anyone."

In a perfect world, Agassi would win the Open, as Sampras did in his finale in 2002, or at least charge into the semifinals, as Connors did in 1991 at the age of 39. When the end does come, Agassi no doubt will bow toward the four corners of the stadium and blow kisses to spectators, as is his custom. For the last time he will feel waves of love pour over him from worshipful fans, like surf breaking over a reef.

There probably won't be a dry eye in the place, including those of the American Original.

Epilogue: Despite excruciating back pain that forced him to receive anti-inflammatory injections after every match, Agassi gutted out victories over Pavel and Baghdatis (who succumbed to muscle cramps in the fifth and final set) before being ousted by Germany's Benjamin Becker. Agassi received a four-minute standing ovation from the crowd after the match and delivered a retirement speech.

Acknowledgments

The press box at a football or baseball game, and press row at a boxing match, are assemblies of relentlessly driven individuals who I imagine are very much like me. No, check that; I *know* they are very much like me, at least in some respects. So I close this anthology with a tribute to all sports writers, be they friends, colleagues or competitors for the reading public's attention. Everyone in our little fraternity knows not only the undeniable benefits of having prime seats so many others would love to fill for memorable or even mundane sporting contests, but there is a cost to be paid for that privilege: tight deadlines, frequent short-notice travel, time away from our families.

Someone once asked me what the best thing about my job was. I mentioned that, for me, it was the lack of the mind-numbing sameness of the 9-to-5 grind that mark so many other professions. In any given week, day or even hour, I might be called upon to quickly pack a bag and rush to the airport so that I might cover a breaking-news event. And when that person inquired as to the biggest downside of a line of work that sometimes seems to be in a perpetual state of flux, I said, "Same thing." See, people with 9-to-5 jobs have a certainty of scheduling, and very often weekends off. They can coach, say, their children's youth-league games (I never felt I had the flexibility to do so) and assure family members and friends of their attendance for special occasions. My participation in such was always iffy, and I recall the stern look of disapproval my wife gave me a few days beforehand when I told her I had to leave on Christmas morning for a flight to Seattle to cover a college holiday basketball tournament.

Growing up in New Orleans, my first sports writing role model was Peter Finney, now deceased, who was a towering figure of sports journalism in my hometown, cranking out peerless prose for 68 years. I met Peter when I was just 16 and landed the plum assignment of copy boy in the *Times-Picayune* sports department for one charmed summer. Peter not only gave me the benefit of his insight and wisdom then, as did another generous *T-P* writer, George Sweeney, also now gone, but I was blessed to maintain a cordial professional relationship with both up to the time of their deaths. It marked a rite of passage, if you will, when they came to see me as a peer and not as the pesty, inquisitive kid I had been when I first met them.

Others who proved influential in my meandering career journey were the late, great Edwin Pope, Miami's Peter Finney equivalent, with whom I worked when I was on the sports staff at the *Miami Herald*, and the late Lee Baker, my sports editor at the *Jackson (Miss.) Daily News*, where my colleagues included the gifted Orley Hood (RIP) and Buck Bennett.

Upon joining the truly special sports staff of the *Philadelphia .Daily News* in 1984, I was privileged to work under such capable executive sports editors as Mike Rathet and Pat McLoone, and alongside Hall of Fame writers Stan Hochman, Bill Conlin and Phil Jasner, all, sadly, now deceased, as well as Ray Didinger, who thankfully still graces the Philly sports scene as a radio and TV commentator. The late Bill Lyon was not a "teammate" with the *PDN*, but his marvelously crafted sports columns for the *Philadelphia Inquirer* will forever place him on a pedestal for longtime readers.

While on the boxing beat for the *PDN*, from which I retired in April 2012, I was spurred to maintain and hopefully build upon the legacy established by predecessors Hochman, Larry Merchant, Tom Cushman (RIP), Jack McKinney (RIP) and Elmer Smith, who set lofty standards anyone following in their footsteps would be challenged to approach. Covering fights and fighters also brought me into regular contact with the incredible Jerry Izenberg, now the sports columnist emeritus for the *Newark Star-Ledger*, who remains at the top of his game at 90 years of age, a level of excellence and longevity that anyone would envy. Shout-outs also must be given to writers I, along with so many others, enjoy reading: Thomas Hauser, Ron Borges, Mark Kriegel, Springs Toledo, Don Stradley, Carlos Acevedo and Arne K. Lang. There are others, too numerous to cite individually here, and I hope they realize they are and deserve to be on anyone's roll call of top-tier fight writers.

232

Now that my nearly 52 years in sports journalism – and life, for that matter – signify much more past than future, I will ask and answer a question I sometimes I have posed to myself: If I had to do it all over again, would I make the same career choice?

Hell, yes. I really wouldn't have wanted to go down any other path. And I thank every reader who has come along with me for any part of the trip.

About the Author

Bernard Fernandez, a native of New Orleans, is a long-time resident of Drexel Hill, Pennsylvania. He now splits his time between his hometown and his adopted hometown. A five-term president of the Boxing Writers Association of America, he has been inducted into the Pennsylvania (2005), New Jersey (2013), Atlantic City (2018) and International (2020) Boxing Halls of Fame. He also is a recipient of the Nat Fleischer Award (1998) for Excellence in Boxing Journalism and the Barney Nagler Award (2015) for Long and Meritorious Service to Boxing.

Photo by Alex Alvarez

Made in the USA
Middletown, DE
26 February 2022